An A–Z of Pasta

To pasta makers and pasta eaters

An A–Z of Pasta

Stories, Shapes, Sauces, Recipes

Rachel Roddy

Photography by Jonathan Lovekin

PENGUIN
FIG TREE

FIG TREE

UK | USA | Canada | Ireland | Australia
India | New Zealand | South Africa

Fig Tree is part of the Penguin Random House group of companies
whose addresses can be found at global.penguinrandomhouse.com.

First published 2021
001

Photography copyright © Jonathan Lovekin except pp. 139,
161, 255, 271, 299 © Rachel Roddy
Designed by Saffron Stocker
Printed in Italy by Printer Trento S.r.l.

The authorized representative in the EEA is Penguin Random House Ireland,
Morrison Chambers, 32 Nassau Street, Dublin DO2 YH68

A CIP catalogue record for this book is available from the British Library

ISBN: 978–0–241–40250–4

www.greenpenguin.co.uk

MIX
Paper from
responsible sources
FSC
www.fsc.org   FSC® C018179

Penguin Random House is committed to a
sustainable future for our business, our readers
and our planet. This book is made from Forest
Stewardship Council® certified paper.

Contents

Introduction 7

Some Suggestions 8

Quantities 11

The A–Z of Pasta **12**

Index 341

Acknowledgements 351

Introduction

Every day millions of us are united in doing the same thing. We take a packet of pasta from the shelf, we tip the shapes into boiling water, we make something to eat.

Pasta, a small word for a universe of shapes. The word comes from the Latin *pasta*, which comes from the Greek πάστη (paste) = a mix of flour and water. From this paste, hands, and then machines, formed shapes – long, short, twisted, pierced, dragged, filled, fresh, dried. Anything from 350 to 600 depending on who you talk to, with 1,300 dialect names, and new shapes being invented every year. The story of these shapes is the story of Italy. For Italians, pasta is more than just a food, it is a symbol, a flag, a way of life and culture. It is a universe with many galaxies, the gravitational pull of passion and opinion, the occasional black hole, and a constellation of stars (recipes).

Only a genius or an idiot would try to concentrate *all* this into a book. I am neither, at least not in this context, so I haven't tried. Neither am I Italian, a scholar, or a chef. However, I have, as a food writer and home-cook living in Italy and surrounded by good teachers, spent the last 16 years in Rome learning about, cooking and eating pasta. And while I am acutely aware of my limits, I also know my worth. I have done what I always do and written stories about 50 shapes. Some stories are practical, others historical, geographical, some more earnest than others, and they always end with recipes. The idea is the 50 stories, arranged alphabetically according to the first letter of the shape, are like pieces of a jigsaw in that they fit together to form not *the* picture, but *a* picture of pasta. Individual pieces also stand alone, useful unto themselves. At the very least, you are holding a book of marvellous recipes.

Pasta may be more than just a food, but it is a food, shapes cooked in water in order to make something to eat, and that is what this book is about.

Rome, November 2020

Some Suggestions

Arranging this book alphabetically meant we had to allocate sauces to shapes. This was a satisfying way to honour classic pairings (lots more about pairing in C – Casarecce) but also a minefield, as most sauces are polygamists pairing beautifully with lots of shapes, which we have noted as alternatives you will discover as you work through the book. However, if you are anything like me you may well have grabbed a packet from the shelf and are now wondering what to cook. With that in mind, before we start at A – Alfabeto, here are some suggestions, a quick reference for much-loved packets, ideas for specific occasions, vegetarian dishes marked with a v.

Suggestions for shapes

Fusilli
Lamb *ragù*
Onion *ragù* (v)
Broccoli with anchovy crumbs
Peperonata (v)
Sardines with fennel and anchovy
   crumbs

Linguine
Onion and anchovy
Courgettes, egg and Parmesan (v)
Clams/*vongole*
Pesto alla genovese (v)
Leeks, cream and saffron (v)

Maccheroni
Macaroni cheese (v)
Midsummer pasta with roasted
   vegetables, mozzarella and basil (v)
With peas, bacon and ricotta
Baked macaroni with meatballs and
   aubergine
Four cheeses (v)

Orecchiette
Broccoli with anchovy crumbs
Braised lentils (v)
Chickpea and chestnut soup (v)
Bursting tomatoes and anchovy
   crumbs
Trapanese pesto of almonds, tomato
   and basil (v)

Pappardelle
Duck *ragù*
Onion *ragù* (v)
Radicchio, fennel, cream and
  Parmesan (v)
Funghi porcini (v)
Leeks and mussels

Penne
Arrabbiata – tomato and lots of red
  chilli (v)
Four cheeses (v)
Sausage, porcini mushrooms and
  leeks
Norma – tomato, aubergine and
  salted ricotta (v)
Courgettes, pancetta and pecorino

Spaghetti
Simple tomato and basil sauce (v)
All'amatriciana
Puttanesca
Cacio e pepe – pecorino and black
  pepper (v)
Carbonara – egg, guanciale and
  pecorino

Tagliatelle
Ragù bolognese
Chicken livers and sage
Bursting tomatoes and anchovy
  crumbs

Butter and Parmesan (v)
Bean soup (broken) (v)

Suggestions for occasions

Very quick
Cacio e pepe – pecorino and black
  pepper (spaghetti alla chitarra) (v)
Aglio, olio e peperoncino – garlic,
  olive oil and chilli (spaghetti) (v)
Burro e parmigiano – butter and
  Parmesan (fettuccine) (v)
Salmone e mascarpone – smoked
  salmon and mascarpone (farfalle)
Scampi e limone – prawns and
  lemon (capelli d'angelo)
Burro e alici – butter and anchovy
  (fettucine)

Quick
Alfabeto in brodo (v)
Simple tomato and basil sauce
  (spaghetti) (v)
Pesto alla genovese (trofie) (v)
Puttanesca
Carbonara – egg, guanciale and
  pecorino (rigatoni)
Four cheeses (penne) (v)
Sardines, fennel, lemon and anchovy
  crumbs (fusilli)

Satisfying supper

Ragù di agnello con tante erbe – lamb *ragù* with lots of herbs (fusilli)

Macaroni cheese (v)

Spaghetti with clams

Pasta al forno – baked pasta with rich tomato sauce and mozzarella (v)

Minestra di ceci e castagne – chickpea and chestnut soup (v)

Fregula with clams

Spring and summer dishes, for a crowd

Pasta di mezz'estate – midsummer pasta (v)

Pesto alla genovese – with potatoes and green beans (trofie) (v)

Vignarola – Roman braised spring vegetables (strappati) (v)

Chicken with orzo

Spinach and potato gnocchi with cream, Parmesan and basil (v)

Autumn and winter dishes, for a crowd

Lasagne alla bolognese (lasagna)

Pumpkin cappellacci (v)

Vincisgrassi – rich baked pasta with porcini, prosciutto and béchamel

Pappardelle with duck

Ziti con la genovese – ziti with onion and beef sauce

Quantities

Recipes serve 4, except where noted otherwise. Regarding the quantity of pasta, a sweep through Italian guidelines and opinion finds the general advice is 60–100g of dried pasta, 100–120g of fresh pasta, 120–150g of filled pasta, 100–130g of gnocchi per person. The lower end of this range can seem modest, until you remember that pasta is often served as a *primo*, literally, a first course, with a meat, fish or vegetable *secondo* coming after. Obviously if there is nothing coming after, a more generous serving is called for, and of course what constitutes generous varies as much as the nature (richness/robustness) of different types of pasta and sauces.

However, we need a rule of thumb. So, with a few noted exceptions, I suggest 400g of dried pasta, 480g of fresh, 600g of filled for 4 people. But this is only a suggestion, which does beg the question, what to do with the 100g of penne left in the bag? If you do decide to throw the contents of the whole 500g bag in to the water, just be aware the sauce may need a bit of help, a little more oil or cheese, an extra ladle of pasta cooking water, so it all comes together. Leftover pasta is brilliant, as it can be made into a frittata (see page 281).

— a —

Alfabeto

There are just 21 letters in the Italian alphabet, no J, K, W, X or Y. Less to remember, but frustrating if you are called Joy, because searching for your name is integral to eating a bowl of broth with letters.

There is no better way to begin this A–Z than with alfabeto, tiny pasta in the shape of letters. Surely invented to engage children, and considered by some a gimmick, alfabeto is made of durum wheat and water. It is a *pastina*, part of a huge family of tiny shapes that includes puntini (dots), stelline (stars), tempestine (little storms), anelli (rings), fregula (balls) and quadrucci (little squares), some of which we will meet later in the alphabet. Unlike other small shapes that hold their own in soups, alfabeto really are tiny. Smaller than a currant or a crumb picked up with a damp finger, they stand up to nothing! And why should they, when they are best in a bowl of broth.

To write about alfabeto, or any *pastina*, is to write about Italian *brodo*, as the two are inseparable. Closer to consommé than stock, *brodi* are liquids to which meat or vegetables, or both, have given flavour, and of course come in cubes and granules too. Several pasta shapes are served 'in brodo', the most famous being belly-button meat-filled tortellini, which we will come to later. Whatever the form, the pasta is cooked directly in the *brodo*, and sometimes grated Parmesan is swirled in at the end, which clouds and enriches. While alfabeto suspended in *brodo* is something given to children, it is by no means just for children. It is a simple joy, although don't expect to find Joy in it.

Alfabeto in brodo
Serves 4

Bring 1 litre of vegetable or chicken broth (see below and next page) to the boil, add 200g of alfabeto and cook until al dente, which takes 4–7 minutes depending on the brand. Ladle into bowls, passing round grated Parmesan. Alfabeto can be substituted with any *pastina*. Spaghetti or dried tagliatelle snapped into short lengths are also lovely in broth.

Golden vegetable broth
Makes 1.7 litres of broth

First up, I should note how much I like granules and cubes. But when I do make this vegetable broth, I am never not surprised at how good it is, the essence of vegetables and, as the name suggests, golden, thanks to the onion skins. To my mind all broths need salt added at the start in order to cook properly, but if you don't agree, add it at the end.

2 onions, unpeeled, halved
4 sticks of celery, quartered
3 carrots, peeled and quartered
1 small bulb of fennel, quartered
1 medium potato, peeled and halved
5 cherry tomatoes, halved
1 bay leaf
5 black peppercorns
3 cloves
salt

Put all the ingredients into a large heavy-based pan and cover with 2 litres of cold water.

Bring to the boil, then reduce the heat to low. Using a slotted spoon, skim off any froth or residue that has risen to the surface (don't worry too much about getting every bit), then cover the pan and simmer gently for an hour and a half.

Strain through a fine sieve, pressing down on the vegetables to extract every bit of flavour. Taste, and add more salt if you think it needs it.

A note about salt
There are two pots of salt by the cooker. One of **sale grosso**, coarse, rubbly sea salt ideal for salting pasta water, in it a spoon that holds almost exactly 10 grams. The other pot is of **sale fino**, fine salt, also sea salt, for everything else. I am a great believer in *adding little, often*, that is adding tiny, cautious pinches of salt throughout cooking, which is inextricably tied to the other cooking advice to live by, *taste, taste, taste*.

Brodo di pollo
Chicken broth
Makes 2 litres of broth

Chicken broth, not too clear or strained of fat, is one of my great pleasures and soothers. This is my mother-in-law's recipe, although she removes the chicken skin. Again salt at the start is important, and the simmering must be calm and steady. The chicken will have given much by the end of cooking. But not all – the poached meat can, and should, be pulled from the bone and eaten with mustard or green sauce.

800kg chicken thighs
veal bone (optional)
salt
1 onion, peeled and
    halved
1 carrot, peeled and
    halved
1 stick of celery,
    halved
1 bay leaf
a few peppercorns

Put the chicken and veal bone into a large heavy-based pan, cover with 2.5 litres of cold water, and add a large pinch of salt. Bring to the boil, then reduce the heat to low and, using a slotted spoon, skim off any scum that has risen to the surface.

Add the vegetables, bring back to the boil, then reduce the heat to low, cover the pan and simmer gently for an hour and a quarter.

Strain through a fine sieve, pressing down on the vegetables and meat to extract every bit of flavour.

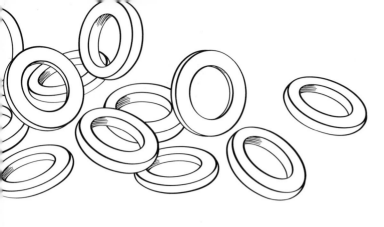

— a —

Anelli

A favourite bag to pull from the shelf, the little rings pressed up against the plastic like kids' faces against a car window. I have a pasta-map tea towel. On it anelli float like tiny life-rings in the stretch of sea between Sicily and the heel of Puglia, the two regions in which they are most typical. For my Sicilian partner Vincenzo they are a shape of his childhood, one that holds personal and collective history. They are part of my childhood too, hooped-tinned memories. The pasta encyclopedia defines anelli as a factory-made, durum wheat and water dried *pastina* that comes in various sizes and goes by various names – anelli, anelletti, anellini, anelloni d'Africa. While anelli are typically served in broth, they are also well dressed with tomato sauce and fried aubergine, layered with cheese and baked for a *timballo*, which I will come to shortly.

Pasta shapes are edible hubs of information: flour and liquid microchips containing huge amounts of data, historical, geographical, political, cultural, personal, practical. Each shape can also be defined physically by its geometry, makeup, and category. And while this book isn't a catalogue, certain terms will come up often so it seems a good idea to clarify a few things before we move on.

Fresh pasta or dried pasta. All pasta starts off fresh, and therefore soft, whether it's a strand of spaghetti extruded in a factory, an ear of flour and water orecchiette, or a ribbon of egg tagliatelle you have made yourself. In referring to **dried pasta** I mean pasta shapes that have been made specifically – usually in a factory – to be dried so they last indefinitely. **Fresh pasta**, whether flour and egg, or flour and water, is made to be eaten while it is still fresh and soft.

Pasta, from the word *impasto* – a magma of flour and liquid – can be made from any flour; the Italian pasta lexicon includes shapes made from chestnut flour, acorn flour, rice flour, corn flour, broad bean flour and buckwheat. The hard king and tender queen, though, are **hard or durum wheat semolina flour** and **soft wheat 00 flour**. Simple, and really all we need to know as shoppers and eaters, although as cooks a bit more information is useful.

Hard or durum wheat, *Triticum durum, grano duro,* is the hardest variety of wheat. High in protein, durum's hardness mustn't be confused with what we consider 'hard' wheat in English, that is, high-protein bread flour, but rather refers to the fact that it is stubborn and resistant to milling, eventually reducing to a granular texture the colour of pale egg yolks. Ground coarsely it becomes semolina suitable for puddings, or the basis for African and Levantine couscous. Ground twice it becomes flour, *semola rimacinata* in Italian, durum wheat semolina flour in the UK. Hard wheat flour absorbs water greedily, producing a dough with real substance, which is why it is ideal for making flour and water pasta. It is the legally stipulated flour for factory-made dried shapes in Italy. **Soft wheat flour, *Triticum aestivum, grano tenero,*** is a separate species from hard wheat. Low in protein, its softness means it is a pushover, milling easily into powdery flour, its precise grade of milling noted in numbers, 00 being the finest, then 0, 1, 2 increasingly coarse. Soft wheat produces a more elastic dough, so is used to make fresh and fresh egg pasta. It is worth sticking your hands simultaneously into two bags, one of hard wheat semolina flour, the other soft wheat flour, to understand the difference. Hard wheat semolina flour is gently gritty and like very fine sand compared to the infinite smoothness of soft wheat 00 flour.

Factory-made and home-made. Leaky definitions, with many shapes being both, especially now people have powerful domestic extruders producing shapes once exclusive to factories, and traditionally home-made shapes being made on an industrial scale. Overwhelmingly though, dried pasta is factory-made, while fresh shapes, both flour and water and flour and egg, are home-made or made on a smaller scale.

Extruded or **Cut** or **Dragged. Extruded shapes** are made by being forced through a die, which means many of the tubular and rounded flour and water dried shapes, also all the long ones with a rounded cross-section – spaghetti, linguine, bucatini, ziti. **Cut shapes** are made by cutting the dough, whether fresh or dried – tagliatelle, pappardelle, mafalde, lasagne. **Dragged shapes** are formed by a dragging motion.

Most useful, maybe, are the **6 categories of pasta shapes** which take in all the above, fresh and dried, all flours, factory-made and home-made.

1. *Pastine.* Very small pasta shapes that are generally cooked in broth, therefore requiring a spoon. *Pastine* can be fresh or dried, and are made with hard or soft wheat, and other flours too. Most *pastine*, though, are factory-made hard wheat and water dried shapes.

2. *Pasta corta,* **short pasta.** Short shapes, both factory-made and home-made, so quills of penne and spirals of fusilli, also lozenge-shaped fregnacce.

3. ***Pasta lunga*, long pasta.** Long shapes, both factory-made and home-made, spaghetti obviously, tagliatelle, fettuccine, pappardelle, also flour and water pici and lagane.

4. ***Pasta ripiena*, filled pasta.** Stuffed or filled shapes, so ravioli and tortellini, also rolls of cannelloni and all the layered, baked pastas.

5. ***Strascinati*, dragged shapes.** Shapes made by being dragged across a surface either with a finger or implement. Orecchiette, the ear-like pasta from Puglia, is probably the most famous of these, but there are many others.

6. ***Gnocchi.*** Shapes with a dumpling form, which may or may not be ridged or indented.

Some shapes straddle two categories. Gnocchi ricci, for example, are gnocchi but also dragged, while maccheroni, fusilli and lasagne can mean many things. Also bear in mind that many shapes have many names, that while classifying pasta is helpful it is not an exact science and at times as slippery as a just-cooked ribbon of fettuccine.

So back to the second shape of this alphabet, anelli, pressing up against the side of the bag like eager faces. As I mentioned, they can be served in broth, which you can then cloud with cheese, or brothy soup. Or they can be par-boiled, dressed with sauce, pressed into a tin, and baked into a *timballo* that you invert with a triumphant ta-dah.

Timballo di anelli siciliano
Anelli baked with tomato, aubergine and cheese
Serves 6

Timballo is also a name for a drum. In Sicily this *timballo* is traditionally made on the 15th of August, Ferragosto, the workers' holiday that dates back to Emperor Augustus's *Feriae Augusti,* and to the Assumption of the Virgin. Often, it is taken to the beach along with a whole watermelon that is buried in the sand near the water to keep cool. By Sicilian standards this is a modest *timballo*. It can be embellished, the tomato replaced with meat *ragù*, bolstered with tiny meatballs or crumbled sausage, and you could add peas or the Sicilian favourite – slices of hard-boiled egg. However you make it, season generously at every stage. You can make individual servings, known as *sformati* for their easygoing form, the benefit of which is a high proportion of edges and crust.

1 onion, peeled and small diced
salt and black pepper
8 tablespoons olive oil
1 x 400g tin of plum tomatoes
500g tomatoes
a pinch of red chilli flakes
a handful of fresh basil
1 large aubergine (plus oil for frying)
400g anelli, alternatively ditalini, tubetti, mezze penne
120g Parmesan or caciocavallo, grated
butter
fine breadcrumbs
400g mozzarella or scamorza, diced or ripped into little pieces

You will need a 28cm, 10cm deep round tin – ideally with a loose base – or a ring tin. Or 6 small dishes, or – as is typical in Sicilian *rosticcerie* – aluminium trays.

First make the sauce. In a large heavy-based pan, fry the onion and a pinch of salt in the olive oil over a medium-low flame until soft and translucent.

Use scissors to chop the tinned tomatoes. Peel the fresh ones by plunging them into boiling water for 60 seconds, then into cold water, at which point the skins should split and slip away easily. Chop the tomatoes roughly, separating away most of the seeds, then add to the pan, along with a good pinch of salt, chilli and a sprig of basil. Bring to the boil, then reduce to a simmer for 30 minutes. Allow to cool a little.

Cut the aubergine into 1cm cubes. Either rub with oil and bake in the oven (set to 200°C), or deep fry in a few centimetres of hot oil, then blot on kitchen paper and sprinkle with salt.

Bring a large pan of water to the boil, add salt, stir, then add the anelli and cook until al dente. Drain.

Mix the pasta with the sauce, aubergine, half the Parmesan and a few grinds of black pepper.

Butter the tin, then dust carefully with breadcrumbs. Half fill the tin with pasta and sauce, then make a layer of mozzarella or scamorza, pressing them into the pasta. Arrange a few leaves of basil on top and sprinkle over the remaining Parmesan, then cover with the rest of the pasta and press down firmly.

Dust the surface with more crumbs and dot with butter. Bake at 180°C in the middle of the oven for 30 minutes for a single *timballo* or 12 minutes for smaller ones, or until the crumbs are golden and the top is bubbling. Wait 10 minutes before inverting the large *timballo* on to a serving plate.

Anelli in zuppa brodosa di funghi e patate
Anelli in mushroom and potato broth
Serves 4

Like other *pastine*, anelli are often served in *brodo*, beef, chicken, vegetable (see page 13), maybe with the addition of parsley or grated Parmesan. I have also enjoyed them served in broth with peas (see quadrucci recipe, page 242) and in *brodo di cozze*, mussels. Another option is serving them in a brothy mushroom and potato soup, as far as I know traditional only in our house. Soothing, with mellow but insistent umami flavour, this is a recipe I love. The mushrooms and potato need to be small diced so as to fit on the spoon with the anelli.

20g dried porcini
4 tablespoons olive oil
1 small onion, peeled
and diced very
finely
300g cultivated
mushrooms, small
diced
200g potatoes, peeled
and small diced
salt
200g anelli, fregola,
ditalini, quadrucci,
maltagliati
grated Parmesan, to
serve

Soak the dried porcini in 200ml of warm water for 30 minutes. Lift the porcini out, chop and set aside. Strain the porcini liquid and make up to 1.2 litres with warm, salted water.

In a heavy-based soup pan or casserole, warm the oil and fry the onion gently until translucent. Add the diced mushrooms, potatoes, porcini and a pinch of salt and fry, stirring, until the mushrooms have softened and collapsed.

Add the porcini stock and a pinch of salt and bring to an almost boil, then reduce to a simmer for 15 minutes or until the vegetables are tender. Taste for salt.

Bring back to the boil, add the anelli and cook until al dente. Serve, passing round grated Parmesan.

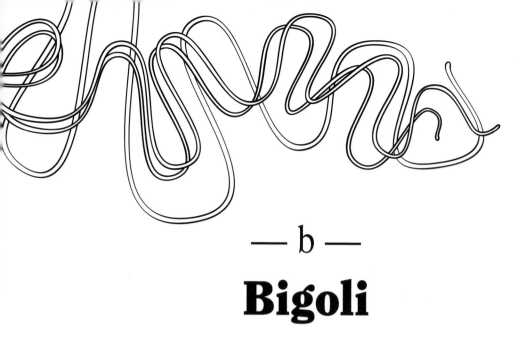

— b —

Bigoli

Maybe you pulled the packet of pasta off the shelf and from there decided the sauce. Or was it the idea of sauce that came first, and from there you settled on the shape? Perhaps the craving for a shape and sauce arrived together like an airdrop, or brainwave – *bigoli in salsa* – I want bigoli with a soft, slightly grey, sweet-salty mush of onion and anchovies. Whatever it was, the next step is to put the water on.

1. Get the pan out and – I know this is going to sound pretentious, or annoying, or both, so apologies in advance **– remember that cooking pasta is an everyday art.** What I mean is that like any art, cooking pasta is a skill acquired by experience, study and observation, and it is ongoing. I learn every time, when I make penne with cheese for the third time in four days for my picky child, or assemble an epic lasagna. As with any art, there is no place for snobbery. Sadly there is plenty, which is a shame because it gets in the way of the most democratic and generous food there is, and lunch.

2. While the suggestion that water for cooking pasta should

be as salty as the Mediterranean Sea is evocative, it is also a question! How salty is the sea? Answer – salty, you wouldn't want to swallow even a mouthful of it. How salty is that? A formula is more useful. People who cook pasta well use the formula, even if it looks as if they are freewheeling, **1 litre of boiling water and 10g of coarse salt (5g of fine) for every 100g of pasta.** I find it useful to have a pasta pan so familiar I know the water levels for 3, 4 and 5 litres, and a spoon that holds 10g of coarse salt. If as a rule you cook a 500g packet of pasta it is not a bad idea to weigh out 50g of coarse salt as an example, then stare at it. Be prepared, some people will think you are trying to kill them if they see you carry 5 spoonfuls between salt pot and pan, and they will also think you are using too much water, therefore trying to destroy the planet. Reassure them you are not, that there is science in this ratio, that pasta doesn't contain salt so obtains it during cooking, which is essential to flavour. Pasta knows exactly what it is doing, and only absorbs as much as it needs.

3. You've added the salt, stirred and the water is at a rolling boil. **Add the pasta and stir.** In the case of long shapes this means allowing the strands to fan out like a peacock's tail, then, as they start to soften and sink, use the back of a wooden spoon to ease them into the water, and stir. Stir a couple of times more during cooking to prevent sticking.

4. **Start your timer or glance at the clock when the water comes back to a rolling boil,** as that is the start of cooking. I set my timer for 2 minutes before the end of the recommended cooking time on the packet. This allows

plenty of time for manoeuvring, to taste and judge the level of doneness, to lift the pasta out if cooking is going to be completed in with the sauce.

5. **Al dente,** literally 'to the tooth', or bite, the descriptor for how pasta 'should' feel when cooked, firm and with slight resistance, although not chalky. There is a scale of al dente, and where you sit on it is up to you. Timings on pasta packets are usually quite good, but I always taste, also because I am trying to find a middle point between the al dente I like and the slightly more extreme al dente my partner likes.

6. I tend not to think of it as draining pasta, **rather, three ways of getting the pasta out of the water.** Because most of the time I don't drain, but scoop or lift pasta out of the cooking water with **1 – a spider sieve, 2 – a pair of tongs** and put it directly into the sauce. If I drain, I save a big cup of cooking water, then drain into **3 – a colander in the sink.** In the case of bigoli and salsa, use tongs to lift it straight into the salsa, either in a bowl, or straight into the pan.

Bigoli is a shape typical of the Veneto region. First mentioned in a twelfth-century rhyme, bigoli was a long pasta made from a mix of hard and soft flours, often with a proportion of wholemeal, which is why it was sometimes labelled a poor man's pasta. It was in 1604 that a pasta maker called Bartolomio Veronese registered his invention, a *torcio bigolaro* or *il bigolaro*. Clamped to a table or a stool, *il bigolaro,* with its press, cylinder and die, produced long, 2mm thick strings, with a rough sauce-catching texture – *bigoli al torcio.* Bigoli is sometimes referred to as wholemeal spaghetti, which it is, only not like that, its flavour and porous texture quite different. Factory-made bigoli is tamer than home-made or artisan bigoli, but it still retains a defining bite.

Bigoli is married to one sauce, which is simply referred to as salsa, everyone knowing that means onion and anchovy, maybe tuna, cooked slowly into an almost cream. *Bigoli in salsa* is the focus of my many cravings and the answer to the question, what shall we have for lunch? Perfect! Grab 2 onions and a tin of anchovies. Put the water on, when it boils add salt, stir and *butta la pasta*, throw the pasta (in the pan).

A note about anchovies

Italians have 32 ways to say anchovy. Almost three dozen names (many in dialect) for this small, slender fish with silvery sides, firm flesh and no chin. Even though they swim numerously in the Mediterranean, Indian and Pacific oceans, anchovies remain rare for many because they are so fragile, deteriorating quickly out of water. It is a consolation that as wonderful as fresh anchovies taste, they are even better preserved. Packing anchovies under salt, *acciughe sotto sale*, to cure them has been common practice in Italy since the ancient Romans, a way of preserving an otherwise ethereal fish, the by-product of which was a fermented fish sauce called garum. They are processed quickly, decapitated (but not gutted and boned) and layered with coarse salt. Salting changes the nature of the flesh completely, transforming it from soft and fragile to firm and taut, like soft leather, and the flavour from gentle with a slight bitterness to rich, salty and searing, making it both the greatest ingredient and the deepest seasoner.

To prepare salted anchovies for eating you need to brush away the salt, rinse and then open them out like a butterfly in order to ease away the bone. Once boned, blot, lay in a shallow dish, cover with olive oil and use within 3 days. A faff, but you are rewarded with fat, pink fillets of a quality and flavour usually found in only the most expensive tins.

Tins of anchovies with a key and roll-back top and tiny jars are simply anchovies cured in salt that have been prepared and covered in oil, making them ready to eat. Quality varies dramatically, as does cost. It is worth buying anchovies in olive oil, but if this isn't possible, pour the vegetable oil away, replace it with your own fresh olive oil and leave them to sit for a while.

Bigoli in salsa
Bigoli with onion and anchovy
Serves 4

In my experience recipes often underestimate the time it takes to cook down the onion, which is anything from 15 to 30 minutes, with the assistance of a spoonful of hot water every now and then. The aim is not to brown, or even colour the onions, but to cook them until they are so soft they break down into a soft mush or cream. Pour yourself a glass of wine, pick your podcast. Bigoli is the classic shape but spaghetti, spaghettoni, linguine and bucatini work too.

3 salt-packed anchovies or 6–8 oil-preserved anchovies
2 onions (200g weight)
6–8 tablespoons olive oil
salt and freshly ground black pepper
400g bigoli, spaghetti, spaghettoni, linguine or bucatini

If you are using salt-packed anchovies, clean as noted on page 27; if they are not in olive oil, blot the oil-packed ones. Bring a pan of water to the boil for the pasta.

Peel and halve the onions and finely slice lengthwise into slender crescents. Put the onions, olive oil and a pinch of salt into a frying pan over a medium-low heat and cook slowly for 15–30 minutes, stirring and adding a bit of hot water every now and then.

Add the anchovies, and cook, stirring, over a low heat so they disintegrate and the mush is now grey-brown. Add a few grinds of pepper. Cook the bigoli until al dente, then use tongs to lift the pasta out of the water, or drain, and either toss directly in the pan, or in a bowl, and serve immediately.

Bigoli in salsa – a variation with tuna and peas. Once the onion is soft, and along with the anchovies, add 100g of tuna, 100g of peas and a handful of finely chopped fresh parsley.

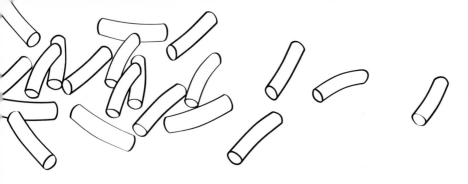

— b —

Brichetti

A rare shape, also a common one. Rare in that you only really find brichetti in and around Genoa, where it shares a dialect name and form with matchsticks. Common in that you can make something incredibly similar by breaking spaghetti. And if anyone ever suggests that it isn't acceptable to break spaghetti, gently point them in the direction of any of the 1,064 regional *minestra* recipes that call for spaghetti spezzati, that is, broken or snapped. Or maybe just change the subject.

And brichetti is really just an excuse to write about minestrone, because at this point in the alphabet there should be a big pan of soup.

Every region of Italy has at least one typical minestrone. A big soup, probably with beans then thickened with pasta, rice or bread, and adapted by every person who makes it. The one on the next page from Genoa, capital of the crescent-shaped north-west region of Liguria, is particularly good and generous. It does feel like soup made backwards. While most minestrone are like cautious swimmers entering the sea, a steady march of ingredients into the pan, this is a fling, all the diced vegetables plunged straight into boiling water, later joined by pasta and then right at the end, the oil and seasoning in the form of a pounded green sauce. It was Genovese merchant ships that carried the first dried pasta, made by the Arabs in Sicily, all over the Mediterranean and to Genoa, which became a cradle of pasta making. Apparently brichetti were made specifically for *minestrone alla genovese,* short strands of a story, in a spoon, for lunch.

Minestrone

Serves 4

A steady march into the pan, but not a fixed one. An immutable plan is never a good idea with soup, there are too many variables (not least tomatoes). My neighbour describes it as 'the cook's itch' – 'keep itching', she reminds me, that is tasting, tweaking as you like. You probably already know the Parmesan rind trick, that last half inch of hard cheese on the rind softens in the soup and as it does adds flavour. Minestrone is always better the next day.

2 red onions, peeled and diced
2 carrots, peeled and diced
2 sticks of celery, diced
4 tablespoons extra virgin olive oil
40g butter or pancetta
salt
200g potatoes, peeled and diced
300g other vegetables: fennel/peas/turnip/ artichoke heart/ leek/pumpkin
200g Savoy cabbage or kale
120g tinned plum or fresh tomatoes (around ½ a tin)
a large Parmesan rind
400g cooked beans, borlotti or cannellini
200g brichetti, broken spaghetti, ditalini, quadrucci, broken tagliatelle

In a large heavy-based pan, over a medium-low heat, gently fry the onions, carrots and celery in the olive oil and butter (or pancetta) with a pinch of salt, stirring every now and then, for about 8 minutes, or until soft and fragrant.

Add the potatoes to the pan, stir and cook for 5 minutes. Chop the other vegetables, shred the cabbage/kale, add all these to the pan and cook for another 5 minutes. Add the tinned tomatoes (resist the urge to put in more than half a tin) and Parmesan rind, stir, then add 2 litres of water or bean cooking broth, cover and leave to simmer gently for 1½ hours.

Add the beans. Stir and cook for another 30 minutes. If you find the minestrone is looking a little too thick, or dry, add a little more water. Cooking can be paused at this point.

I add the pasta directly to the minestrone, bring it back to the boil and cook for a further 10 minutes, which means keeping an eye on it and, if it looks too dense, adding a little more salted warm water. Pasta can also be cooked separately and added to the soup, or some of it if you are keeping half until the next day.

A note about extra virgin olive oil
While butter, pork fat, and other oils play a part, extra virgin olive oil is the foundation of my cooking, maybe the most important ingredient and a big part of not a very big budget. While special bottles for occasional use are wonderful (especially in October and November when the olive oil is pressed), I am more interested in having decent, fragrant, flavourful everyday extra virgin olive oil I can use raw and for cooking – ignore all myths about it not being suitable, it is ideal, if you don't heat past smoking point. It is worth shopping around for extra virgin olive oil, buying from a particular maker if you can, also in bulk, then keeping the can in a cupboard and decanting into a dark bottle with a stainless steel pourer.

Minestrone alla genovese
Minestrone soup from Genoa
Serves 4

The fact there is no initial fry and everything is simply boiled produces a brothy soup and vegetable consistency that can be disconcerting the first time you make it. I urge you to try though, for the simple and substantial taste, for another approach to minestrone making, one I become more and more fond of, especially in summer. Traditionally this was a farmer's breakfast, so made the night before, packed up in order to be taken out into the fields and eaten cold. These days it is served hot, although generally not too hot. I think a 10-minute rest before serving is best, which gives it time to thicken as the pasta swells, and allows the flavours to firm up. Half the pesto of basil, garlic, pine nuts, cheese and anchovies should be stirred in just before it comes to the table so the scent is a lively fanfare of sorts. The rest blobbed on each serving, along with a swirl of your best-tasting olive oil.

2 courgettes, sliced in rounds
2 sticks of celery, strings pulled away, sliced
1 large onion, peeled and sliced
1 small cabbage, halved and sliced into strips
100g green beans, trimmed and each cut in 3
1 medium potato, peeled and diced
2 tomatoes, peeled and roughly chopped
200g fresh borlotti or cannellini beans (or 250g cooked by you or tinned)
salt and black pepper
2 cloves of garlic
25g pine nuts
4 anchovies (optional)
50g fresh basil leaves
8 tablespoons olive oil
40g grated pecorino or Parmesan, or a mix
300g brichetti, broken spaghetti, ditalini, quadrucci, broken tagliatelle

Bring 2 litres of water to the boil, add salt and then add all the vegetables prepared – courgettes, celery, onion, cabbage, green beans, potato, tomatoes, fresh borlotti beans if you are using them and salt. Bring to the boil, then reduce to a simmer, cover and cook for an hour, adding the cooked beans after 30 minutes.

Meanwhile make the pesto by blending first the garlic, pine nuts and anchovies if you are using them, then two-thirds of the basil, then the oil and cheese – this can be done in a food processor or a mortar with a pestle (which is traditional).

During the last 15 minutes of cooking time add the pasta, and cook until it is tender. Swirl in the remaining whole basil leaves, a few grinds of pepper and half the pesto just before coming to the table. Top each serving with a spoonful of the remaining pesto.

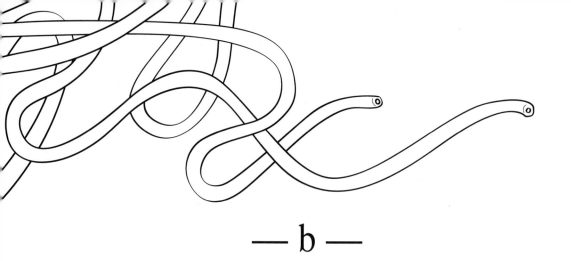

— b —

Bucatini

Bucato means pierced, which is exactly what bucatini is, a thick-spaghetti-like pasta with a hole running down its length. Its ancestors are the early, fresh pierced pastas (in Italian, *buco* means hole). Its modern form is a durum wheat and water factory-made dried shape. When cooked al dente, bucatini retains its shape surprisingly well: you *can* wind it around your fork, but it may well break loose, which is why it is known as unmanned-hose pasta in our house, for its habit of flicking back at you unexpectedly. Bucatini is a popular shape all over the South, but I know it best here in my adopted city of Rome and my partner's home town of Gela, in Sicily.

The *trattoria* that inhabits the bottom, left-hand corner of our building is called Il Bucatino, leaving no doubt as to a shape they like to serve. Like many *trattorie* in Rome it is run by a family whose roots are in neighbouring Abruzzo, a rugged and green region bookended by mountains and sea, and defined by good food. It makes sense that it was shepherds, high in the mountainous hinterland between Abruzzo and Lazio, who first fried guanciale then tossed it with pasta and pecorino cheese to make what is now known as *gricia*. It was much later, when an immigrant from the Americas arrived and settled, that *gricia* (and many other dishes to boot) went from *bianca* (white) to *rossa* (red) and this variation became known as *amatriciana*, named for the historic town tragically scarred by earthquakes. Il Bucatino's kitchen window opens on to a communal courtyard which acts like a vortex and spins the sound of the dishes being sprayed clean, snappish exchanges between waiters and cooks, and the scent of guanciale in a hot pan through the vent above our front door. Both *bucatini all'amatriciana* and *bucatini alla gricia* are served in high-sided, fluted white bowls. Il Bucatino also provides bibs, and it isn't some novelty for tourists, but a precaution for anyone who knows.

A note about Parmesan and pecorino

Parmesan, Parmigiano-Reggiano, is a cow's milk cheese that takes its name from the cities of Parma and Reggio Emilia, both in Italy's Emilia-Romagna region. Its ancestor, Grana Padano, which means granular cheese made in the Po valley, can be dated back to 1136 and the abbey of Chiaravalle near Milan and its industrious monks. There is no doubt the evolution of Parmigiano is extraordinary, that in the hands of long-established makers and now a large workforce of Sikhs from Punjab it has become a superstar cheese although it wasn't until the second half of the twentieth century that it was diffused all over Italy. It is rich, ripe and rounded, its grain like crystal shards that take on more definition as they age, 18, 24, 36, 48, 60, 72 months and beyond. There is a galaxy of Parmigiano-Reggiano worth exploring with a good guide, a local deli or the comprehensive online database of the Consorzio del Formaggio Parmigiano-Reggiano. For the purpose of this book, though, I suggest you look for Parmigiano-Reggiano DOP (in English Protected Designation of Origin, which protects its integrity and production) that is at least 24 months old. **Grana** or **Grana Padano** is an alternative to Parmesan. It is not a lesser cheese, just different, and often less expensive as it is sold younger. Look for Grana DOP that is at least 12 months old.

Pecorino simply means sheep's milk cheese and there are hundreds of varieties from all over Italy, the ancestors of which are some of the most ancient cheeses. In this book, however, I mostly refer to **pecorino romano,** sharp, salty, undeniably sheepish, also persistent, ringing in your mouth and stinging the tiny cut on your tongue long after the craggy crumb has dissolved. Pecorino romano (90 per cent of which is made in Sardinia) can be a table cheese, especially when young (5 months), but is mostly considered a grating cheese: its piquant saltiness means it is a great seasoning and melts accommodatingly, which is why it is indispensable in the quartet of classic Roman pasta, *amatriciana, gricia, cacio e pepe* and *carbonara*. Again it is worth exploring pecorino with a good guide. But for the sake of this book, look for pecorino Romano DOP that is 8 months old.

Grating. The painful truth is the star side of the box grater is the best one. It produces fat crumbs that melt differently to those made by a microplane, and this is particularly important when the crumbs are an ingredient in, say, *cacio e pepe*. There are strong opinions about where you should and shouldn't put grated Parmesan and pecorino, which like most strong opinions are turned on their head by other strong opinions. More than having strong opinions I am simply a fan of both and I know I use them too often, that I should pause, ask myself if olive oil and a pinch of red chilli flakes might work better. Often Parmesan and pecorino are tossed along with the sauce so they help with the binding. And of course if you can't get Parmesan or pecorino, use whatever cheese you have/enjoy.

Bucatini all'amatriciana
Bucatini with tomato, guanciale and pecorino Romano
Serves 4

There are strong opinions about this Roman dish. I trust those of Alessandro Venturi, a young Roman chef living in York, where he serves some of the best Roman food you could hope to eat from his food truck. His method includes a couple more steps, but you are rewarded for the extra work. You can use tinned tomatoes (many prefer them) but I like the brightness of fresh tomatoes for this sauce studded with pork, enriched and sharpened by pecorino cheese. A note about shapes – though this is the bucatini chapter, the shape used with this sauce in the town of Amatrice is spaghetti, while rigatoni is also popular, as are a fresh dragged gnocchi ricci and potato gnocchi (see pages 138 and 132).

200g guanciale, or pancetta and a little olive oil
50ml white wine
500g ripe tomatoes, peeled and roughly chopped, or a tin of peeled plum tomatoes, chopped
a pinch of red chilli flakes
400g bucatini, or spaghetti/rigatoni, gnocchi ricci or potato gnocchi
120g pecorino (ideally Romano)

Bring a large pan of water to the boil for the pasta.

Cut the guanciale or pancetta into 3mm thick/2cm long batons. In a large frying pan, over a medium-low heat, fry the guanciale at a gentle sizzle until it renders its fat and is just starting to turn golden and crisp at the edges. Using a slotted spoon, lift the guanciale on to a plate and tip the fat into a bowl.

Put the empty pan back on the heat, add a little white wine to deglaze – which will sizzle – then add half the guanciale and 6 tablespoons of guanciale fat, then the tomatoes and chilli flakes. Bring to just before a boil, then reduce to a simmer for 20 minutes, or until it thickens into a rich sauce. Meanwhile cook the pasta until al dente.

You need plenty of space to mix properly, so if the pan isn't big enough use a big, wide, warm bowl. Lift the pasta directly on to the sauce with a spider sieve or forked spoon, add two-thirds of the pecorino and then either toss or better still jolt the pan/bowl so the underneath pasta comes up as a wave and the sauce, starch and cheese come together. Divide between serving dishes, topping each serving with more cheese and some of the crispy guanciale.

Bucatini alla gricia
Bucatini with guanciale and pecorino Romano
Serves 4

Also known as *amatriciana bianca* (white *amatriciana*) for its lack of tomato, *gricia* is a haiku of ingredients and demonstration of guanciale at work, how its rendered fat forms a silky coat to which the grated pecorino clings, forming a sauce on the surface of the pasta. Suggesting something other than bucatini as the pasta shape would be like going into the Adidas shop and asking the way to Nike. (That said, I also like rigatoni, mezze maniche and spaghetti.) *Gricia* demands a glass or two of white wine.

200g guanciale, or 200g pancetta plus 2 tablespoons olive oil
salt and black pepper
400g pasta – bucatini, rigatoni, spaghetti, penne, mezze maniche
120g pecorino Romano, grated

Cut the guanciale or pancetta into 3mm thick/1cm long strips. Bring a large pan of water to the boil, add salt, stir, add pasta, stir, and cook until al dente.

While the pasta cooks, in a spacious frying pan, over a medium-low heat, fry the guanciale (or pancetta with olive oil) gently so it renders its plentiful fat and is just starting to crisp at the edges.

Once the pasta is ready, lift it directly into the hot guanciale pan and toss. Pull from the heat and add two-thirds of the cheese, a few grinds of pepper and toss and swish again – better still, jolt the pan so that the underneath pasta comes up as a wave, so everything comes together. Divide between bowls and top with the remaining cheese and plenty of freshly ground black pepper.

*Given the choice I would choose rigatoni for my *gricia*, but then I would choose rigatoni over most shapes.

A note about guanciale and pancetta

Like pepper-dusted decorations, the lozenges the size of small loaves hanging in Italian *salumerie* or delis are **guanciale**, whole pig cheeks cured in salt. Look at a cross-section and you will see guanciale is mostly fat, streaked with pink meat. But what gorgeous, seasoned fat! That renders into sweet, rounded melted fat and a nugget of meat. Purists are adamant that only guanciale will do for certain dishes, it is just a shame that fanaticism and one-upmanship so often get in the way of simply saying 'try this', because it is a marvellous ingredient, seasoning, binding, giving richness, bringing everything together. **Pancetta** is cured pork belly, which comes as flat (*tesa*) and rolled (*arrotolata*) pieces, or ready diced in boxes. Pancetta is an even mix of fat and cured meat, again deeply seasoned, although not as sweet as guanciale. As we know, though, fat is flavour and pancetta doesn't render as much, which is why it is sometimes suggested that you add a little olive oil to the pan when you fry pancetta.

Bucatini con i broccoli arriminati
Bucatini with cauliflower, saffron and anchovies
Serves 4

The method for this recipe will come up again in the book, the vegetable cooked until tender in water, drained and then dragged around a frying pan containing olive oil and, on this occasion, anchovies, onion and saffron, pine nuts and currants. Currants, by the way, are like teeny, seedy and almost tannic bites, completely different from raisins or sultanas which are the reason many people are put off at the mention of dried fruits in savoury food. Again a big pan is useful here, and using the starchy pasta cooking water as an ingredient to loosen the sauce. The breadcrumbs are essential for contrast and crunch against the soft sauce and wayward bucatini.

1 large
    cauliflower
8 tablespoons
    olive oil
1 onion, peeled
    and sliced
salt
4 anchovy fillets
30g currants
30g pine nuts
5 saffron strands
400g bucatini, or
    casarecce,
    mezze
    maniche,
    paccheri,
    fusilli
50g breadcrumbs

Trim the tougher outside leaves from the cauliflower, saving the tender ones, and cut away the base. Break into large florets and cook along with the leaves in well-salted boiling water until tender. Lift from the water with a slotted spoon and set aside, keeping the water for the pasta.

In a large frying pan, over a medium-low flame, warm 6 tablespoons of the olive oil and the onion with a pinch of salt, stirring until the onion is soft. Add the anchovies, currants and pine nuts and cook for a minute more.

Break the florets into smaller ones, chop any leaves into manageable pieces and add to the onion pan, stir for a minute, then add 2 ladles of the cauliflower cooking water and allow to simmer for 5 minutes. Dissolve the saffron in a little cauliflower water and add during the last minute, then pull off the heat and allow it to sit – it should be soft with just a little liquid.

Bring the cauliflower water back to the boil, add the pasta and cook until al dente.

Meanwhile in another pan, toast the breadcrumbs in 2 tablespoons of olive oil, with a pinch of salt, until golden brown and smelling like digestive biscuits. Put the cauliflower back on the heat to warm through, adding some pasta cooking water if it seems at all dry.

When the pasta is al dente, drain or lift directly into the cauliflower pan and toss and swish so the ingredients come together. Divide between plates and top with the toasted crumbs.

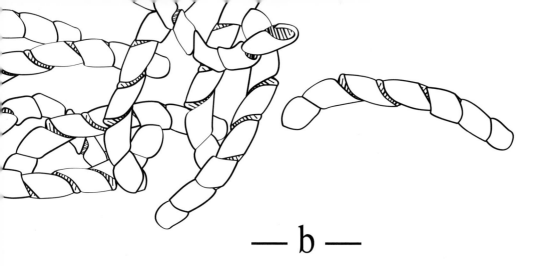

— b —

Busiate

Busiate is a long, twisting pasta that is pierced down the middle. Pasta's history is a long, twisting story that begins with wheat. A complicated story too, and a nebulous one, even for historians and archaeologists. But most of all it is a fascinating story, a page-turner even, especially in the hands of Giuseppe Prezzolini, Emilio Sereni, Silvano Serventi and Françoise Sabban, Oretta Zanini de Vita and Massimo Montanari, whose work I hope this book will lead you to. I am not a historian or a scholar. I am also aware of my limits and apologize in advance to historians and scholars for the following wrestled telling of the story and epic journey of wild grain to the pasta shapes we cook and eat every day, spaghetti with clams with a pinch of epic.

If the story of pasta is the story of the domestication of wheat, it begins 12,000 years ago, on the plateaux of the Near and Middle East, the so-called Fertile Crescent, particularly – and this is something I remember from school – the ancient land of Mesopotamia. It is here Sumerians are thought to have first domesticated the wild seeds of eight neolithic founder crops – barley, lentil, pea, chickpea, bitter vetch, flax, emmer wheat, einkorn wheat – ingredients for a heroic-sounding soup, and the beginning of true agriculture. From this nexus, agriculture moved, each area of the world developing its grain of choice, rice in Asia, corn in America, sorghum on the African continent and wheat in the Mediterranean. The French historian Fernand Braudel defines these as the 'plants of civilization'. New societies were constructed around the chosen one, agriculture, economy, exchange, politics, culture, ritual, city and civilization built around grains.

The Polish-Swiss botanist Adam Maurizio observed that the story of pasta must be written in parallel with the story of the consumption of cereals. Trusting Maurizio, we should note the consumption of cereals has four stages. The first is that it is consumed like any other wild fruit or berry, raw. The second is that it is toasted or boiled. The third is that it is milled. The fourth is that the milled cereal is kneaded with water, creating a mass of dough that can be shaped and cooked. Archaeological evidence shows all four of these stages in prehistory. But cooked to what? Bread? Pasta? Both?

There is evidence wheat has been cultivated in Italy, in particular Puglia, Sicily and Abruzzo, since 6500 BC. To understand the evolution and mysterious channels of Maurizio's four stages in Italy – who first toasted grains, who boiled grain into a soupy pulp, who made bread and who made pasta – is to understand the various indigenous populations, as well as their interactions with other civilizations, Sumerians, Phoenicians, Greeks, Arabs, Vikings, Normans, Bourbons, looking for trade or conquest of new territory. In short, to wrestle with the history of Italy (the divisions of which looked nothing like they do now) and Italy in relation to the world. A nice reminder we are all connected, a mind-boggling task. And of course history was written by those who wrote, which was very few. Most food, prepared by illiterate people (the majority), by definition lacks any sort of documentation. Archaeologists can provide evidence of toasted grains, pots used to boil, mills and baking stones, murals on the walls of Etruscan tombs, but words are words, and with them we encounter minefields of meaning.

Happily, food historians have negotiated (and debated) the minefields of meaning to find a circle of identity around a food called *tracta*, mentioned in ancient Greek and Roman texts, also drawing on sources from the Babylonian and Jerusalem Talmuds and a food called *triqta*. They conclude that *tracta* can be interpreted as flour, either hard or soft wheat, mixed with water to form an early form of pasta, either soft or dried, which could be boiled in water or fried, used in layers like modern lasagne, broken into small pieces to thicken liquid foods, or crumbled into sauces. As cooks and eaters we recognize all these things, and have more evidence that things are easier to understand when the end point is lunch.

Following *tracta* we meet the Greek *làganon* / Roman *lagana*, which derives from *lasanon* and *lasanum*, Greek and Latin words for pots. Lagana may or may not be precisely the same thing as *tracta*, but is certainly extremely similar, and so another early pasta. An important piece of the jigsaw is the Roman poet Horace, who lived from 65 BC to 8 BC and wrote that after wandering round the Roman Forum one night, he grew tired and went home to a bowl of *porri et ciceris laganique catinum*, leeks, chickpeas and *lagana*. Tempting, and an important testimony of *lagana*/pasta as a common food.

While *lagana* was evolving with the Greeks and Romans, the Arabs were evolving and perfecting the art of drying their own form of pasta, in strings. Again historians return to the Babylonian and Jerusalem Talmuds, and mention of a food called *itryya*, also the Yiddish *vrimzliash*. What we know is that between 902 and 1165 during the overlapping Arab and Norman rule of Sicily the art of drying pasta, *tria*, was evolved and industrious. We have the enchanting description by the Arab geographer Al-Idrisi in 1154 as part of a book documenting the geography and rituals of the island he authored for Sicily's then Norman king, Roger II.

'In Sicily there is a town called Trabia, an enchanted place endowed with perennial waters and mills. In this town they make a food in the form of strings in quantities such as to supply in addition to the towns of Calabria, those of Muslim and Christian territories.'

And what do we take from all this? In the words of Corrado Barberis, the origin of pasta is multitudinous, it isn't Italian, or Greek, or Arab, or Jewish, but all of them, with the metamorphosis in Italy, which provided the necessary conditions. The physical evolution of pasta, though, can be looked at simply. Wheat was milled into flour and mixed with liquid to make a big lump, a *gnocco*, from which came parents *lagana* and *tria*, who between them gave birth to hundreds of children. This book is about some of them.

Enter busiate, born in Sicily around 1000 AD, amidst the overlapping Arab

and Norman rule of Sicily, which means it has characteristics of both parents, but especially the pierced pastas of the Arabs. It is considered the oldest Sicilian home-made pasta, formed by rolling a rope of dough about 10cm long and then pressing a *busa*, a stiff reed, into the dough and rolling the rope vigorously so the dough surrounds the reed, which is then slipped out, leaving a hollow tube. Busiate were eaten both fresh and dried, which made them ideal for transportation, as sailors' food but also as cargo, which is why they diffused, along with strings of dried pasta *itryya*, all over the Mediterranean so efficiently, most notably to Genoa, which was to become a centre of pasta production.

Busiate is still a homemade shape, one which varies according to the cook. At the Anna Tasca Lanza cooking school, for example, rather than a pierced rope busiate is more like a ringlet or a ribbon round a maypole. It is also a factory-made shape and one worth seeking out, the long spiral the most magnificent sauce-catcher imaginable, especially with *pesto trapanese,* or Sicilian *ragù* of pork and aubergine, scented with fennel seeds and a touch of epic.

Busiate al ragù bianco di maiale e melanzane e finocchio
White ragù with pork, aubergine and fennel
Serves 4

White as opposed to red *ragù* does not include tomatoes (although it is blushed, as so many Sicilian dishes are, with a spoonful of tomato concentrate). Pork and fennel seeds are a magical combination and busiate the shape that catches this delicate *ragù* best.

5 tablespoons olive oil
1 red onion, peeled
    and diced
250g ground pork
salt and black pepper
1 teaspoon fennel
    seeds
150ml white wine
1 teaspoon tomato
    concentrate,
    diluted in 100ml
    warm water or
    light stock
2 medium aubergines,
    cut into 2cm cubes
oil for frying
400g busiate, fusilli,
    cavatelli, radiatori,
    pici, linguine
fresh basil

In a frying pan, warm the olive oil and fry the onion over a medium-low heat until soft and translucent. Add the pork and season with salt, pepper and fennel seeds, then fry until the pork has lost all its pinkness.

Add the wine and the tomato concentrate dissolved in water/stock and reduce to a lively simmer for 40 minutes, or until the pork is cooked through and the sauce thickened and tasty.

Meanwhile, either rub the aubergine cubes with olive oil and bake until golden and tender, or fry in at least 5cm of hot oil until golden.

Bring a large pan of water to the boil for the pasta, salt, add pasta and cook until al dente. Add to the sauce, along with the aubergine and a handful of ripped basil.

Busiate con pesto trapanese
Busiate with basil, tomato and almond pesto
Serves 4

From the verb *pestare*, to pound (originally with a pestle in a mortar), pesto means a 'pestato' pounded sauce, the most famous of which is basil, pine nut, garlic, olive oil and pecorino *pesto alla genovese* (see page 318). Apparently this recipe is a result of homesick Genovese sailors moored in the Sicilian port of Trapani making their beloved pesto with what was available locally – almonds, basil, tomatoes. Trapanese has a looser consistency than Genovese pesto, and looks like green and red speckled tweed which clings to the spiral of busiate. I have given specific quantities as a guide, but it is an easygoing pesto that can, and should, be made by eye and taste. It doesn't contain cheese, but welcomes a grating of salted ricotta on top of the final dish.

350g ripe tomatoes
2 cloves of garlic
100g blanched
    almonds
60g fresh basil leaves
black peppercorns
salt
150ml olive oil
400g busiate, fusilli,
    cavatelli, radiatori,
    also spaghetti,
    linguine

If you want, peel the tomatoes by plunging them into boiling water for 60 seconds, then cold water, at which point the skins should split and slip away easily. Chop the tomatoes roughly, separating away most of the seeds and any tough bits.

In a food processor, blend the garlic, almonds, basil, 2 peppercorns and a pinch of salt until you get a rough paste. Add the oil and blitz, then add the tomatoes and blend again. The final texture depends very much on your taste.

If you're using a (large) pestle and mortar, first pound the garlic and pinch of salt, then add the basil and pound again. Add the oil bit by bit, rotating until the sauce is creamy. Stir in the tomatoes and pound again – quite how much depends on whether you want texture or a smooth sauce. Scrape into a large warm bowl or deep platter.

Bring a large pan of water to the boil for the pasta, salt, add pasta and cook until al dente. Add to the pesto, stir and serve, passing round salted ricotta.

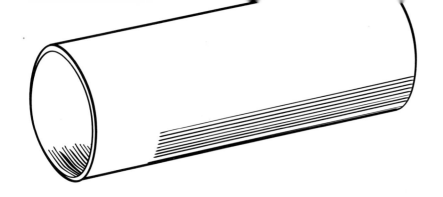

— C —

Cannelloni

As a child, I was sometimes given flour and water to play with as a distraction while Mum cooked. At first, combining the two haphazardly was enough, letting the mixture squelch through my fingers and swirling my hands through the sticky mess. Soon though, I learned; real satisfaction was to be gained by mixing enough of each to make a pliable dough every bit as satisfying as plasticine or putty. After pressing and pummelling I would pinch bits from the ball and roll them into worms, balls and rings for my fingers. I was making pasta.

As an adult I forgot this. Until the age of 35 I avoided making pasta. The story I told myself was it was complicated, ambitious and mysterious, that it required either shiny equipment or Italian DNA. I found evidence to back up my story, pictures of exquisite pasta made by chefs with sleek stainless steel counters and by agile grannies, a four-page description of the method, decided I preferred dried pasta and assumed making pasta meant trouble.

It took a morning with my friend Paola for my story to collapse. To be reminded that making pasta is essentially simple, that it is mixing enough flour and liquid to make a rough dough which is neither too sticky nor too dry, then practising, better still *playing*, in order to find the moves and pummels needed to transform the rough dough into a pliable one. Exactly what I had done instinctively aged 6.

Fresh pasta, two small words for a universe of shapes, many of which are child's play. Others that aren't. It is these more challenging shapes for which it is even more imperative that we remember our childish hands and head: the essential nature of pasta is simple. Take some flour and water, take some flour and eggs, combine, knead, rest, shape. Or go and buy some, this book is also about that.

~~~~~~~~~~~~~~~~~~~~~~~~~~~~~~~~~~~~~~~

To make fresh egg pasta
This is the foundation recipe for a fresh egg pasta dough, suitable for all the fresh egg pasta recipes in this book – cannelloni, cappellacci, capelli d'angelo, fettuccine, pappardelle, quadrucci, tagliatelle, tagliolini, lasagne, ravioli, tortellini. I might mention variations in the relevant chapters, but for now, this is it. The first time you make this, treat it as a game. Notice how the egg and flour comes together, how dry and scraggy it feels to start but how it softens as you knead. Weather, humidity, the flour, age of eggs and how dry your hands are all play a huge part in making pasta, the first step is to notice. Also identify your work-spot, keeping in mind you need a kneading area (wood is ideal because the surface friction does some of the work) and also a spot to spread out/ hang the rolled sheets.

The proportions are 2:1, with natural variations. For every 100g of soft white flour (00 or 0) you need 1 medium egg, 53–58g. So if you are making pasta for 4, you need 400g of flour and 4 eggs. The traditional way to work is on a wooden board – making a mountain of flour then turning it into a volcano by swirling a crater in the centre with your fist and breaking the eggs into it. You can also work in a bowl, or in a food processor. Back with the crater, use a fork to break the egg yolks and whisk them gently before starting to incorporate the flour by knocking it from the inside edges of the crater and into the eggs. Once you have added enough flour that the eggs no longer run away, you can abandon the fork for hands (or one hand and a dough scraper) and continue to mix, bringing the flour and eggs into a soft scraggy ball.

Do not be tempted to add any more liquid at this point – put some music on, plant your feet firmly, and start kneading. How you knead is up to you – *whatever works*. I like using the heel of my hand to bring the bottom of the dough up and over and then rotate in a sort of rocking roll, until the dough starts to soften and smooth out – timings vary but this will take at least 5 minutes. If after kneading for a few minutes the ball is still looking dry or flaky, flick a few (just a few) drops of water on to the board then knead them into the dough – the aim is a smooth, firm but pliable dough with an almost talcum-like silkiness to touch. Once you are happy, leave the dough to rest, covered by a cloth, cling film or upturned bowl for at least 30 minutes otherwise it will not relax and will keep bouncing back when you roll.

We will come to hand rolling later – for now the machine. Clamp it to the work surface and set it to the widest setting. Cut the dough into four, take a quarter and put the other three back under the bowl. Flatten the first lump of dough into a patty and send it through the rollers. Then fold the strip of dough like an envelope and pass it through again, envelope again, then pass again. It will be the size of a small book.

Set the machine at two and pass the dough through, but this time without folding, allowing it to come out of the machine and settle in folds, then extend it. Do the same with the third setting, and so on until you have rolled it through all the settings and have a long strip, which you can cut to make it more manageable. If it feels sticky, dust with flour. Repeat with all the other lumps of pasta. While there is no need to rush, the swifter you are the less chance there is of it drying out. How you cut the sheets depends on the shape you are making.

~~~~~~~~~~~~~~~~~~~~~~~~~~~~~~~~~~~~~

C is for cannelloni. From the word *canna*, cane or tube, plus the suffix *-oni* signifying largeness, so big tubes made from sheets of pasta. While its ancestor is clearly those first sheets of lagane and lasagne, cannelloni is a relatively recent shape. There are rare mentions in eighteenth-century cookbooks, but even then it isn't entirely clear if the cannelloni is one we would recognize now. Twentieth-century post-war cookbooks, such as Ada Boni's 1929 *Il talismano della felicità*, however, are full of tubes, almost every region having a version, often as a feast-day recipe.

I have included three recipes in this section. The first is from the northern region of Piemonte, each tube stuffed with spinach and pork. The second from Sorrento, just down the coast from Naples, and the tubes are filled with mozzarella and ricotta. The third from Lazio with a meat stuffing. For all three you can make your own pasta, buy sheets of lasagne or use dried cannelloni tubes, the preparation of which I have singled out for the third version. As the author, I am obliged to love everything. But in the case of cannelloni I am also an enthusiast, of its satisfying, easy-going form and neat portioning; of how each bite is an open-ended parcel; and of how it looks in the middle of the table.

Cannelloni alla piemontese
Cannelloni with pork, spinach and Parmesan
Serves 4

For this cut your fresh egg pasta into 12 sheets, each 20 × 10cm. The dish needs to be big enough to contain 12 rolls in a single layer.

300g spinach
400g roast pork or
    veal
100g cooked ham
2 eggs
100g Parmesan,
    grated
salt and black pepper
grated nutmeg
a batch of fresh egg
    pasta (see page 51),
    cut into 12 sheets,
    each 20 × 10cm
butter for dish

For the béchamel
500ml milk
50g butter
50g flour

Wash the spinach, discarding any discoloured or very tough stems. Lift it, dripping wet, into a pan and wilt down over a medium-low heat – keep turning it so it doesn't burn. Drain thoroughly and chop.

Using a sharp knife, mince both meats as finely as possible and then add the spinach and mince again. This can also be done in a food processor, but pulse rather than blend – you want things minced and well combined, but still with texture.

Put the meat and spinach into a bowl and add the eggs, half the cheese, salt, pepper and nutmeg and mix thoroughly.

Make the béchamel (see page 58).

Bring a large pan of salted water to the boil and prepare a large bowl of cold water. Drop the pasta sheets a few sheets at a time into the boiling water, leave for 1 minute, lift from the pan into the cold water for 20 seconds, then lay on clean tea towels.

To roll the cannelloni, put a heaped spoonful of the filling at the top of the longer edge of each sheet and then roll closed.

Smear the baking dish with butter, then arrange the cannelloni on top, pour over the béchamel, and sprinkle with the rest of the grated Parmesan. Bake at 200°C for 30 minutes.

Cannelloni alla sorrentina
Cannelloni in the Sorrento style
Serves 4

A three-cheese filling of mozzarella, ricotta and Parmesan is matched with tomato and basil sauce here. Like all assembled pasta dishes destined for the oven, this one benefits from a rest – two actually. The first when you have shaped the cannelloni, for at least 2 hours, or overnight. The second after it is baked, for at least 30 minutes, so the flavours settle.

For this cut your fresh egg pasta into 12 sheets, each 20 × 10cm. The dish needs to be big enough to contain 12 rolls in a single layer (or you can use two dishes). For a dried tube alternative see page 58.

a batch of fresh egg pasta (see page 51), cut into 12 sheets, each 20 × 10cm

For the sauce
6 tablespoons olive oil
2 cloves of garlic
a pinch of red chilli flakes
800g peeled tomatoes, fresh or tinned, chopped
a few fresh basil leaves
salt and black pepper

For the filling
300g ricotta, drained
2 eggs
200g mozzarella, drained overnight and diced
3 heaped tablespoons chopped fresh flat-leaf parsley
60g Parmesan, grated, plus extra for on top
a few fresh basil leaves
salt and black pepper
grated nutmeg

Sauce – in a large, deep frying pan, warm the olive oil, garlic and chilli. Once the garlic is fragrant, add the tomatoes, basil and a pinch of salt. Use the back of a wooden spoon to break the tomatoes up. Allow to simmer for 15 minutes.

Filling – in a large bowl mash the ricotta and then beat in the eggs. Add the mozzarella, parsley and Parmesan and season with salt, pepper and nutmeg to taste.

Bring a large pan of salted water to the boil and prepare a large bowl of cold water. Drop the sheets a few at a time into the boiling water, leave for 1 minute, lift from the pan into the cold water for 20 seconds, then lay on clean tea towels.

To roll the cannelloni, put 2 spoonfuls of the filling at the top of the longer edge of each sheet and roll closed. For dried rolls, see page 58.

Spread a little tomato sauce at the bottom of a Pyrex or baking dish, arrange the cannelloni on top, sprinkle with grated Parmesan and a few fresh basil leaves, then pour over the rest of the sauce. Bake at 200°C for 30 minutes.

Cannelloni alla laziale
Cannelloni in the Lazio style

Serves 4

From Livio Jannattoni's wonderful *La cucina romana e del Lazio*, this cannelloni is filled with rich *ragù*. While you can use fresh sheets here, I have described the method for dried cannelloni tubes that can also be applied to the other two recipes. Dried tubes can be flour and egg, or flour and water, the latter having more substance. Some cannelloni tubes don't require parboiling, but as with lasagne I am distrustful, finding you need a very liquid sauce for the dried tubes to cook properly, so prefer to play it safe by dipping them in boiling water for 5 seconds, blotting, then stuffing.

4 tablespoons olive oil
75g butter
1 onion, peeled and finely diced
1 stick of celery, finely diced
1 carrot, peeled and finely diced
70g prosciutto, diced
300g ground beef
30g porcini, soaked in 100ml warm water for 30 minutes
a glass of white wine
1 tablespoon plain flour, mixed with a bit of porcini water so it is a paste
300g tinned whole plum tomatoes, milled or mashed with potato masher
12–16 dried tubes of cannelloni
50g grated Parmesan
salt and black pepper

For the béchamel
200ml milk
20g butter
20g flour
grated nutmeg

Make the filling. In a large heavy-based pan over a medium-low flame, warm the olive oil and a third of the butter and fry the onion, celery, carrot and prosciutto until soft and translucent. Add the beef and stir until it breaks up and has lost its pink colour, then add the drained porcini and stir again.

Add the white wine and allow it to bubble vigorously, then add the flour paste, stir so that it amalgamates, then add the tomatoes. Cook over a low flame, stirring occasionally until it is rich and very dense – about an hour. Leave to cool slightly.

Make the béchamel. Warm the milk. Melt the butter in a heavy pan, stir in the flour and cook, stirring vigorously to create a light biscuit-coloured roux, for 2 minutes. Pull the pan from the heat and use a balloon whisk to gradually whisk in the warm milk, salt, pepper and a little nutmeg. Return to a low heat, whisking or stirring with a wooden spoon until the sauce comes to a simmering boil. Continue cooking for another 12 minutes, always stirring, until the sauce has the consistency of double cream.

To par-boil the tubes, bring a large pan of salted water to the boil and prepare a large bowl of cold water. Drop the dried cannelloni tubes in and par-boil as instructed, lift into the cold water for 20 seconds, then lay on clean tea towels.

To fill the cannelloni tubes, use a teaspoon and the end of a wooden spoon, leaving a third of the filling for the top.

Generously butter a large Pyrex or baking dish and arrange the cannelloni on top. Mix the remaining *ragù* with the béchamel and pour over the top of the tubes. Top with the grated Parmesan, dot with butter and bake at 200°C for 30 minutes.

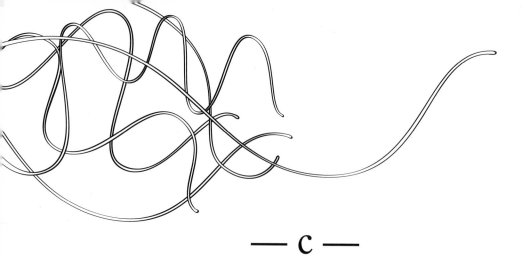

— C —

Capelli d'angelo

A sheet of pasta is full of potential. Let's say it's a sheet of flour and egg pasta you've made, 18cm wide and 30cm long. Fold the long ends in so they meet in the middle. Now bring the new folded ends in so they too meet in the middle producing a sort of envelope. Cut horizontally into strips 3–4cm wide and you have made pappardelle, 1cm wide – fettuccine, 8mm wide – tagliatelle, 3mm wide – tagliolini, 2mm wide – fine tagliolini. Cut into strips 1mm or less, and congratulations! You have a steady hand and have made capelli d'angelo, pasta so thin it looks like an angel's hair.

Fresh capelli d'angelo that is, cited in Rome since the seventeenth century when nuns made pasta as nourishment for new mothers. Then there are dried capelli d'angelo, a whisper of a form that seems almost translucent curled in nests. Unlike other shapes they came in paper trays that protected them from harm – transportation, stacking, being tossed into a trolley. Not, though, against restless hands. I remember as a teenager pressing the brittle nest through the plastic and hearing them crack and shatter, a physical memory that still feels subversive and satisfying. Then I learned capellini spezzati is a shape you can buy, thin threads broken for you. Although why would you buy them ready shattered when the pleasure you get from cracking them is so great?

Between 0.78mm and 0.88mm wide, dried capelli d'angelo really are thin, and so suited to broths – vegetable, maybe with ribbons of herbs, chicken, to which I don't hesitate to add shredded chicken meat, or fish, which is my broth of choice, here.

Making fresh capelli d'angelo

You can buy sheets of pasta and cut them. Or make your own, in which case the standard fresh egg pasta dough is ideal – see page 51. Or if you would like a variation, use a mix of soft 00 flour and hard wheat semola (see page 17) for softness and substance. Bring 200g of soft 00 flour, 200g of semola and 4 eggs into a dough, knead, rest, roll, fold into an envelope if you have rolled by machine, a log if by hand, and then cut with steady cuts. My knife skills are deeply average and even I can cut pasta 1mm thick, or thereabouts. And I enjoy it. The key is making a firm dough and decisive cuts, never lifting the knife too high so the cuts feel like tiny rhythmic steps. Rather than using dried capelli d'angelo for these next two recipes, I would look for slightly wider dried capellini (which means little hairs and is usually about 1mm), linguine or tagliolini. The two sauces that follow are in keeping with the idea that this shape goes well with fish and light creamy sauces.

Maccheroncini di Campofilone con scampi e limone
Fresh capelli d'angelo with prawns and lemon
Serves 4

As far back as the sixteenth century, in a town called Campofilone in Le Marche, *maccheroncini* – remember that for centuries the word maccheroni was the generic term for all pasta – was described as so thin it was like angel hair. Nowadays Maccheroncini di Campofilone is protected by an Indicazione Geografica Protetta or IGP (PDO – protected designation of origin in English), which defines how it's made and in which specific area geographically.

This recipe is inspired by a dish served at an elegant fish restaurant called Chalet Galileo, whose windows open on to an almost white beach in Civitanova in the region of Le Marche. Prawns cooked swiftly in olive oil, with white wine and scented with lemon zest, are netted for the second time in fresh egg pasta. Cooking times for the prawns and the pasta are brief, so the dish comes together incredibly quickly. A bright, swift tangle of a supper.

olive oil
1 small clove of garlic,
   peeled and sliced
a pinch of red chilli
   flakes
400g small prawns,
   peeled
120ml dry white wine
salt
400g fresh egg pasta,
   cut to approx.
   1mm thick,
   alternatively
   tagliolini or
   spaghettini
zest of 1 unwaxed
   lemon
1 heaped teaspoon
   chopped fresh
   flat-leaf parsley

Bring a large pan of water to the boil for the pasta.

In a large frying pan, warm the oil, garlic and chilli gently to infuse the oil. Add the prawns, stir, then raise the heat, add the wine and a pinch of salt and allow to bubble for 3 minutes while you cook the pasta – which will only take a minute or so.

Drain the pasta, or lift directly into the prawn pan, add the lemon zest and parsley, then toss for the last time, and serve.

Capelli d'angelo with leeks, cream and saffron

Serves 4

Leeks, cream and cheese is a familiar and lovable combination – saffron, warmly metallic, is a welcome addition. Another reminder that capelli d'angelo cooks incredibly quickly – no sooner than you have dropped it in the water, be ready to drain or lift it directly into the sauce.

2 leeks
3 tablespoons olive oil
125ml white wine
400ml single cream
50g Parmesan, grated
a few threads of
    saffron
salt and black pepper
400g capelli d'angelo,
    tagliolini or
    spaghettini

Bring a large pan of water to the boil for the pasta.

Trim the leeks back so there is only the white and palest green part, split down the side so you can wash them thoroughly. Slice into thin rounds.

In a large frying pan, warm the oil and leek and cook over a medium-low flame, stirring, until the leek is soft. Add the wine and let it bubble vigorously and mostly evaporate.

Lower the flame, add the cream and half the Parmesan and allow to bubble for 10 minutes, by which time it should reduce by a third and thicken. Add the saffron, salt and pepper.

Meanwhile cook the pasta, just 40 seconds in water, then the last 20–30 seconds of cooking time in with the sauce – if it looks stiff, loosen it with a little cooking water. Serve, with the remaining Parmesan sprinkled on top.

Capelli d'angelo in brodo di pesce
Capelli d'angelo in fish broth
Serves 4

A delicate but distinctly flavoured broth for a delicate shape. As is possibly clear by now, I am a fan of small or very thin pasta in broth, as a meal, or served in smaller portions as a first course, a dish that comes together quickly and provides a soothing start to a meal. You can leave the capelli d'angelo whole or *spezzare* – break them. Either way, there are no two ways about it, you need to get close to the bowl and slurp.

1 white onion, peeled and diced
1 carrot, peeled and diced
1 stick of celery, diced
5 stalks of fresh flat-leaf parsley, chopped
the stalks from 1 bulb of fennel, diced
1 bay leaf
5g salt
10 peppercorns
400g fish heads
300g dried capelli d'angelo, whole or broken

Put the onion, carrot, celery, parsley and fennel stalks into a pan along with the bay leaf, salt, peppercorns, fish heads and 1.5 litres of water. Bring to a gentle boil, reduce to a steady simmer, then cover and leave simmering for 30 minutes. Strain through a fine sieve, then strain again. Taste for salt.

Bring the stock back to the boil and add the capelli d'angelo, which will cook in a minute. Serve with red chilli flakes for those who want them, and toasted bread rubbed with garlic and zigzagged with olive oil.

A note about chilli

Peperoncino is the generic Italian name for piquant and hot members of the Capsicum family, all of which came to Italy from the Americas in the fifteenth century. Peperoncini took root in the south of Italy, which is why we see such prevalence and deft use there, particularly in Calabria where they have been called the *spezia dei poveri,* spice of the poor. While Italy doesn't grow anything like the galaxy of peppers found in, say, Mexico, there are numerous varieties with different natures which alter when dried, although generally at the milder end of the spectrum. For the most part, peperoncini are used moderately for gentle heat and spice in Italian cooking. The most common way of cooking with them is to add a small piece (say 2.5cm) of fresh or dried peperoncino (generally whole but sometimes chopped or crumbled), along with the garlic to the olive oil, then fry both gently to coax out flavour and heat – like garlic, peperoncino turns nasty if burned. *Fiocchi di peperoncino rosso* – dried red chilli flakes – are an alternative but are best added later with other ingredients, notably tomato, so they don't burn. I keep a jar of crumbled dried peperoncino mixed with olive oil to spoon over pasta or soup at the end – it is maybe my favourite way to add peperoncino to dishes. I've seen it suggested that Italian peperoncini aren't interchangeable with other chillis! An absurd idea! They are. The most important thing is that you are in tune with the heat and how you think it works for the recipe and you.

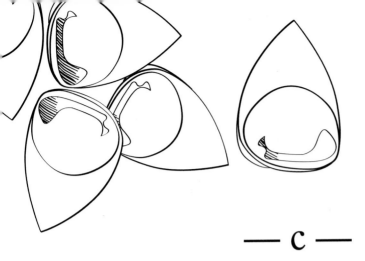

— C —

Cappellacci

Within the pasta universe, there is a galaxy of *pasta ripiena*, stuffed shapes. It is a bewitching galaxy, home to some of the most intricate and sculpted forms, many of which can be traced back to the 1500s when stuffed pasta entered into Italian gastronomy, with style, in the north of Italy. In the beginning, stuffed shapes were the preserve of the wealthy, of royal courts and aristocracy, meaning their evolution is well documented by great cooks and writers of the day, such as renaissance chef Bartolomeo Scappi, and Cristoforo di Messisbugo, the steward of the house of Este in Ferrara. Pasta shapes are – like any food, from apples, to Parmesan, to Monster Munch – the result of environment, climate and customs. Add to this great wealth, politics, court chefs, lavish entertaining and all the skill and vanity that encompasses, and the rich intricacy of many stuffed shapes makes sense. Over time, stuffed shapes trickled down into regional and humbler kitchens, being modified and adapted in the process, but for the most part remained shapes for feasts and celebrations, which in turn gave them a deep significance. Years ago, my neighbour Vera showed me how to make the *cappelletti alla romana*, little hats Roman-style, she had made for Christmas lunch for six decades. She served them to me bobbing in amber broth. Vera died six years ago, but I can still see her knowing fingers pressing dough around a filling of pork, mortadella, chicken and pecorino, the back of her hand brushing a stray hair from her forehead, still naturally black, at 75. So much gentle pride.

Choosing shapes for this alphabet was hard, especially those from the stuffed pasta galaxy. While I am aware of what I have left out, I'll admit relief at concentrating on just four filled shapes, cannelloni, cappellacci, ravioli and tortellini. As a home cook who is intimidated by (also not particularly interested in) sleek exhibition pasta making, I have enjoyed embracing the domestic easy-going side of my four fixed stars in the stuffed pasta galaxy.

~~~~~~

Pasta ripiena, stuffed pasta

While I have picked four, this seems a good time for a field guide to *pasta ripiena*, stuffed pastas. Or some of them at least, which is still a minefield as there are so many regional variations and names, but here goes. **Agnolotti** – diffused but typical of Piedmont. While shapes and fillings vary, they are typically an elongated square and filled with meat. **Agnolotti col plin** are smaller (*plin* means 'pinch') and folded so they have a little ledge that makes them stand up; again fillings vary, but leftover braised meat and greens are notable. **Anolini** – discs or half discs, typical of the cities of Piacenza, Parma (where they are filled with *stracotto*, meat braised until incredibly soft, also the region of Le Marche. **Casonei** – a very old shape, discs of dough filled and closed in various ways, half-moons or a sort of pinched bag, fillings vary, but the meat filling of Brescia is notable, also cheese and pears. **Culurgiones** are from Sardinia and vary in shape, but often resemble a slightly elongated fig with a central seam of pleats; fillings also vary, but potato, pecorino and mint is one to look out for. **Marubini** – like flying saucers, but also squares and half-moons, typical of the city of Cremona where they are filled with braised meat. **Pansotti**, quite literally pot-bellied, typical of Liguria and often stuffed with potato and served in walnut sauce. **Scarpinocc** – comes from the dialect for shoe, hence the shape (also reminiscent of a squashed sweet), typical of Lombardia and typically filled with breadcrumbs, cheese and spices. **Tortelli** – the name traces back to *torta*, the Latin word for something filled, most likely a pie, so these are little filled things, sometimes squares folded into triangles, other times circles folded into half-moons. Tortelli are widespread but most common in Emilia-Romagna, where they are filled with cheese. And now it is my duty to note that many of these names are interchangeable and subject to regional variations, dialect, and the weather.

Which brings us to cappellacci, big hats, the big brothers of cappelletti (little hats). This plump and generous shape is typical of the city of Ferrara, where the filling is a velvet purée of pumpkin and cheese, the sauce butter and sage. Just writing their name makes me want to jump on a train and spend the day in Ferrara, half red-brick Renaissance city, half medieval labyrinth dense with shops, cloisters, old palaces, ordinary houses and places to eat curls of fried dough and slices of prosciutto, *cappellacci di zucca*, *salama* with mashed potato, and drink Lambrusco by the litre. But until I can, I will make them at home.

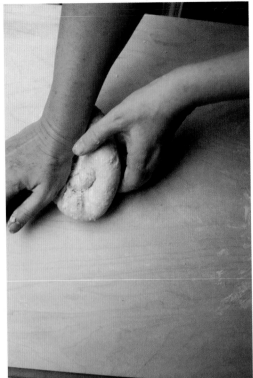

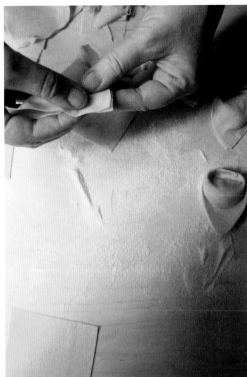
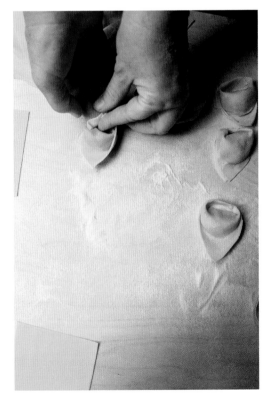
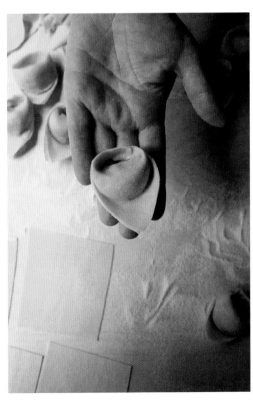

Cappellacci di zucca
Pumpkin cappellacci
Serves 4

Or *cappellacci ferraresi*, a monument of a dish since the 1700s, also a ritual dish for
Ferrara's Jewish community.

The pumpkin needs to be a variety with thick, compact flesh that bakes into firm, silky
pieces. In Ferrara this is typically Barucca, a particularly dense and sweet variety, so
substitute Mantova pumpkin, Hokkaido or butternut squash. Then when you are mixing
the filling, it should be soft but firm enough to sit in an upright pile on the spoon.

For the filling
1.2kg pumpkin or
    butternut squash,
    peeled and cut into
    5cm chunks
salt and black pepper
80g Parmesan, grated
2 amaretti biscuits
1 egg
grated nutmeg

For the pasta
400g flour
4 eggs

For the sauce
100g butter
12 sage leaves

Make the filling by spreading out the pumpkin or squash on a
baking tray rubbed lightly with oil, sprinkling with salt and roasting
until soft and ever so slightly caramelized at the edges – about 30
minutes at 180°C. Mash with the Parmesan, crushed amaretti, egg,
salt, pepper and a grating of nutmeg. It should be firm – if it is not,
add another couple of crushed amaretti.

Make pasta according to the recipe on page 51. Lay out the pasta
sheets, then cut them into 8cm squares. Put a heaped teaspoon of
filling in the middle of each square, fold into a triangle and press
closed firmly, then close the end of the triangle around your finger
to make a cap shape (see page 71). Put them on a clean tea towel or
flour-dusted tray, making sure they don't touch each other or they
will stick.

To cook, bring a large pan of water to the boil, add the salt, stir and
then carefully drop the cappellacci into the pan a few at a time. If
the dough is rolled to the thinnest setting, they will only take 2–3
minutes. Lift out with a spider sieve or large slotted spoon, wait to
let the water drip off and put on a platter.

While the pasta is cooking, melt the butter in a small saucepan or
frying pan over a low heat. Increase the heat, add the sage leaves
and allow to sizzle gently. Pour over the pasta.

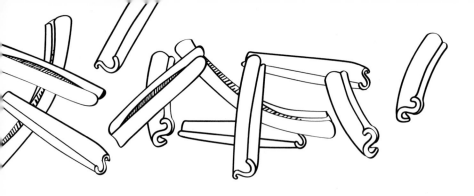

— C —

Casarecce

What sauce to match with casarecce? Bearing in mind it is a durum wheat and water, factory-made dried pasta shape that looks like a twist that has folded back on itself.

Any.

Any sauce. On this I take my lead from the great Oretta Zanini de Vita, scholar and author of the astonishing *Encyclopedia of Pasta* and wise home cook, and her theory that 'any sauce goes pretty well with any shape and anyone who says otherwise is probably overthinking'.

And yet…

And yet, there are a few things to remember when matching shapes and sauces, while bearing in mind that for every suggestion the opposite will also be true.

~~~~~~

Shapes
1. **The first isn't about matching at all,** but the texture and surface of the pasta. Better quality pasta means better quality texture, that is rough and porous, which catches

sauce. In the case of hand-made pasta this is created by the surface it is rolled or dragged on; in the case of dried pasta by extrusion through bronze dies, which sounds fancy and expensive, but is neither – simply an effective process. Good pasta feels and looks like the finest sandpaper on the outside and medium sandpaper inside. It is the difference between pouring tomato sauce down a glass window, or a gently sandblasted wall: which catches more sauce?

2. **Form leads to flavour.** Pasta shapes are all made of flour and liquid, the hundreds of shapes practically the same in substance, but the different forms have a hugely different feel (and this is different to their geometry) and you could argue flavour. Think about (and forget any prejudice) a quill of penne as opposed to a 3cm wide ribbon of fresh egg pappardelle, a strand of spaghetti as opposed to a little twisted slug of trofie. What is your personal and entirely subjective feeling about a shape, how does the form feel therefore taste, what would you put with it?

3. **Geometry plays a part.** Tiny shapes are better suspended than swamped, so are good for soup or broth, which means a spoon, unless the result is so dense you return to a fork (orzo – I'm talking to you). Shells and tubes are Venus fly traps waiting to catch or hide things: beans, batons of guanciale or small florets of cauliflower. Dragged and caved-in shapes, for example ears of orecchiette and indented cavatelli, are also waiting to catch vegetables or vegetable *ragù*. Spiral shapes, fusilli and busiate, radiatori, vesuvio, are also looking to ensnare chunky sauces and *ragùs*. Long pasta too can be a catcher, spaghetti and

clams, spaghettini with chunks of tomato, ribbons of fettuccine with porcini mushrooms, pappardelle with chestnut-coloured duck *ragù*. Geometry, though, does double back to texture, as so much depends on that. Tomato sauce is a classic companion for spaghetti or penne, but even the densest, richest sauce will struggle to cling if there is nothing to cling to.

4. **Cheese is not simply an ingredient,** but an enabler, bringing things together. Penne and peas are not particularly well matched, either physically or emotionally, but give them a handful of grated Parmesan or a spoonful of ricotta, or both, and the next thing you know they've eloped and got married.

5. **Geography is a guide.** Keep in mind that many classic pairings were not the result of being matched but evolved together in the hands of home cooks using what was available. The pair were made and eaten so often they became a habit-ritual and ritual became tradition, and now that's just the way it is. Hard wheat and water dried pasta shapes are historically typical of southern Italy, where the fat is principally olive oil, vegetables are omnipresent and cheese is made from sheep's milk, which is why we see so many harmonious combinations of all those. The same is true of the North, where soft flour and egg pasta is typical, and the cooking fat is butter (which does cling particularly well to egg pasta). In central Italy, where fresh and dried pasta traditions meet, so do the fats, also pork. Use pairings evolved through geography and consolidated over time as points of reference for other combinations.

6. **Which brings us back to Oretta** and her idea, which is much more suited to the spirit of home cooking (by its very nature anarchic, resourceful, personal) than any finger-wagging dogma. An idea neatly illustrated by *cacio e pepe*, the Roman sauce of pecorino cheese and a nose-tickling amount of black pepper loosened with water into a sauce. A canonical shape is tonnarelli, a long, fresh pasta which (depending on who you talk to) is made of flour and water, or flour and egg.

And yet.

Cacio e pepe is served by many with spaghetti or bucatini, also gnocchi, while others (me included) prefer *cacio e pepe* coating tubes of rigatoni or mezze maniche, while some use it as a coat for ravioli.

Which brings us to the single most important factor in matching a shape and sauces: you and what you like.

So in answer to the question what sauce to match with casarecce?

For me, many sauces, but especially broccoli cooked 'Roman style', first in boiling water and then dragged (strascinati) around a pan with plenty of olive oil, smashed garlic and red chilli so it forms almost a cream. Also a version of peperonata, peppers, tomatoes and onions, cooked until so soft and velvety it clings keenly to the factory-made dried pasta shape that looks like a twist that has folded back on itself.

Casarecce con broccoli
Casarecce with broccoli
Serves 4

1.5kg broccoli (around
    2 heads of
    calabrese or
    1 romanesco)
2 cloves of garlic
1 dried red chilli,
    crumbled
6–8 tablespoons extra
    virgin olive oil
4 anchovies (optional)
salt and black pepper
400g casarecce
75g soft white
    breadcrumbs
olive oil, for frying

Split the broccoli into medium florets. Pare away the tough skin from the stalk and cut it into thick strips. If the broccoli has tender leaves, chop them roughly. Wash the broccoli. Bring a large pan of well-salted water to the boil, then add the broccoli and cook until they can easily be pierced by a fork, about 5–7 minutes, depending on the broccoli's age and freshness.

Peel, then, depending on your preference, crush, slice or dice the garlic, or leave it whole. Finely chop the chilli and seeds. In a large frying pan, over a low flame, warm the olive oil, garlic, chilli and anchovies if you are using them, allowing them to sizzle gently; do not let them burn or they will be bitter. You can remove the whole garlic at this point.

Use a slotted spoon to lift the broccoli from the water into the frying pan – don't worry about the excess water, it is helpful. Keep the pan of water for the pasta. Raise the flame, move the broccoli around the pan so each piece is coated with oil, add a pinch of salt, then allow the broccoli to stew for a few minutes, stirring and mashing with a wooden spoon, during which time it will break up, taking on an almost creamy aspect.

Bring the broccoli cooking water back to a fast boil and add the pasta. In a small frying pan, fry the breadcrumbs in olive oil with a pinch of salt until golden, then blot on kitchen paper.

Once the pasta is al dente, use the slotted spoon to lift it into the frying pan, add a ladleful of pasta cooking water and mix well over a low heat for 2 minutes, shaking the pan so the starch is released, therefore binds. Add a grind of black pepper.

Divide between bowls and serve with the pan-toasted breadcrumbs, also cheese if you wish.

Casarecce con peperonata
Casarecce with peperonata
Serves 4

Peperonata, a classic Italian dish of red peppers stewed with onion and tomato until it is soft, thick and richly red, pairs well with casarecce. By the end of cooking the peppers are soft and the tomatoes saucey enough to dress the pasta in the colour of a desert sunrise. However, I take it one step further and remove half the peperonata, reduce it to smooth cream with an immersion blender, then return it to the pan. In this way it clings carefully to the twists, while some peppers remain distinct.

1 large white onion
4 tablespoons olive oil
a knob of butter
salt
4 large red peppers
6 good ripe tomatoes
(or two dozen tiny plum ones)
400g casarecce, fusilli, busiate, linguine, pappardelle
grated Parmesan or pecorino, to serve

Peel and slice the onion. In a large heavy-based pan, over a medium-low flame, fry the onion in the olive oil and butter, with a pinch of salt, until soft and lightly golden.

Cut the peppers into 2cm thick/6cm long strips, discarding the stalks, seeds and pith. Add the sliced peppers to the pan, stir, then cover the pan and leave over a low flame for 15 minutes.

Peel and roughly chop the tomatoes and add them to the pan. Leave the peperonata to cook uncovered for 30–40 minutes at a blipping simmer, or until all the liquid has evaporated away, the peppers are extremely soft and the whole stew is rich and thick. Take out half the stew and blend until smooth, then return it to the pan.

Cook the pasta in plenty of well-salted boiling water, drain and toss in a bowl with half the peppers, saving the rest for another day. Serve the pasta, passing round grated Parmesan or pecorino for those who want it.

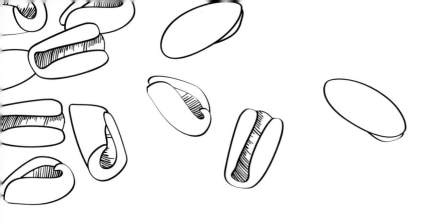

Cavatelli

If you want to teach yourself to make flour and water pasta, cavatelli is a good place to start. The name comes from the word *cavato*, caved in, which is exactly what you do when you press the tip of your index finger or thumb into a nugget of dough, then drag your fingers and the dough, towards you. First attempts are usually a bit rum, but by your fourth or fifth try the dough will curl over itself, maybe even flip towards you. You have produced a hollowed-out curl. You have made a cavatello.

One version at least: the genealogy of cavatelli is nearly as bewildering as the dozens of regional variations from all over southern Italy, particularly Molise, Puglia, Basilicata, Calabria and Sicily. To make things even more complicated, the line between cavatelli and other dragged shapes such as strascinati and capunti is a blurred one. This is babel for historians, a minefield for food writers, thrilling for those who like to eat, sending us off on imagined or real searches for Puglian cavatelli with olive oil laden turnip tops, Calabrian cavateddi with hot red peppers, or cavasuneddi with sausage, mint and tomato from Ragusa in Sicily.

What is clear, though, is that these small pasta sculptures are domestic works of art that came about through ingenuity and the need to make something to eat. We should approach making cavatelli as people have for hundreds of years, finding a way to cave a nub of dough. As well as one finger, I have been taught to make cavatelli by dragging the nugget of dough with rounded knife and ice scraper-like tool; by using two fingers (which makes it look like a canoe); also rolling it away from me over a ridged board, some rough wood, the star side of the grater and the inside of a wicker basket. The aim of all is to create both a cave and a sauce-catching surface. Because at the end of the day, catching the sauce, that is the aim.

Akin to its ear-like cousin orecchiette, hard wheat and water cavatelli, with its stout and sturdy nature and textural bite, pairs well with vegetable sauces, particularly green vegetables like broccoli and turnip tops. To get vegetables to work as sauces, though, they need to be cooked until soft, coated generously with olive oil and seasoned with chilli, or garlic, or anchovy, the dish finished with cheese. Cavatelli also work brilliantly with ground meat and tomato sauce, and pounded ones such as *pesto alla trapanese* (almonds, basil, tomatoes, olive oil and garlic) and almond and sage pesto.

To make flour and water dough

This is the mothership recipe for a hard durum wheat flour (*semola rimacinata* in Italian, durum wheat semolina flour in the UK) and water dough, suitable for all the flour and water pasta recipes in this book – cavatelli, lagana, pici, trofie, orecchiette. There are also variations, which I will mention in the relevant chapters, but for now, this is it. The first time you try this, treat it as a game, notice how the coarse semola and water comes together, how dry and scraggy it feels to begin with, then how it softens as you knead. Weather, humidity, the flour, how dry your hands are, all play a huge part in this; the first step is to start to notice. Also identify your work-spot, keeping in mind you need a kneading area (wood is ideal because the surface friction does some of the work) and a spot to spread the shapes once you have made them.

The proportions are 2:1, so for every 100g of durum wheat

semolina flour (semola), 50ml of warm water. So to make pasta for 4 you need 400g of semola and 200ml of warm water. Working on wood is best as it creates heat and friction, but you can also work in a bowl, or in a food processor. Working on a board, tip the semola into a wide mountain and add the water bit by bit, pinching it into the flour so it doesn't run away. Once you have added all the water, bring it into a rough ball, then knead, in the most comfortable way for you (I use the heel of my hand to fold the dough over itself and then push and rotate). Avoid adding extra water until you have kneaded for a while. If it still feels dry or flaky after 2 minutes, a few drops or light spray of water on the board may well be enough. Knead for at least 6 minutes, or until the dough is smooth and silky – when you hold it against your cheek, it should feel lovely. Rest under an upturned bowl for 30 minutes before shaping according to the recipe.

To shape cavatelli

Cut a thick strip from the ball (and put the rest back under the bowl so it doesn't dry out). Using the hollow of your hands, roll the strip into a 1cm rope. Cut the rope into 1cm nuggets and then shape on your chosen surface, pressing your thumb or index finger into the nugget and dragging, either away or towards you, so it curls and caves.

Cavasuneddi or cavatelli con salsiccia, menta e pomodoro
Cavatelli with sausage, mint and tomato
Serves 4

2 cloves of garlic,
    peeled and crushed
4 tablespoons olive oil
400g sausage meat,
    crumbled
150ml white wine
400g ripe tomatoes,
    peeled and roughly
    chopped
a sprig of fresh mint
salt
450g fresh, 400g dried
    cavatelli,
    orecchiette, fusilli,
    casarecce
grated pecorino and
    red chilli flakes, to
    serve

In a capacious pot over a medium-low heat, fry the crushed garlic in the olive oil. Add the crumbled sausage and stir until all pinkness has gone.

Pour in the wine and raise the heat. When the wine has evaporated, add the tomatoes and cook for another 5–10 minutes, or until the sauce has thickened. Finally, add the mint leaves and salt to taste.

Cook and drain the cavatelli, put them into the pot with the sauce and let them simmer for a few minutes, stirring and adding some of the cooking water if needed. Serve, passing round grated pecorino and red chilli flakes for those who want them.

A note about garlic
While some would have us believe garlic is a fixed star, it varies massively in strength and pungency. This is to do with variety, but more so with age. Garlic is a spring vegetable – young bulbs have white skin and tender cloves with a sweet, sunny fragrance, with which you can be careless with quantity. As garlic gets older its skin turns translucent and flaky and the cloves take on a greater pungency and power. Which is great, but you need to take care, also pull out any green shoot that has developed inside. Too old and garlic can be acrid and a bit of a bully. Be reassured, garlic is no good at hiding, the smell as you open a clove tells you everything. Then prepare accordingly, also to your personal taste. It is all about surface area. Peel and gently crush with the back of a knife or the heel of your hand so the clove is broken but still whole, for a gentle fragrance (whole means it can be pulled out if you wish). Peel and slice thinly for a stronger flavour. Peel and mince for the strongest. In all three cases always put the garlic into a cold pan with cold oil (fat) and then on a gentle heat. To start, warm rather than fry garlic, to encourage and coax out the flavour, then progress to a gentle sizzle but not much more; too hot and the garlic will burn and, regardless of how young or carefully prepared, it will turn into a bitter bully. Store garlic out of the fridge.

Cavatelli con pesto di salvia e mandorle e ricotta salata
Cavatelli with sage and almond pesto and salted ricotta
Serves 4

A recipe from the Anna Tasca Lanza cooking school in the heart of Sicily, a place that has taught me much. Like sage itself, this pesto is strong-flavoured and rugged, not one to be eaten by the spoonful straight from the pestle or mixer. It meets its match though, in stout, satisfying cavatelli. A ladleful of pasta cooking water loosens and tempers the pesto, while the heat wakes the garlic and the lemony side of the sage. If you wanted you could add some crumbled and pan-fried sausage or cubes of roasted pumpkin. Salted ricotta is, as the name suggests, ricotta that has been preserved in salt, which transforms its texture, from soft to firm, and compact enough to be grated, or pared into crumbly-edged slices. Salting transforms the flavour too: creamy and shy wobbles are given sharp, salty edges, with that sheepishness becoming more pronounced. It is great here.

400g dried cavatelli, or 450g fresh, or orecchiette, fusilli, casarecce, spaghetti, linguine, bucatini
1 clove of garlic
100g peeled almonds
a pinch of salt (ideally coarse)
50g sage
100ml olive oil
a knob of butter
grated salted ricotta, to serve

Bring a large pan of water to the boil, add salt, stir, add pasta and cook until al dente.

Make the pesto.

In a pestle and mortar. Put the garlic, almonds and a few grains of coarse salt in the mortar and pound with the pestle until they are reduced to a rough paste. Add the sage and pound either with a firm push and twist or a wider rotating movement, until you have a paste. Add the oil and mix again.

In the food processor. Pulse the almonds, garlic and a few grains of salt until a paste. Add the sage and oil and pulse again.

Scrape the pesto into a warm serving dish, add a ladleful of pasta cooking water and a knob of butter and stir (it will seem quite loose).

When the pasta is cooked, drain (saving some pasta cooking water), then tip on to the pesto and toss rigorously. The pesto will coat the pasta and get absorbed – it should be soft and saucey, so add a little more pasta cooking water if need be. Serve, passing round grated salted ricotta for those who want it.

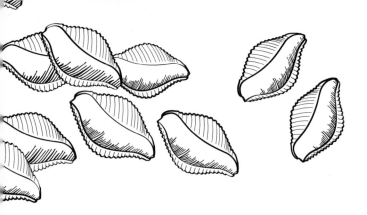

Conchiglie

Like the conch-shaped seashells they mimic, conchiglie are designed to contain. What exactly depends on their size, which like their natural counterpart varies tremendously. The smallest, often called conchigliette piccole, can be as small as coffee beans and so ideal for broth – the suffix *-ette*, by the way, signifies a smaller form of something, you'll meet it often in the alphabet. The largest, conchiglioni, are the size of a squeezed-out lemon half and ask to be stuffed. Medium-sized conchiglie suit spoons, and are a fitting shape for soup or *minestra*.

Minestra, plural *minestre*, is a small word for a multitude of preparations, including soups, but also pasta, rice and bread dishes that are brothy and so united by an action of being *minestrata*, administered, or less medicinal, shared by ladling from a pan into a bowl, and needing a spoon. When you look at a menu in an Italian restaurant (bearing in mind the separatism of Italian eating and that pasta or rice is served as a *primo* or first course, then the meat or fish as a *secondo*) you will notice that the pasta dishes are also divided into two sections. *Pasta asciutta*, dry pasta, which doesn't mean dry, but pasta served with a sauce, so eaten with a fork, and *minestra* – pasta cooked or served in enough liquid to require a spoon.

The queen *minestra* is *pasta e fagioli* or pasta and beans, essentially a thick bean soup with pasta, a version of which can be found in every region, varying in the hands of every home cook. Its popularity makes absolute sense, it is easy-going, generous, cheap, good. A particularly good bean for *pasta e fagioli* is the mottled borlotti, which is plump and almost velvety in texture. In summer if you can find fresh borlotti, mottled beans hiding in mottled pods, lucky you, otherwise you can use dried beans, which need soaking, or trusty tins. I am possibly starting to sound like a broken record saying this is a template that invites improvisation, but it really does. Make a bean soup that is as tasty as possible, then cook little shells in it.

Pasta e fagioli
Pasta and beans
Serves 4

Tinned beans work brilliantly here, and the more expensive jars that sometimes come with paper hats are even better. The incentive for using fresh or soaking your own beans is the cooking water, which, cloudy with starch from the beans and salted, is a sort of stock. If you are soaking your own, check the date of packing because they should not be more than a year old – old beans rarely soften and there are few things worse than making the effort to soak and being rewarded by mean bean-bullets. This version is simple, a foundation of oil, garlic and rosemary, just enough tomato to give flavour but not dominate, partly blended into softness but still with whole beans, that know where to hide (in a shell).

400g fresh borlotti beans (this is about 1kg of beans in their pods) or 250g dried borlotti, or 600g tinned
5 tablespoons extra virgin olive oil
2 cloves of garlic, peeled and lightly crushed
a big sprig of fresh rosemary
200g fresh tomatoes, peeled and crushed
salt and black pepper
220g conchiglie, other small tubular pasta or broken tagliatelle
olive oil, red chilli flakes and grated Parmesan or pecorino, to serve

If you are using dried beans, soak them for 12 hours or overnight. Drain, then cover them with enough cold water that it comes at least 10cm above the beans and cook at a simmer until tender, which usually takes about an hour and a half. Leave the beans to cool in their cooking liquid.

If you are using fresh beans, pod them, then cover them with enough cold water that it comes at least 10cm above the beans. Bring to a very gentle boil and then reduce to a simmer for 30 minutes or until tender. Leave the beans to cool in their cooking liquid. If you are using tinned beans, drain and rinse them.

Meanwhile, in a large, deep sauté pan or casserole, warm the olive oil over a low flame, add the crushed garlic and the rosemary, then fry them gently until fragrant. If desired, you can remove the garlic at this point. Peel the tomatoes, then roughly chop them and add them to the pan. Raise the heat just a little and cook the tomatoes for 10 minutes, or until soft and saucey. Add the beans and a couple of ladlefuls of liquid, either bean cooking water, or water, then let the pan bubble away for another 10–15 minutes. Season with salt. At this point you may like to blend half the soup for a creamier consistency.

Add another couple of ladles of liquid and then the pasta. Continue cooking, stirring attentively until the pasta is tender. You may need a little more liquid. Serve with a zigzag of olive oil, red chilli flakes and grated Parmesan or pecorino.

Conchiglie con piselli, pancetta e ricotta
Conchiglie with peas, bacon and ricotta
Serves 4

Moving from a spoon to a fork, pasta shells with peas, bacon and ricotta. Shells know their job and don't need help catching, but ricotta helps anyway. This is a pleasing combination that children adore, except my child. Adults too. Use the pasta cooking water to loosen the consistency.

400g conchiglie, lumache, penne, fusilli, casarecce
200g peas (either fresh or frozen)
2 tablespoons olive oil
100g pancetta or bacon, cut into batons
200g ricotta
50g Parmesan, grated
salt and black pepper
unwaxed lemon zest or nutmeg

Bring a pan of water to the boil, add salt, stir, tip in the pasta and cook until al dente.

Cook the peas in simmering water until tender, which will vary depending on age and size, then drain.

Warm a tablespoon of olive oil in a small pan and fry the bacon batons until the fat melts and they are just starting to turn golden. Add the peas and stir so each one is coated with fat.

In a large bowl, mash the ricotta with the Parmesan and a little of the pasta cooking water. Taste and season with salt (the Parmesan will also season), pepper and either lemon zest or a little nutmeg.

Once the pasta is done, drain, save some pasta cooking water, and tip into the ricotta bowl. Add the peas and bacon and toss. Add a little pasta cooking water if you think it needs loosening.

Conchiglioni ripieni di ricotta e spinaci al forno
Conchiglioni stuffed with spinach and ricotta
Serves 4

And to the biggest of the shell family, which need par-boiling for 3 minutes less than the recommended cooking time, before you stuff them with ricotta and spinach, and any other cheese that you think might work. The shells are topped with béchamel and tomato sauce that swirl into a savoury red and beige ripple. Arranged in a wide shallow dish this is a lovely thing to plonk in the middle of the table, along with a bottle of wine or two, a big salad and plate of prosciutto for after, ice-cream for after that.

400g conchiglioni, alternatively lumaconi
250g spinach
200g ricotta
1 egg
60g Parmesan, grated
100g smoked scamorza or mozzarella
50g other cheese, e.g. fontina, Taleggio, Gruyère, goat's cheese
salt, black pepper and nutmeg
250ml tomato sauce (see page 270)

For the béchamel
500ml whole milk
40g butter
40g plain flour

Bring a large pan of water to the boil, add salt, stir, add the conchiglioni and cook for 3 minutes less than the recommended cooking time. Drain in a colander and douse with a little cold water to stop cooking.

Pick over the spinach, removing any tough or damaged leaves, and then wilt down completely, drain thoroughly and chop roughly.

In a large bowl mix the spinach with the ricotta, egg, a third of the Parmesan and both other cheeses. Season generously with salt, pepper and nutmeg.

Make the béchamel (see page 58). Warm the tomato sauce. Spread a little béchamel on the bottom of an ovenproof dish. Fill the par-boiled conchiglioni with some of the spinach and ricotta mixture and arrange the shells in the dish open side up.

Pour the tomato sauce over the filled shells, making sure some falls in the gaps, then pour over the béchamel, swirling the two together. Sprinkle the remaining Parmesan over the top. Bake at 180°C for 20 minutes, or until the top is bubbling and blistering.

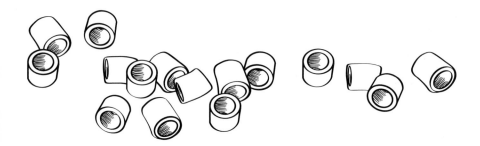

— d —

Ditali

Un dito is a finger, *un ditale* a thimble-ring for sewing, ditali is thimble-ring-shaped pasta. A durum wheat and water, factory-made shape typical of Campania but now diffused, the circumference of ditali varies from brand to brand, some large enough even for my thick index finger, others like beads for a child's sweet necklace. Manufacturers also make ditalini (*-ini* being diminutive) and ditaloni (*-oni* augmentative), meaning there are a gamut of thimble-ring forms. Even the largest ditali and ditaloni fit in a spoon though, which makes them ideal for *minestre*, any *minestra*, but especially those with lentils.

In fact, for me ditalini and lentils are so inextricably linked, it is hard for me to see one without the other, which is narrow-minded I know, but convenient for lunch or supper. And ditalini are great with pumpkin, too.

Pasta con la purea di zucca
Ditali and pumpkin
Serves 4

A rare move beyond lentils is ditalini with pumpkin, which is cooked in a pan until it is so soft it is almost a purée – almost but not quite. I have purposely kept this recipe simple, but it invites improvisation, the addition of crumbled blue cheese or sausage, a handful of brittle and musty fried sage.

2kg pumpkin, Mantova or other dense variety, or butternut squash
6 tablespoons olive oil
20g butter
3 cloves of garlic, peeled and chopped
a pinch of red chilli flakes
2 teaspoons finely chopped fresh flat-leaf parsley
400g ditali or ditalini, or tubetti, fusilli, penne, cavatelli, orecchiette
grated Parmesan, to serve

Working carefully, cut away the skin from the pumpkin or squash, scoop away the seeds and strings and cut into 2cm pieces.

In a large deep frying pan, warm the olive oil, butter, garlic and chilli and fry gently for a minute or two, then add the cubes of pumpkin and toss so each one glistens. Then add a 1cm depth of water to allow it to bubble and cover for 10 minutes or so, or until the pumpkin is soft. Lift the lid and let any water bubble away and the pumpkin take just a bit of colour – the pieces should be soft and slightly saucey. Add the parsley.

Cook the ditalini in plenty of fast-boiling water, drain, saving the pasta cooking water. Mix the pasta with the pumpkin, adding some water to loosen the mixture.

Serve, passing around grated Parmesan and more red chilli flakes for those who want them.

Ditalini e lenticchie
Ditalini and lentils
Serves 4

Lentils, lentils, tiny, tinkling, useful, no-need-to-soak small brown or slate grey Italian lentils – look out for those from Castelluccio. I have also used masoor dal (brown lentils), which needed soaking in cold water for 30 minutes and also longer cooking. Puy are not suitable here. The way I cook lentils for pasta is almost identical to the way I cook them with sausages, fried eggs or grilled cheese. That is adding lentils to an already softened confetti-like mix of diced onion, celery, carrot, garlic, rosemary and bay, stirring and then covering with water and cooking until the lentils are soft and the consistency wavy. The pasta goes in for the last 12 minutes of cooking, and also more lightly salted warm water, so that the lentils and pasta cook together into a dense soup stew. Steady and good food.

300g small brown lentils
5 tablespoons extra virgin olive oil
1 medium onion, peeled and finely chopped
1 medium carrot, peeled and finely chopped
1 stick of celery, finely chopped
2 cloves of garlic, peeled and finely chopped
2 bay leaves, or a sprig of fresh rosemary
salt and black pepper
a pinch of red chilli flakes
200g ditalini or other small pasta, especially orecchiette, tubetti, quadrucci, also maltagliati

Pick over the lentils to check for gritty bits, then rinse. Cover the base of a large heavy-based frying or sauté pan with olive oil over a medium-low heat, add the chopped vegetables, bay leaves or rosemary and a pinch of salt, and cook gently until the vegetables are soft, but not coloured.

Add the lentils to the pan along with the chilli, stirring for a minute or two until each lentil glistens with oil.

Cover with 1.5 litres of water (which should rise about 2.5cm above the lentils), bring to the boil and reduce to a simmer. Cook the lentils, stirring occasionally, until they are tender – the time will depend on how old they are.

Once the lentils are tender, add the pasta and cook, stirring until it is al dente – you may need to add a bit more lightly salted hot water.

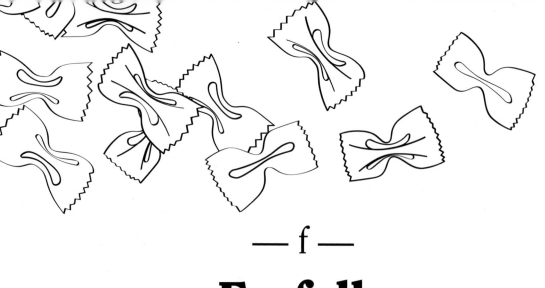

— f —

Farfalle

Every week the resident Pasta Agony Uncle Vincenzo answers one of the many letters he receives.

Dear Vincenzo,

I am a huge pasta fan and consider myself open-minded and adventurous with all shapes and sauces. I know firmness matters, that al dente, with bite, is the aim, and over-cooking a sin. What then, am I to do about farfalle, the butterflies? When I cook them until al dente, the middle pinch is still hard, and causes discomfort. If I continue cooking until the middle pinch is al dente, the wings are floppy which causes frustration, anger and, at times, shame. Please help! Please advise! I want to love farfalle as much as I love all the other shapes.

Yours hopefully,
Carl Hoddrey

PS – is it OK to call them bowties too?

Dear Carl,

Thank you for your letter, and honesty. Firstly, I want to reassure you that you are not alone. Farfalle, butterflies, also known as stricchetti in Emilia-Romagna, and gasse in Liguria, are tricky. Pinched to thickness in the middle, cooking is never going to be even. The first step is acceptance.

Your instinct is right, focus on the whole shape when judging al dente, not the middle point. Also keep in mind that due to its geometry farfalle are best cooked until the least extreme point of the al dente scale. Keep time, keep tasting. Also take note of brands, better quality means better quality wing and pinches.

And experiment! Try cooking farfalle, or better still farfalline, in a brothy minestrone or *minestra* such as green bean, white bean and tomato. *Minestra* doesn't demand al dente in the same way a sauce does. Once you are comfortable, progress from broths to gentle creamy sauces, lemon and cream, ricotta and black pepper. Remember farfalle come in a range of sizes, including diminutive farfalline, and larger farfallone, which are excellent with sausage *ragù*, the pinched fold serving a purpose and collecting sauce.

Then when you have a quiet afternoon, make farfalle. Roll out a sheet of egg pasta, cut into oblongs about 5cm long and 2½cm wide and pinch them into butterflies, then serve with smoked salmon and mascarpone. Fresh egg pasta farfalle are different creatures from dried ones, more forthcoming and pinching into softer pleats, which really do collect sauce. Also the contrast between the middle and the edges is somehow more welcome with fresh farfalle. Also proof that from time to time, a little hard core is a good thing.

Wishing you all the best and please let me know how you get on.

Vincenzo

PS – yes.

Minestra di fagiolini, fagioli, pomodori e farfalline
Minestrone with tomato, and two kinds of beans
Serves 4

Adapted from a Calabrian recipe, this is high summer soup for when tomatoes are sweet and beans tender. It is a brothy and simple soup that may appear too watery, but isn't thanks to full-flavoured ingredients and the enriching addition of grated Parmesan, olive oil and maybe red chilli flakes. As mentioned, don't rush this one. Allow it to rest, giving flavours time to emerge and farfalle to settle in.

500g fine green beans, topped and tailed
6 tablespoons olive oil
2 cloves of garlic, peeled and finely chopped
400g ripe and sweet cherry tomatoes, diced
a big handful of torn fresh basil
salt
250g cooked white beans
250g farfalline, or other small shape
75g Parmesan, grated
a pinch of red chilli flakes or black pepper

Bring a pan of water to the boil, add salt, stir, and then drop in the beans for 10 minutes, or until they are just cooked al dente (not crunchy or floppy), and drain.

In a deep frying pan or casserole over a medium-low flame, warm the olive oil and the garlic, then add the tomatoes, basil and a pinch of salt and allow to bubble gently for 15 minutes.

Add the green and white beans to the tomatoes, along with 1 litre of warm water and another pinch of salt, then simmer for 15 minutes.

Add the pasta, raise the heat and boil until the pasta is al dente. You can at this point pour the soup into a tureen or leave it in the pan. Add half the cheese, a few grinds of black pepper or sprinkle of red chilli flakes, and stir. Serve, passing round the rest of the cheese and a bottle of olive oil so everyone can swirl a bit on top.

Farfalle con salmone e mascarpone
Farfalle with salmon and mascarpone
Serves 4

Ripped by a friend from the March 1979 issue of the magazine *La Cucina Italiana*, I think this quick dish is gorgeous and timeless. Dried farfalle work, but fresh farfalle are even better. Buy sheets of fresh egg lasagne, cut them into squares and pinch.

400g farfalle, linguine, tagliatelle
200g smoked salmon
125g mascarpone
20g butter, at room temperature
zest of 1 unwaxed lemon
salt
fresh dill, snipped, and more lemon zest for on top

Bring a large pan of water to the boil, add salt, stir and add the pasta, stir and cook until al dente.

While the pasta cooks, use scissors to cut the salmon into short strips and put into a large warm serving bowl along with the mascarpone, butter and lemon zest. Use a small ladle or big spoon to lift out some pasta cooking water and add in order to loosen everything into a cream. Taste and add salt if it needs it.

Drain the pasta, reserving some water, then tip on to the sauce and toss gently, adding more cooking water if you think it needs it. Serve, sprinkling with dill, and grating over a bit more lemon zest if you wish.

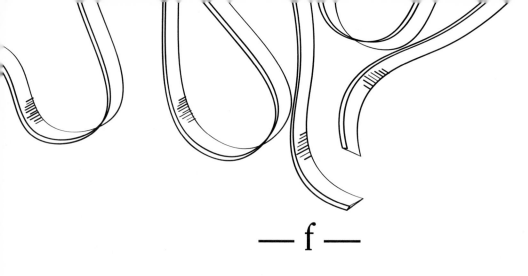

— f —

Fettuccine

It is 9 o'clock on Saturday morning. We are at Gatti & Antonelli, one of Rome's numerous *pasta all'uovo*/fresh egg pasta shops. The queue is almost as long as the veined marble counter that runs the length of the shop, the smell a milder version of the one you meet in pasta factories, hopeful and sappy, like fresh sawdust and a clean baby. Beyond the counter, a glass door reveals the laboratory with its gargantuan, strangely thrilling versions of familiar equipment, mixers and rollers, cutters and shapers. Behind the counter two women with white coats and blue hairnets serve efficiently, lifting long and short pasta from shallow boxes into paper trays. Timing matters. Behind the women is a yellow sign headed Cotture, Tortellini – 8, Agnolotti – 7, Ravioli – 8, Fettuccine – 3. The numbers are minutes, the recommended cooking times for Gatti's fresh egg pasta in *acqua abbondante a bollore lento* – abundant water at a slow boil. Many in the queue have come for the *agnolotti ripieni di carne*, the speciality of the house. I have come for fettuccine.

Glance quickly and long slender fettuccine seem the identical twins of tagliatelle. Look closer and you find fettuccine are (mostly) a bit wider, 1cm or thereabouts as opposed to the exacting 8mm of its northern relative, and thicker, therefore with more substance, rather like a Roman. Fettuccine means 'little ribbons' and they are direct ancestors of wisp-thin capelli d'angelo. In the hands of strong-armed home cooks, wisps became ribbons, hand-rolled and served on a Sunday, usually with a rich meat *ragù*, often including giblets and mushrooms, and certainly finished with grated pecorino. These days fettuccine can be fresh or dried, vary in size and thickness, and have migrated all over the country and globe. They remain most beloved in central and southern Italy, and especially Lazio and its capital, Rome, where the fresh ones are the pride of numerous *pasta all'uovo* like Gatti and in the middle of the table on a Sunday.

My turn has come; 400g of egg yolk yellow fettuccine scooped from the box into a white tray which is then wrapped in a white paper stamped with Gatti, making it seem like a gift, which it is. The glamorous signora behind the cash desk reminds me that cooking time is 3 minutes, but that I should start the timer only when the water comes back to the boil. By the time we leave the queue is even longer than the counter and folding back on itself like a belt, or a ribbon of fettuccine.

To make fettuccine at home

Roll **classic egg dough** for 4 by hand or with a machine (see page 51). How thinly you roll depends on what you are serving it with. Meat *ragù* works well with sturdy fettuccine, butter and Parmesan with thinner ribbons. Thickness also depends on personal preference – you decide. Cut the rolled dough into 30cm lengths, rub with semola flour and fold both ends over the dough so they meet in the middle once, then again so you have an envelope. With a sharp knife cut the folded dough into 1cm wide fettuccine. For a much more relaxed fettuccine, simply cut the sheet into ribbons ad hoc – these are called *fettuccine ignoranti*, ignorant fettuccine. I love them.

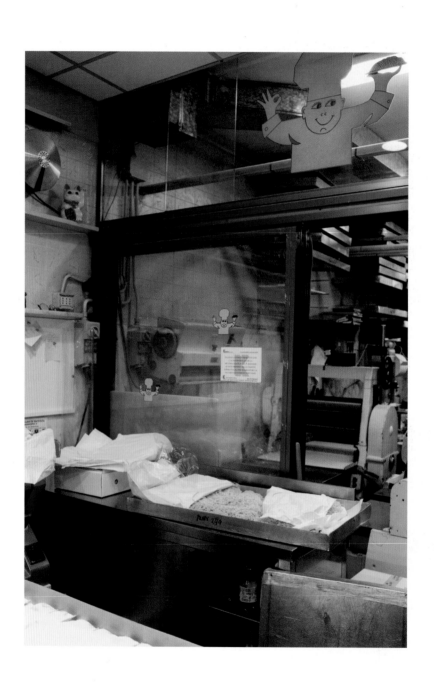

Fettuccine con fegato di pollo e salvia
Fettuccine with chicken livers and sage
Serves 4

Known as *fettuccine con le rigaglie* in Rome, *rigaglie* being the generic term for chicken giblets, this version just uses the liver. Paired with more sage than most recipes, just a little ground beef (but this is optional), tomato and a little vermouth or Marsala that tempers the bitterness of the velvet liver and moleskin mustiness of sage.

250g chicken livers
30g butter
2 tablespoons olive oil
2 shallots, peeled and finely diced
1 clove of garlic, peeled and finely diced
50g pancetta, diced
10 whole sage leaves
120g ground beef (optional)
salt and black pepper
1 heaped teaspoon tomato concentrate, dissolved in 150ml vermouth or Marsala
500g fresh fettuccine, tagliatelle or pappardelle, or 400g dried
100g pecorino or Parmesan, grated

Bring a pan of water to the boil for the pasta. Trim the chicken livers of any sinew or discoloration. Wash and pat them dry, then cut each liver into 6.

In a heavy-based frying pan, over a medium-low flame, warm the butter and olive oil and fry the shallots until soft and translucent. Add the garlic, pancetta and sage and cook, stirring, for a few minutes. Crumble in the ground beef, add salt and a grind of pepper and cook, stirring, until the beef has lost all signs of pink.

Raise the heat, add the chicken livers and fry, stirring, until the livers have lost any red colour. Add the tomato dissolved in vermouth/Marsala and reduce to a lively simmer – long enough for the liver to take on flavours, but not so long as to get rubbery.

Meanwhile, salt the boiling water, add the pasta and cook until al dente. Drain the pasta, keeping some pasta cooking water.

Tip the pasta into the chicken livers, sprinkle over some cheese and toss, adding a little pasta cooking water if it needs it.

Fettuccine, burro e parmigiano
Fettuccine, butter and Parmesan

Serves 2

A combination taken to the extreme in a dish called *fettuccine Alfredo*, fettuccine with a good amount of butter, cheese and plenty of black pepper, eaten from a bowl on your lap while watching a film, is ace. I usually make this for 2 but it can easily be doubled. While you cook 220g of fresh fettuccine or 200g of dried, put 60g of diced butter and 4 tablespoons of grated Parmesan in the bottom of a bowl. When it is done, add the hot pasta on top, add 3 or 4 more tablespoons of Parmesan and as many grinds of black pepper as you like, and use two forks to scoop from below and toss so everything is well mixed.

Fettuccine, burro e alici
Fettuccine with butter and anchovy
Serves 2

What I want to eat a lot of the time. While you cook 220g of fresh fettuccine or 200g of dried, warm a thick slice of butter with 4–8 anchovy fillets in a frying pan so the butter melts and the anchovies disintegrate. When the pasta is al dente, lift it into the pan, toss and divide between bowls.

Fettuccine con funghi porcini
Fettuccine with porcini mushrooms, butter and garlic
Serves 4

If you can't find porcini, you could use field mushrooms and 20g of dried porcini soaked in a little warm water. The key to this dish is the triangle of butter, olive oil and garlic into which the mushrooms collapse, creating a thick liquor which coats the ribbons of fettuccine, which meets the slices of mushroom. Symmetry, baby!

500g mushrooms – these could be fresh porcini, a mix of button or field mushrooms with porcini, or with 20g dried porcini, soaked in warm water for 20 minutes
4 tablespoons olive oil
100g butter
1–2 cloves of garlic, peeled and gently crushed (split but still whole)
450g fresh fettuccine, or 400g dried, tagliatelle, pappardelle
1 heaped teaspoon chopped fresh flat-leaf parsley

Clean the mushrooms using a cloth or a little knife to brush, scrape or pare away any grit or earth from the stalk, then use a damp cloth to wipe the stalk and cap. Cut the mushrooms into 2mm slices, cutting the cap and stem separately, if you prefer.

In a large frying pan, warm the oil, butter and the garlic, until the garlic is fragrant. Add the mushrooms, raise the flame and cook, stirring, for a few minutes until they absorb the fat, then reduce the flame and cook for 6–8 minutes, or until they are cooked through – the time needed will depend on the mushrooms – but still with plenty of buttery sauce.

Meanwhile cook the fettuccine until al dente.

In the last 30 seconds, add salt, pepper and parsley, raise the heat and stir. Add the fettuccine, toss vigorously so the starch from the pasta meets the mushroom juices and serve immediately.

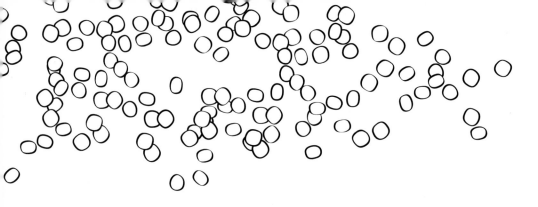

— f —

Fregula

As packets of pasta go, fregula is a particularly pleasing one to pull from the shelf and hold. And squeeze, the hundreds of tiny balls rolling and rising under the pressure like a beanbag under a bottom, a momentary stress ball for your hand. Another pleasure is tipping a hailstorm of them into the metal bowl if you want to weigh them, grabbing a fistful if you don't.

The birthplace of fregula (often Italianized as fregola) is the island of Sardinia. Politically one of Italy's 20 regions, Sardinia is one of the 5 with broader autonomy. It is a true continent with its own language and forthright culinary traditions, within which fregula plays a role. First documented in the fourteenth century, fregula is made from durum wheat flour (semola) and water. It is made using the same technique as is used to make North African couscous: water is sprinkled, a little at a time, over flour in a wide-bottomed dish, which is then rubbed in a rotary movement until – like a snowball gathering layers as it rolls – balls form. The fregula is then toasted. It is a technique that requires agile hands, patience and practice, one that for years was the first and most important dowry of a wife, or as my Sardinian friend Manuela noted, the burden. The name fregula derives from the Latin *ferculum*, commonly *fregolo*, both of which mean crumb. Whether made by skilled hands or swift, burden-lifting machines, fregule are roughly spherical, their porous surface ready to absorb flavour and sauce.

Fregula is a *pastina*, a tiny shape usually cooked in broth or brothy soup.

Fregula stands alone though, as being particularly stout and, thanks to the toasting, nutty. It can also be boiled and used with sauce, or treated like rice and cooked by an absorbing method – *risottata*. After lamb broth, the most famous pairing is with small, blue-grey triangular clams called *arselle*, whose essence-of-the-sea liquor, mixed with garlic, chilli and tomatoes, makes for a sapid *minestra*, brothy enough to justify the use of a spoon, but only just. Fregula varies in size, from 2mm peppercorn size to 6mm pea. It also varies in quality, some brands passing off spaghetti cut into very short lengths (you can tell).

Fregula con la salsiccia e zafferano
Fregula with sausage and saffron
Serves 4

In this recipe fregula is treated like rice in a risotto, so the broth is added gradually, each addition given time to absorb before the next is added. Saffron shows its power here, not only standing up to, but putting a spell on, the sausage. Like risotto the final consistency is key, so rich and dense, but not stiff, some movement is nice, as is a Sardinian red called Cannonau to drink with the end result.

1 clove of garlic, unpeeled
6 tablespoons olive oil
120g sausage meat
4 sun-dried tomatoes, diced
2 stalks of thyme
a small piece of chilli
1 litre stock, meat or vegetable
350g fregula
a few strands of saffron
60g pecorino, grated

Don't peel the clove of garlic, just smash it with the heel of your hand and put it into a deep frying pan with 3 tablespoons of olive oil over a medium-low flame and allow to fry gently. If you wish, remove the garlic from the pan.

Crumble the sausage meat into the pan, along with the sun-dried tomatoes, thyme and chilli, and fry, stirring, for 2 minutes.

Put the stock into a small pan at the back of the stove – it should be simmering hot. Add the fregula to the sausage and stir for a minute. Then, as you would a risotto, start adding the stock to the fregula pan ladle by ladle, keeping everything at a lively simmer, stirring as you go. It will take about 12 minutes for the fregula to cook and produce a brothy dish.

Add the saffron, pecorino and the remaining 3 tablespoons of olive oil to the pan and serve.

Sa fregula cun cocciula
Fregula with clams or arselle
Serves 4

The self-contained, almost circular nature of this recipe is satisfying. Steamed open, the clams produce a deeply flavoured liquor, which is enriched with oil, garlic, chilli and just a few sweet tomatoes. This is then used to cook the fregula, which absorbs the liquor back, mostly – the final dish should be brothy enough for a spoon. Right at the end you add the clams back along with a handful of parsley. It doesn't need toast rubbed with garlic and drenched with olive oil, but is better for it. It is one of my favourite things to eat.

1kg clams or arselle
7 tablespoons olive oil
250ml dry white wine
2 cloves of garlic, peeled
red chilli or red chilli flakes
a sprig of fresh flat-leaf parsley
12 sweet cherry tomatoes, or 3 or 4 (200g) tinned plum tomatoes with no juice
salt and black pepper
250g fregula
1 heaped tablespoon chopped fresh flat-leaf parsley

Wash the clams under running water, then leave to soak for 20 minutes in tepid, salted water. Drain.

In a deep frying pan with a lid, warm 2 tablespoons of olive oil, add the clams, raise the flame, add the wine, then cover the pan. Stay near the pan and shake it from time to time, listening out for the sound of the clams opening and when they do, lift the lid and lift them out. Once you have pulled all the open clams out, remove the pan from the heat and strain the liquor though a fine sieve. Pick two dozen clams in their shells and set aside, then pull the rest of the flesh from the shells and also set aside. Measure out the clam liquor and add enough boiling water to make up 800ml of liquid.

Finely chop the garlic, a small piece of chilli (if using) and the parsley, put into the frying pan along with the remaining 5 tablespoons of olive oil and fry gently over a medium-low flame. Add the tomatoes and a pinch of salt and leave to bubble away, stirring, for 6 minutes.

Add the clam broth and raise the heat so it boils, then add the fregula and cook, stirring, until it is al dente. The final dish should be soft and soupy (although not watery), so if it seems dry or too stiff as the fregula cooks, add more water or wine. In the last minute of fregula cooking time, add the clams and clam flesh, and the parsley. Serve.

Variation with mussels
The procedure is exactly the same, just substituting clams for mussels and leaving out the tomatoes.

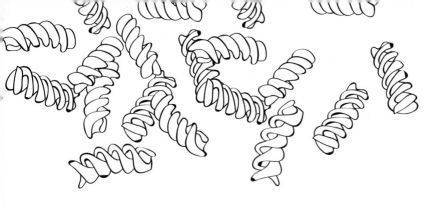

— f —

Fusilli

Watching any pasta shape being extruded is a hypnotic thrill. But with fusilli, the succession of short spirals twisting from the die before being chopped is particularly psychedelic, whether from a domestic worktop extruder or a two-ton factory one. One day I will watch an extruder forming fusilli while smoking a joint and listening to the Incredible String Band. As with any invention that has become commonplace, we take a pasta machine that can extrude perfect spirals for granted. It was Guido and Aurelio Tanzi, Italian brothers living in New York, who in 1924 finally perfected a machine capable of making fusilli of uniform size and pierced with a hole. Just shy of 100 years later factory-made fusilli, single or double spiral, is the third most popular shape in Italy.

The ancestors of factory-made fusilli are some of the most ancient flour and water forms, Sicilian busiate and Sardinian busi, names echoing the *busa*, the thin reed around which the dough was wound. From these founding shapes myriad forms evolved using various objects – knitting needles, stalks of plants, bicycle spokes, wooden rods – all over the south of Italy. On the coast of Campania, shapes were made by winding dough around a spindle-shaped iron rod (*ferretto*) called a *fuso*, hence the dialect name *fusillo*. These fusilli, though, were different from the factory form, more like long scrolls than the tight spirals the brothers perfected centuries later.

Fusilli, whether scrolls or spirals, are designed to catch sauce. Like many early rolled forms, fusilli was traditionally a feast-day shape. When I quiz my

Sicilian parents-in-law, the daughter of a tomato farmer and son of a baker, about pasta, and especially when I try to entangle them in (my) nostalgia, they remind me that as children they, like 80 per cent of Italy's then rural population, ate mostly vegetables and bread. Pasta was for feast days, even more of a feast if meat was involved.

Lamb *ragù* with fusilli and lots of herbs is one of my favourite recipes to cook, the roar of marjoram, rosemary and sage at all stages of chopping and cooking made even better by a glass of wine and an album, psychedelic or otherwise.

Ragù di agnello con tante erbe
Lamb ragù with lots of herbs
Serves 4

Years ago, a girl behind the perfume counter in John Lewis told my mum that for impact you should layer scent. I much prefer the analogy in cooking, adding the first batch of chopped herbs early, the remaining whole ones later, and then a final handful just before serving. Three layers for impact. This is a Friday-night dish for us, a bottle of red wine while we cook, another with it, and a big salad beside, cheese and more wine for after. If you prefer you can omit the tomatoes and make it in *bianco*, white (as opposed to red), in which case you will need to add more wine.

1 onion, peeled and finely diced
1 small carrot, peeled and finely diced
1 stick of celery, finely diced
6 tablespoons olive oil
a sprig of fresh flat-leaf parsley
2 sprigs of fresh marjoram
2 sprigs of fresh rosemary
8 fresh sage leaves
salt and black pepper
700g boneless lamb suitable for stewing, e.g. neck, cut into 2cm cubes
200ml white wine
1 x 400g tin of peeled plum tomatoes
1 small dried red chilli, crumbled
500g fusilli, alternatively rigatoni, paccheri, tagliatelle, pappardelle
grated pecorino, to serve

Put the diced onion, carrot, celery and the olive oil into a large heavy-based pan. Finely mince half of each of the herbs and add to the pan along with a pinch of salt. Fry gently, over a low heat, until soft and fragrant – about 7 minutes.

Raise the heat a little, add the lamb, and cook, stirring until browned on all sides. Raise the heat another notch and add the wine, letting it bubble for 2 minutes.

Add the tomatoes, two-thirds of the remaining whole herbs, the chilli and a good pinch of salt, then lower the heat, cover and simmer gently for an hour and a quarter, lifting the lid to stir from time to time and adding more wine if it seems dry.

Cook the pasta in plenty of fast-boiling salted water. Drain, tip into a bowl, sprinkle over a handful of grated pecorino and the remaining herbs, finely chopped, tip on the sauce, toss well and serve immediately, handing round more grated pecorino for on top.

Fusilli al ragù di tonno
Fusilli with tomato and tuna ragù
Serves 4

Fresh tuna and fresh tomatoes make a gorgeous couple, always, also in *ragù*.
The recipe, a great favourite, can be adapted to use tinned tuna, also embellished
with more herbs, olives, capers.

500g fresh tomatoes
6 tablespoons olive oil
1 small onion, peeled
   and sliced
a sprig of fresh basil
1 clove of garlic,
   unpeeled
300g fresh tuna,
   diced, or 200g
   tinned tuna, in
   olive oil, drained
white wine
salt and black pepper
400g fusilli

Bring a large pan of water to the boil. Peel the tomatoes by
plunging them into the boiling water for 60 seconds, lifting them
out (keep the water for the pasta later) and rinsing under cold
water, at which point the skins should slip away. Chop roughly.

In a large frying pan warm the olive oil and onion and cook gently
until soft. Add the tomatoes and a few leaves of basil and allow to
simmer for 15 minutes, in which time the tomatoes collapse into a
sauce and thicken slightly.

In another pan, warm more oil and the bashed clove of garlic. Once
the garlic is fragrant, add the diced (or tinned) tuna and cook
briskly until cooked through, then spritz with a little white wine,
let the pan sizzle for 20 seconds, then tip the fish and juices into
the tomato pan and check for salt and pepper.

Cook the pasta until al dente, drain or lift directly into the sauce,
toss and serve.

Fusilli with tinned sardines, fennel, lemon and anchovy crumbs

Serves 4

This is a long way from the dish that inspired it, *pasta con le sarde* (pasta with fresh sardines), but has a goodness all of its own. It is also a battle cry for tinned sardines and a reminder of the power of lemon zest. Anchovy crumbs, inspired by the English chef Rowley Leigh, are the business and once made, usually become a habit.

1 small red onion
1 small bulb of fennel
6 tablespoons olive oil
salt
1 small red chilli, crumbled, or red chilli flakes
1 tin of sardines
zest of 1 unwaxed lemon
1 tablespoon chopped fresh flat-leaf parsley
400g fusilli, also bucatini, spaghetti, linguine
1 small tin of anchovy fillets, drained of oil
50g soft white breadcrumbs

Bring a large pan of water to the boil for the pasta.

Peel the onion and slice thinly. Trim the fennel, discarding the tough part of the stalks but keeping the pale part and any feathery fronds, then chop them finely and set aside. Slice the bulb lengthways very thinly.

In a large frying pan over a medium heat, warm the olive oil, onion and fennel bulb along with a pinch of salt and cook, stirring until the vegetables are soft. Add the chilli and cook for a minute or so, then add the sardines, mashing gently so they break into the vegetables. Add the lemon, parsley and the chopped stalk and fennel fronds you saved, stir and put to one side.

Add salt to the pasta water, stir and add the pasta. Cook until al dente.

Make the anchovy crumbs by warming the drained anchovies in a little olive oil, then adding the crumbs and frying them over a lively flame until they have absorbed the anchovy oil and are golden.

When the pasta is almost ready, put the fennel and sardines back on the heat. Lift the cooked pasta directly into the sauce, stir well, then divide between bowls and top with the anchovy crumbs.

— g —

Garganelli

You will need the broadest hair comb you have (washed obviously), and a wooden spoon to make garganelli.

And while you're looking, do you have a rolling pin (any rolling pin) and a wooden surface, a wicker basket and grater, a rough piece of wood, an ice or paint scraper, a butter knife with a rounded end, a small liqueur glass with sharp edges, round biscuit cutters, a bicycle or umbrella spoke, metal knitting needle, wooden skewers, a pizza cutting wheel, a knife with a slender blade?

The idea that you need to buy special equipment to make pasta, or to hold back from trying until you have a specific tool, is not just a shame, it's at odds with the very nature of pasta. Looking back at the evolution of shapes, we find the results of hands working with everyday objects. Caved, ridged shapes made by rolling lumps of dough against baskets or graters, dragged ones made by scrapers, hollows in a rope created by the spoke of an umbrella, the edges of parcels defined and sealed with the twist of a sharp-edged glass, ridged tubes formed by rolling a square of dough obliquely over a comb and round the handle of a wooden spoon.

Parts of the body and animals have inspired many shapes and in the case of garganelli it was both, deriving either from *garganel* – a chicken neck – or *garganello*, a small oesophagus, both Romagnolo dialect, both conjuring a vivid picture, also a physical one for when we next swallow. Ridged tubes of garganelli are typical of the Romagna part of Emilia-Romagna, and also Le

Marche and Umbria. There are legends of course, the cook of a rich man who misjudged allocation of the cappelletti filling so had to improvise with a tea-towel and stick, the housewife whose cat ate the filling and so she rolled squares over a loom comb, both not entirely believed or doubted. Because believing or doubting isn't the point of folklore, rather reaffirmation that the creation of garganelli was an act of resourcefulness, imagination, beauty and humour.

In Bologna Francesca and her parents have a small cotton loom, 15 by 60cm, once intended for handkerchiefs: it is ideal for forming garganelli, a ridged surface over which to roll squares of dough round a stick. The day they taught me to make tortellini, we also rolled some garganelli. Many homes in Romagna still have specific *pettini per garganelli*, loom combs to make their Sunday lunch. The dough for garganelli is soft flour and egg, often with the addition of a little grated Parmesan and nutmeg. Once shaped they are served in many ways, notably in chicken broth with a swirl of Parmesan, *alla romagnola* with tomato, sausage, nutmeg and Parmesan, with *ragù alla romagnola* (a wondrous thing), or with braised vegetables and Parmesan which catches in the ridges made by your *pettine*, whatever it looks like.

To make garganelli

This is a standard egg dough, with the addition of Parmesan and nutmeg. 400g of 00 flour, 4 eggs, 2 tablespoons of grated Parmesan and a grating of nutmeg. Working as usual (mountain way or in a bowl, see page 000), mix the flour, Parmesan, nutmeg and eggs into a rough ball, knead until smooth and firm, rest and then roll (by hand or a machine) into a thin sheet. Cut into 5cm squares. To shape, position a square on the comb (or pasta board or basket), then place the wooden spoon handle (pencil, baton, or suitable tube) diagonally at one corner, lift the end up and round the spoon handle and then roll forward, so as to create a tube or quill, pressing to seal. Cook in plenty of fast-boiling salted water.

Ragù alla romagnola
Romagna-style ragù
Serves 4

Alla romagnola, so typical of the Romagna half of the now united Emilia-Romagna, also the birthplace of garganelli. Quicker to make than other *ragùs*, it is extraordinarily rich and sumptuous thanks to the addition of chicken liver, Marsala and béchamel, which acts as the milk does in a Bolognese *ragù*, only better, softening edges, enriching. This is a Friday night dish, a bottle of wine for the cook and whoever else is sitting at the table keeping them company, slicing salami or keeping the crisp bowl full, music and smells filling the room with Friday fog.

1 small onion, peeled
1 carrot, peeled
1 stick of celery
a few stalks of fresh
    flat-leaf parsley
50g butter
100g beef
200g chicken livers
Marsala
300g ripe tomatoes
grated nutmeg
50g pancetta or
    prosciutto
450g fresh garganelli,
    tagliatelle,
    pappardelle, 400g
    dried, alternatively
    fusilli or rigatoni
grated Parmesan, to
    serve

For the béchamel
200ml milk
15g butter
15g flour

Make the béchamel (see page 58). Finely dice the onion, carrot, celery and parsley stalks – this can be done in a food processor.

In a large heavy-based pan, warm the butter and chopped vegetables and cook until they are soft and translucent.

Finely chop the beef and livers and add to the pan, stirring so they lose all their pink, then add a good freestyle pour of Marsala, which should bubble.

Peel and roughly chop the tomatoes, mash a few times with a potato masher, then add to the pan and simmer for 5 minutes. Add the béchamel and a grating of nutmeg and allow to bubble at a steady simmer for 45 minutes, adding a little warm water or broth if at any point the pan seems dry. By the end of cooking the sauce should be rich and thick. At the very end, fry the pancetta or prosciutto in a little oil until crisp and add to the sauce.

Cook the garganelli in plenty of fast-boiling well-salted water, drain, tip on to the sauce and toss. Serve, passing round grated Parmesan for those who want it.

Garganelli con verdura, pancetta croccante e parmigiano
Garganelli with spring vegetables, crisp pancetta and Parmesan

Serves 4

The recipe this is adapted from is called *garganelli in salsa di scalogno*, in shallot sauce. While it does contain lots of shallots, which collapse accommodatingly, there are also peas and lettuce and in my version courgette, hence the name. The vegetables are cooked *in umido*, best translated as a steamy braise. This means they are cooked first in oil and butter, then you add water so they bubble and soften and release their juices, which are then absorbed back as the water evaporates. A circle of flavour and vegetables soft enough to wrap themselves around the tubes. It is a lovely vegetarian dish, so I have kept the crisp pancetta optional.

6 shallots (or 10 spring onions), thinly sliced
butter
olive oil
1 courgette, in thin rounds
150g peas
salt
150ml salted water or light stock
1 small lettuce head, such as romaine or little gem, cut into thick ribbons
100g pancetta, in batons
480g fresh garganelli, 400g dried
50g Parmesan, grated

In a large frying pan, gently fry the shallots/spring onions in butter and oil until they are just getting soft. Then add the courgettes, peas and a good pinch of salt, stir, then add 2 ladles of hot water or light stock and allow to bubble until everything is very soft – about 10 minutes. At the last minute add the lettuce and allow to wilt down.

In a separate pan crisp the batons of pancetta.

Boil the garganelli in plenty of well-salted water. Once al dente, drain and toss with the soft vegetables and a handful of grated Parmesan.

Divide between plates, topping with crisp pancetta for those who want it and passing round more grated Parmesan.

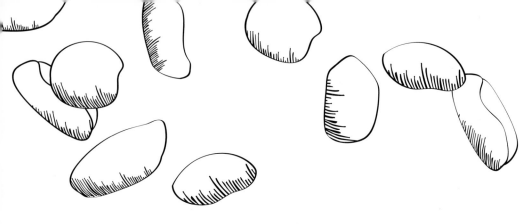

— g —
Gnocchi

Before we come to the important issue of how to make potato gnocchi that don't dissolve like aspirin when cooking, let's return to the idea that in the beginning was the *gnocco*.

The word *gnocco* is Venetian dialect for a tree-knot or lump, but here it is used to describe the mother of all pastas, a huge symbolic lump of dough or '*gnocco*' from which all other shapes evolved. Historians and cookery writers try to chart the evolution of these shapes, which is rather like trying to separate 1,300 threads. But in the beginning the undocumented forms were simply bite-sized lumps, gnocchi. According to the first Italian food historian, Luigi Messedaglia, when Boccaccio describes Bengodi, land of pleasure in his fourteenth-century poem, the maccheroni tossed into a pan of broth balanced on a mountain of grated Parmesan were in fact gnocchi. That is to say, a symbol of great pleasure. Late Middle Age and Renaissance cookbooks give us recipes: flour or breadcrumbs mixed with cheese or eggs to make gnocchi, which were cooked in water, or broth. Later recipes document poverty and imagination: gnocchi made with chestnut, barley, rice and rye flour, bread dough, vegetables, stale bread, especially stale bread, also reminding us that nothing is new. Of the various gnocchi, the ricotta and spinach malfatti of Tuscany (which are muddled with the story of ravioli), chestnut gnocchi, and semolina gnocchi alla romana were particularly significant.

Enter potato. The marvel from Peru, brought by the Spanish to Europe but misunderstood. For centuries Italian farmers refused to cultivate it. It was only in the eighteenth century that potato was first kneaded into gnocchi. Pellegrino Artusi has a potato recipe in his 1891 book *Science in the Kitchen and the Art of Eating Well*, a sure sign the potato had shaken its stigma as a poor man's food. Then, in her 1929 *Il talismano della felicità*, Ada Boni has three recipes: potato gnocchi Genovese style, Piedmont style and alla romana, Roman style. Which brings me back to the all-important question. How to make potato gnocchi that don't dissolve like aspirin when cooking?

Artusi has the answer: the right potatoes. In his words they should be *gialle* (yellow) and *compatte, sode e poco farinose*, compact, firm and not very floury. Floury or mealy potatoes dissolve, even if you add egg. Potatoes for gnocchi should have a compact flesh, borderline waxy, and they should be old. I am convinced older potatoes make better gnocchi, which makes sense as they have less water. Boiling the potatoes whole and then peeling and drying them is also key, because waterlogged potatoes dissolve too. If you would like to make gnocchi a regular thing, consider a potato ricer, because as well as consistency you want lightness and this creates it.

The right potatoes mean that you don't need to add too much flour, which bosses the potato. Also hot potatoes help, which you should work on as soon as you can. I am writing from a Roman perspective and I am not light-handed – my aim is not the ethereal puffs that some describe, rather tender but sturdy potato gnocchi that can stand a bit of rough and tumble both in the making and in the pan. The day for *gnocchi di patate* in Rome is Thursday, blackboards boast them, streets dense with *trattorie* carry the smell of sauces that coat them – tomato, guanciale and pecorino, deep and dark oxtail stew.

Gnocchi di patate
Potato gnocchi
Serves 4

1kg firm, old potatoes
salt
200g plain flour
1 egg (optional)

Scrub but don't peel the potatoes, and boil them whole in salted water until tender. Drain, then put the empty pan back on a low heat until it is dry. Add the potatoes and let them dry for a moment. Once the potatoes are cool only enough to handle them (and the hotter you can handle the better), peel, then pass them through a potato ricer into a bowl, or mash them with a fork.

On a work surface or in a bowl, add flour and egg if you are using it and then bring the ingredients together, kneading until you have a consistent dough that shouldn't stick to your hands – if it does, add a little more flour.

Dust the work surface with flour, pull off an egg-size lump, roll it into a 2cm thick rope, then cut the rope into 1cm pieces. At this point, if you want you can make the distinctive grooves with a gnocchi board or by pressing the gnocchi gently on a cheese grater or the back of a fork. Put the gnocchi on a clean tea towel.

Bring a large pan of water to the boil, add salt, stir, then gather up the tea towel so as to gently drop all the gnocchi in at once. As soon as they bob to the surface, scoop them out with a slotted spoon. Have a warm serving plate and the sauce ready, so when the gnocchi are cooked, you put them straight on the plate, top with the sauce and serve.

The traditional sauces for potato gnocchi in Rome are *al pomodoro*, tomato sauce (page 270), *amatriciana* (page 36), or *coda alla vaccinara* (page 254). Potato gnocchi are also good with pesto (page 318) or *alla bava* (so 200ml cream, warmed with 150g of Parmesan and 50g of fontina).

Gnocchi all'ossolana
Chestnut, pumpkin and potato gnocchi with butter and sage
Serves 4

The balance is right in this recipe, the sweetness of the pumpkin tempered by the potato and balanced by the almost tannic nature of the chestnut flour. I wouldn't double this recipe; it works best for four, or for two and freeze the rest. Serve with sage and butter, or buttery mushrooms.

400g pumpkin flesh, thickly sliced
olive oil
salt and black pepper
400g potatoes (floury, such as Maris Piper)
1 egg yolk
100g chestnut flour
grated nutmeg

To serve
100g butter and 12 leaves of sage, or 200g thinly sliced mushrooms, a clove of garlic and 100g butter
grated Parmesan

Rub the pumpkin with olive oil and salt, put on a baking tray and bake at 200°C until tender and darkening at the edges – about 25 minutes. Boil the potatoes whole, in their skins, until tender and allow to cool enough to handle – then peel.

If you have one, press the potato through a ricer, or simply mash, and do the same with the pumpkin. Add the egg yolk, chestnut flour, nutmeg, salt and pepper. Bring together into a dough.

Cut the dough into 4 pieces, roll each one into a 1cm thick rope and then cut into 1cm gnocchi. Shape by rolling over a board, or the inside of a fork so they are ridged on one side and have an indent on the other.

Prepare the sauce by either melting butter and sage leaves or sautéing sliced mushrooms in butter with sliced garlic.

Cook the gnocchi in plenty of well-salted water until they float to the surface. Use a large slotted spoon or a spider sieve to lift them on to a warm plate, pour over butter and sage or mushrooms and add a handful of grated Parmesan, toss gently and serve.

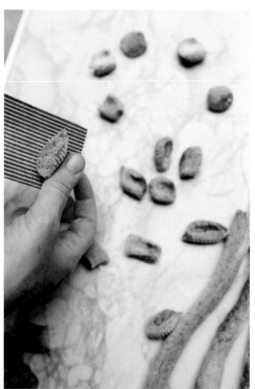

Gnocchi di spinaci e patate con panna, parmigiano e basilico
Spinach and potato gnocchi with cream, Parmesan and basil
Serves 4

This is possibly my favourite of these recipes, dark green spinach and potato gnocchi, dressed with cream, Parmesan and lots of basil. It is from the writer Rita Pane, who lives on the Sorrento coast, the land where lemons grow. Her recipes are notable because they are superb but also because of her point of reference; she suggests the ball of dough is cut into pieces the size of lemons. Basil, cheese and cream are a dream combination, also beautiful – the final dish looks like leaf pattern painting.

400g spinach
600g potatoes
250g flour
1 egg
salt and black pepper
grated nutmeg
200ml cream
100g Parmesan,
    grated
20 leaves of fresh basil

Pick over the spinach and then wash in lots of cold water, twice. Lift the spinach into a pan, with residual water clinging, then put over a medium-low flame and cover. Leave for a few minutes, shaking the pan, so the spinach wilts completely. Drain thoroughly, pressing with a heavy weight. Chop finely.

Peel the potatoes and boil in plenty of well-salted water until tender, drain and then mash or – better still – pass through a potato ricer.

Mix the chopped spinach with the potato, flour, egg, salt, pepper and nutmeg and work into a soft, consistent dough.

Divide the dough into pieces the size of a medium lemon. Working one at a time, roll them into 1cm logs and then cut the logs into 1cm gnocchi. If you like, you can make the distinctive grooves with a gnocchi board, or by pressing the gnocchi gently on a cheese grater or the back of a fork. Dust with flour and sit them on a clean cloth.

When you are ready to cook them, bring a large pan of water to a fast boil, lift up the cloth, let the gnocchi fall into the pan and boil gently for 5 minutes.

In a small pan warm the cream, Parmesan and ripped basil, stirring, until it thickens. Pour a little into the bottom of a platter, then once they are cooked lift the (blotted) gnocchi on top and pour over the rest of the basil cream.

Gnocchi ricci
Curly gnocchi
Serves 4

Ricci means curly, so curly gnocchi is a possible translation for this shape, typical of Amatrice in the central Italian region of Abruzzo. It's a unique shape made by dragging a short length of rolled dough some distance along a wooden board so it curls but also stretches and takes on crêped ridges, the end effect being a bit like a sun-dried tomato, or a cauliflower ear, which make it an exceptional sauce catcher.

It is also a unique dough of two parts, a flour and water dough and a flour and egg dough, made separately, rested, then kneaded together which gives faint marbling. According to the historian Oretta Zanini de Vita, this feast-day shape was saved from extinction when, fearing the knowledge would die with the last two old women, the town organized workshops which rekindled the knowledge of this shape. It was taught to me by a young Roman chef called Alessandro Venturi, who serves it *all'amatriciana* (with tomato, guanciale and pecorino, see page 36) from his food truck in Yorkshire. This is his recipe, an exceptional drag.

For the flour and water dough
200g 00 flour
100ml warm water

For the flour and egg dough
200g 00 flour
2 eggs

First make the flour and water dough. Make a mountain of flour on a wooden board, swirl a crater in the middle and pour in the water and then, using either your fingertips or a fork, work the two together. Once you have a craggy dough, start kneading, usual routine, heel of hand bringing edges up and over, continual rotation. Resist adding more water until you have worked for a while and if you do, wetting your hands or splashing the board may be enough. Cover with a bowl and rest.

Make the flour and egg dough. Make a mountain of flour on a wooden board, swirl a crater in the middle and break in the eggs and then, using either your fingertips or a fork, work the two together. Once you have craggy dough, start kneading, usual routine, heel of hand bringing edges up and over, continual rotation. Resist adding water until you have worked for a while and if you do, wetting your hands or splashing the board may be enough. Cover with a bowl and rest for an hour.

Flatten the two balls into patties, put one on top of the other and then work them together, usual routine, heel of hand bringing edges up and over, continual rotation.

Cut off a thick strip and roll into a 1cm rope. Cut off 2cm nuggets. Pour out a small pile of flour and starting with the nugget of dough in the flour (which is important) and two fingers in the nugget, drag it towards you, pressing it into the wooden board or work surface so it curls up and crêpes, which sounds more complicated than it actually is.

— 1 —

Lagane

Picking up where I left off at B — Busiate with Horace, and his mention of lagane: the year is 35 BC, during the Second Triumvirate, and the Roman poet notes in his *Satires* that he wandered round the Roman Forum, got tired and so went home for dinner: a bowl of chickpeas, leek and lagane, as you do.

Food history is fascinating, even more so when the pursuit of it is driven by appetite and the desire to eat. Horace and his soup of chickpeas and lagane is all very interesting, but many times more so if we can have it too. In Salento in Puglia *ciceri e tria* is a popular dish of chickpeas with boiled *and* fried strips of pasta, also a symbolic meeting of two traditions — the *lagana romana* and the dried strings or *tria* introduced by the Arabs. Meanwhile in the instep of the boot, Basilicata (interestingly the birthplace of Horace), lagane are described as 3cm by 10cm strips of semola and water pasta and cooked various ways, including with chickpeas, salt cod and *peperoni cruschi*, small red peppers that are fried until they are so crisp they shatter. In Rome you can do as Horace did and wander round the streets and do a bit of shopping, wander a bit more in the Roman Forum, then when you get tired walk into any *trattoria* and order *pasta e ceci*.

History and Horace aside, *pasta e ceci* is a winning and comforting combination. The basis is clear: cooked chickpeas are added to some sort of *soffritto* (that is, the finely diced mix of onion, celery and carrot fried in oil), water or chickpea cooking liquid added, everything simmered with pasta added towards the end. Beyond this, the variations are endless and it is up to you. *Pasta e ceci* can be brothy or creamy; can include tomatoes, anchovies, potato and celery; can be scented with garlic, rosemary or sage; the chickpeas can be soaked by you or from a tin, whole, or reduced to a cream; the pasta can be lagane, tubes, or broken tagliatelle. It is a dish that invites improvisation and tweaking according to taste. It is a dish to come home to when you are tired.

To make lagane

Make a batch of flour and water dough (see page 83), rest and then roll into a sheet 2mm thick. Using a sharp knife, cut into 3mm wide strips and these strips into 10cm lengths. Lagane can be substituted with broken tagliatelle, fresh or dried, also egg maltagliati, and for these next two soups ditalini, conchiglie and lumache also work brilliantly.

Pasta e ceci
Pasta and chickpea soup with tinned chickpeas
Serves 4

I have a huge amount of love for this dense, toffee-coloured version of *pasta e ceci*, and it is our lunch or supper at least once a week in autumn and winter. Half blended until creamy, it coats the folds of pasta, or broken bits, or thimbles, anything goes. Double the quantity and it makes an easy-going and generous meal for a crowd, also accommodating, as you can make it during the day, then reheat and add and cook the pasta when it suits you and the crowd. To serve, zigzag with some of your best olive oil.

2 x 400g tins of chickpeas
6 tablespoons extra virgin olive oil
1 onion, peeled and finely diced
1 stick of celery, finely diced
1 small potato (optional), peeled and diced
a sprig of fresh rosemary
1 tablespoon tomato concentrate
a small pinch of dried red chilli flakes (optional)
salt and black pepper
a Parmesan rind (optional)
200g fresh lagane, or 200g dried broken tagliatelle, or any of the shapes noted on page 141

Drain and rinse the chickpeas. In a large heavy-based pan, warm the olive oil, add the onion and celery and cook gently until soft and fragrant.

Add the potato, rosemary, tomato and chilli, stir, and cook for a minute before adding the chickpeas. Add 1.3 litres of water, salt and the Parmesan rind if you are using it. Bring to the boil, then reduce to a simmer for 25 minutes.

Remove half the soup from the pan and either blend or pass it through a food mill, then return it to the pan.

Remove the cheese rind. Taste and adjust salt if need be. Bring the soup to a steady but moderate boil, add the pasta and then – stirring – cook until the pasta is tender, adding a little more water if necessary. Taste to check the seasoning, adding black pepper if you wish. Serve with a little more olive oil poured over the top.

Pasta e ceci
Pasta and chickpeas
Serves 4

There are as many versions as cooks. This is a version inspired by those I have enjoyed here in Rome and it includes rosemary and anchovies at its foundation, which function as a deep salty seasoning anchovy lovers like to say is so subtle you don't notice (but try telling that to a hater). They are easily left out. This version is best with chickpeas you have soaked overnight, providing cooking water which acts as broth. For a tinned version, see the previous recipe.

250g dried chickpeas
2 cloves of garlic
2 sprigs of fresh rosemary
6 tablespoons extra virgin olive oil
3 anchovies, packed in oil
3 plum tomatoes, peeled, seeded and coarsely chopped (optional)
salt and black pepper
200g fresh lagane, or 200g dried broken tagliatelle, or any of the shapes noted on page 141

Soak the chickpeas in plenty of cold water for 12 hours or overnight. Drain and cover with 2 litres of water, add a clove of garlic and a sprig of rosemary. Bring to the boil over a medium heat, and simmer for 1½ hours, or until the chickpeas are tender.

In a large heavy-based pan, warm the olive oil and add the anchovies, the remaining clove of garlic (peeled and gently crushed with the back of a knife), and the other sprig of rosemary. Fry gently until the anchovies dissolve into the oil. Add the tomatoes if you are using them, and break them up with a wooden spoon. Cook for another few minutes.

Use a slotted spoon to add the chickpeas, and then add the chickpea broth, making sure there is 1.3 litres, and a pinch of salt. Increase the heat so the soup boils. Add the pasta and cook until tender, stirring, tasting and adding more broth to keep it to a soupy consistency. Serve with a few grinds of black pepper and a little more olive oil poured over the top.

Ciceri e tria
Chickpeas, pasta and fried pasta
Serves 4

The classic Salentine dish of chickpeas with boiled and fried strips of pasta, according to Luigi Sada's recipe in his book *La cucina pugliese*. The additional step of changing the water halfway through the cooking is a worthwhile one. Instead of removing the onion, celery and tomatoes, which are essentially flavour, I have mashed them into the soup. The contrast of boiled and fried pasta is so pleasing, and a reminder of the joy of fried dough – in fact, put a few fried curls on one side to eat with a glass of wine while you finish cooking. You do need fresh pasta for this, ideally lagane, but fresh tagliatelle cut into lengths works too.

300g dried chickpeas
½ teaspoon
    bicarbonate of soda
salt and black pepper
1 clove of garlic
1 bay leaf
1 onion, peeled and
    halved but with the
    root intact
1 stick of celery, diced
a sprig of fresh
    flat-leaf parsley
2 or 3 cherry tomatoes
olive oil
300g fresh lagane or
    short lengths of
    tagliatelle
dried red chilli flakes,
    to serve

Cover the chickpeas with water, add the bicarbonate of soda and a pinch of salt and leave overnight or for 12 hours. Drain them, then put into a heavy-based pan with the garlic and bay leaf and cover with water. Bring to the boil, then reduce to a simmer for 45 minutes – at which point they will be half cooked.

Drain the half-cooked chickpeas, then put them back into the empty pan. Add the onion, celery, parsley and tomatoes, cover with 1.3 litres of boiling water, and continue cooking until the chickpeas are tender.

Meanwhile fry half the pasta in hot oil until golden and crisp and lift on to kitchen paper to blot.

Pull the vegetables out of the chickpea pan, then add the other half of the pasta and cook, stirring, until it is tender – you may need to add a bit more hot water so it remains nicely soupy. At the last minute, add half the fried pasta and lots of black pepper, stir over a lively flame, and serve immediately with a little olive oil and the rest of the fried pasta on top. Pass red chilli flakes for those who want them.

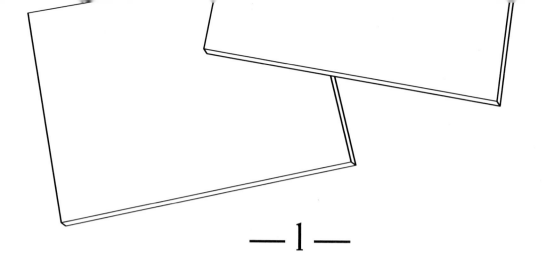

— 1 —

Lasagne

There are few things as beautiful, as inviting, as complete, as a lasagna on its way to the table. And I am not talking about any particular lasagna (yet). But all of them, a succession of layers and golden top, the bubbling edges, and the smell, the smell.

The word takes us back to the Greek *lasanon*, and Latin *lasanum*, both of which mean kitchen pot, which gave the name to those early sheets of flour and water, lagana, lasanea, lasagna. A fourteenth-century cookbook describes dough, made into fingers, boiled and layered with cheese. From this various forms evolved, some documented, most not, using every dimension of pasta from every sort of flour, every filling, domestic ingenuity ruling.

By the 1800s *lasagna al forno* had found form and its place all over Italy, local produce and customs layered into a celebration: the *lasagne da fornèl* with apple of the Dolomites, the meatball and mozzarella *lasagna di carnevale* of Naples, *lasagne incassate* from Le Marche, Bologna's majestic lasagna with *ragù*, béchamel and Parmesan. A note about plurals: lasagna refers to a single sheet (which vary massively in their dimensions), sheets are lasagne, hence the name *lasagne alla bolognese*. However, the whole thing can be singular, *lasagna al forno*, which is more familiar outside Italy.

And nothing has changed. Lasagna still comes in all shapes and sizes, with every imaginable filling, its size and proportions decided by the dish and the person who assembles it. I make lasagna often, usually with one of five fillings

– meat *ragù*, roasted vegetables, various greens, many cheeses, or lentils, to which I might add mushrooms. How I make them, whether using home-made fresh egg pasta, bought fresh pasta or dried sheets, depends on how much time I have.

While the cooking of the separate parts is of course vital, lasagna is all about a system and assembly. For me it is also about a moment of chaos. Regardless of how well organized I am, and whether it is the simplest or the most elaborate, there will be a moment when my entire kitchen is turned inside out and I ask myself if it is worth it (I have on occasion sworn never to make lasagna again, at least not *this one*). But lasagna chaos is like a summer storm, intrusive and violent, and also stopping as dramatically as it started. You clean up, it is just you and a neat lasagna, the sun comes out, the storm is forgotten, or forgiven, or both. Baked and brought to the table, there are few things as beautiful, as inviting, as complete.

Lasagne alla bolognese
Lasagna Bolognese style with ragù, béchamel and Parmesan

Serves 8

While freedom to adapt and vary is a basic tenet of cooking, classic recipes honed over time are too. Here is one for a majestic *lasagne alla bolognese* as taught to me by Rina Poletti, who you will meet properly at the letter T. Home-made, hand-rolled, fresh egg pasta, layered with long-simmered *ragù*, béchamel and lots of grated Parmesan. It feels important to note that the addition of milk to Bolognese *ragù* is traditional for some, but not for others. I love the way it softens and rounds the flavour. Feel free to leave it out. Lasagna is a project. Also extraordinary, and – thanks to the thinly rolled pasta and many layers – surprisingly delicate. I always make double or triple *ragù* because it freezes so well. I love many lasagne, but this one, cut into deep terrazzo tiles, in particular.

For the pasta
pasta dough made from 400g of 00 flour and 4 eggs (see page 51) if you want, with the addition of spinach and cut into sheets, suitable for your dish

For the ragù (this makes approx. 1 litre, which is the right amount for a 2 litre dish)
30g butter
3 tablespoons olive oil
150g pancetta or bacon, minced
1 onion, peeled and finely chopped
1 carrot, peeled and finely chopped
1 stick of celery, finely chopped
salt and black pepper
400g ground beef
300g ground pork
1 bay leaf

Ragù

In a large heavy-based pan, over a medium-low flame, warm the butter and olive oil and gently fry the pancetta, onion, carrot, celery and a pinch of salt until the vegetables are starting to soften and turn translucent.

Crumble the meat into the pan, then raise the heat a little and cook, stirring until the meat has lost all trace of pink and is evenly brown. Add the bay leaf and wine, allow to bubble for a few minutes, then add the tomato passata, salt and pepper.

Reduce the heat to low, cover the pan and cook for 2 hours, lifting the lid every now and then to stir and add the milk bit by bit. By the end of cooking the *ragù* should be rich and mellow-tasting. Check the seasoning.

Béchamel (see page 58).

Pasta – par-boiling
Bring a large pan of water to the boil, add salt and stir. Prepare a big bowl of cold water and lay out clean tea towels. Add the pasta sheets to the boiling water a few at a time, boil for 30 seconds, then lift (I find a slotted spoon and tongs good here), plunge briefly into the cold water and then spread out on the cloths.

120ml white wine
350g passata di
    pomodoro (see
    page 277)
200ml milk

**For the béchamel
(which should be
quite loose)**
800ml milk
60g butter
60g flour
grated nutmeg

Also
butter or olive oil, for
    dish
100g Parmesan,
    grated, plus extra
    for the top

To assemble the lasagna

Butter or oil a 25 x 30cm, 2 litre capacity dish and spread with a little béchamel. Bear in mind you are going to have seven layers, so share accordingly. Make a layer of pasta, encouraging rumples that catch the sauce and create height, spoon over some of the *ragù*, then some béchamel, smearing both thin with the back of a spoon. Sprinkle with Parmesan. Cover with a layer of pasta and repeat until all the ingredients are used up, ending with a layer of pasta, béchamel swirled with just a little *ragù* for colour and a good dusting of cheese.

Bake in the middle of a preheated oven at 180°C for 20–25 minutes, or until it is warmed through and the top bubbling and golden. I sometimes put it under the grill for 1 minute too. Allow to sit for at least 20 minutes before serving in slices.

Lasagna variations and other tips

So after the classic rigour of the previous recipe, let's return to the adaptable ease of lasagna, that is layers of pasta and filling, baked.

Ease starts with a calculation. The best lasagna advice I've received is to calculate. That is measure your dish and work out how many pasta sheets (fresh or dried) will fill it, roughly as scraggy edges are welcome. My dish is 25 x 30cm, 2 litre capacity, and I like 7 layers, which is 14 fresh pasta sheets (standard batch of egg dough) or 28 dried ones. There is lots of debate about par-boiling, forums dedicated to science and opinion. I always do. I par-boil fresh pasta sheets in fast-boiling, well-salted water for 30 seconds, then plunge them into the cold, then spread them on clean tea towels. I par-boil dried sheets according to the instructions on the pack. As for sheets that say par-boiling is not required, I am wary, finding they need a very liquid sauce and long cooking, but not if they are dipped in boiling water for 30 seconds, then cold water, then blotted. You may have a different experience.

I think of lasagna filling in three parts. **First – the main component** – my dish takes a standard portion of *ragù* (see above), 1kg of diced roasted vegetables, 1kg of *vignarola* (see page 290) or wilted spinach and sautéd greens, 1 litre of rich tomato sauce (see page 273), 600g of diced cheese (fontina, mozzarella/Taleggio, or a portion of braised lentils (see page 98). **Second – the white binding** – 600ml of béchamel, or 500g of ricotta loosened with 100ml of milk. **Third – the cheese** – 100g of grated Parmesan or pecorino or a mix. I treat the above as a pick and mix, taking one main component, one white binding, also cheese, putting some of each in each of 7 layers, finishing with a rug of grated cheese.

Lasagna can be made a day or two before; just omit the last layer of cheese, cover and keep in the fridge. But remember to take it out at least an hour before baking and to add the rug of grated Parmesan.

Bake in the middle of a preheated oven at 180°C for 20–25 minutes, or until it is warmed through and the top bubbling and golden. I sometimes put it under the grill for 1 minute too. Allow it to sit for at least 20 minutes before serving in slices.

— 1 —

Linguine

There is a farm that produces pasta in the middle of a wheat field. Finding it was difficult. It was January, snow iced the A24 highway like a freezer shelf and spun into a blizzard as we crossed the Apennine mountain range. And then there was the familiar failure of maps, paper v. virtual, which effectively cancelled each other out. We were saved by the sea, the coast road and San Tommaso (a town) that pulled us into Le Marche.

If Italy is a thigh-high musketeer boot, the region of Le Marche is the back of the knee. It's a crooked oblong, Adriatic Sea to the east, Apennine chain to the west, and bordering Emilia-Romagna, Umbria, Lazio and Abruzzo. Two-thirds of the region is covered with mountains and hills threaded with rivers, much of the rest is alluvial plains, with alluvial soil which is loose and made up of silt, clay, sand and gravel: in short absolutely perfect for agriculture, especially wheat.

Le Marche has been a granary for Italy for thousands of years. It still is. There are many fields of wheat. Eventually we found the right one, the young plants still only a few inches high, but vigorously green against the earth and Tupperware sky. In the middle was, as promised, a wooden building, sleek as a spa but certainly a farm, also a mill, offices and a *pastificio*, a pasta factory called Mancini.

Walking into the main hall reminded me of entering a department store on a cold day, the thick rush of warm air that meets you as you walk through the electric doors; the atmosphere, though, was more like a church. The smell was also thick, and hopeful, as if someone had mixed fresh sawdust, chalk and ground almonds. Hairnets, and thin white jackets made of the same material used for disposable hospital gear, added to the sense of controlled creation. In the middle of the room was an aluminium machine, huge, with various limbs modifiable depending on the shape being made. The shape of the day was linguine (also known as bavette or trenette), so called because the oval cross-section of each strand means it resembles a *lingua*, a tongue, something I find amusing when eating 'tongues with a tongue' – imagine if you made a sauce with tongue too, a twister as good as Peter Piper.

At the top of a staircase we looked down into the mixer, with its churning dough of semola and water, a yet unformed mass of great potential. Making shapes by extrusion requires force and gravity; the dough is compressed into cylinders and then pushed through a bronze die, which in the case of linguine looks like an enormous shower head. However, instead of water, linguine streams down like a yellow cascade. The flow is cut into lengths which are portioned and hooped over rods, at which point they seem even more like string curtains, as they swing out from under the machine.

So much depends on the drying. Also good grain, good water, extrusion through bronze and good practice, but a considered drying process is what defines good pasta. If you have ever tried drying semola and water pasta at home you will know – too fast or hot and it cracks like brittle, too slow or humid, and mould creeps in. The art of drying, *essiccazione*, means balancing temperature – from the initial warmer blast that seals the surface to the slower cooler dry, also humidity, ventilation and time, which can vary from 24 to 56 hours depending on the shape. We were invited to peer into drying chambers to see short-sleeves of mezze maniche and inch-long rigatoni, screws of fusilli and fringe upon fringe of linguine and spaghetti. There was spaghetti in the packing area, too, cut to size and bundled into packets which were bundled into boxes.

Having seen the end, we went back to the beginning. Two giant silos behind the factory contain grain from the previous year's harvest, the annual yield

from the 43 fields that sustained 5 varieties of hard wheat. Milling, which reduces the grains into the granular semola necessary for pasta making, is done as required, meaning flavour and nutrients live on in every tube and little tongue.

Massimo Mancini, Lorenzo Settimi and I sat at a long table, examining uncooked pasta like dermatologists, admiring the pores and rugosity that results from extrusion through bronze. Then we ate and admired how well the sauce clung to the same rough surface, the tender substance of each tube. After lunch, a snaking tour through the muscular hills meant we saw a good proportion of the 43 fields through the car window, also pit-stopped to crouch next to two-month-old plants that will be golden by July and will be future shapes.

The next day, back home, I put a pan of water on to boil, sliced some courgettes and onion and cooked them in olive oil, beat eggs and cheese together and pulled a packet of linguine from the shelf. Before opening I did what I always do, read the sentence written on the back of the orange label, *Esiste un'azienda agricola che produce pasta in mezzo a un campo di grano* – There is a farm that produces pasta in the middle of a wheat field.

Linguine con pesce spada alla messinese
Linguine with swordfish Messina style
Serves 4

A few weeks in southern Sicily puts an end to the myths and finger-wagging rules about never mixing fish and cheese, especially with pasta. At Sakalleo, a fish restaurant in the town of Scoglitti, they add grated cheese to almost every pasta dish; red mullet and bottarga, tomatoes and shrimps, swordfish and mint. It not only binds and seasons, explains the gorgeous owner Giada, it elevates flavours.

Likewise with this swordfish sauce, which is a sort of *alla ghiotta*, glutton style: a lively sauce of tomato, capers, olives, enriched with a handful of pecorino. The sharp piquant cheese melts into the sauce, seasoning but also turning it slightly opaque and thickening, meaning it clings richly to one of its ideal shapes, linguine.

1 heaped tablespoon salted capers
3 ripe tomatoes
1 small white onion, peeled and finely diced
salt
1 stalk of celery, finely diced
6 tablespoons olive oil
white wine
10 green olives, stoned and roughly chopped
400g swordfish, diced
400g linguine, also spaghetti, fusilli, busiate, cavatelli
fresh mint or flat-leaf parsley
3 tablespoons grated pecorino

Cover the salted capers with water and leave to sit and soak for 10 minutes. Drain.

Bring a large pan of water to the boil, turn off the heat, add the tomatoes for 60 seconds, then use a slotted spoon to lift them out and cool under cold water, at which point the skins should slip away. Chop the tomatoes roughly, pushing out the seeds and any tough bits. Keep the water for the pasta.

In a large, deep frying pan, cook the onion and celery in the oil with a pinch of salt over a medium-low heat until soft and translucent. Add a little white wine, allow to bubble a few minutes, then add the tomato, capers and olives and cook for 5 minutes, stirring often until it is saucey.

Add the swordfish and cook, stirring for 4 minutes or until the fish is just cooked through. Taste for salt. Turn off the heat and leave to rest for 30 minutes. Turn the heat back on in the last minutes of pasta cooking time.

Bring the pan of water back to the boil, add salt and then the pasta, stir and cook until al dente. Keep back some pasta cooking water.

Tip the pasta into the sauce, add herbs and pecorino, toss well, adding a little pasta cooking water if you feel it is required. Serve.

Linguine con zucchine, uova e parmigiano
Linguine with courgettes, egg and Parmesan
Serves 4

A family favourite which never fails to feel like ordinary alchemy. It is important that you cut the courgettes thinly, almost as thin as the linguine. The effect is rather like carbonara, in that the egg and cheese meet the fat and starch from the pasta and form a cream sauce. As with carbonara you need to be careful you don't get a scramble; the key is hot courgette and hot pasta so there is enough residual heat for you to bring it all together off the stove.

5 tablespoons extra virgin olive oil
1 medium onion or 4 spring onions, thinly sliced
300g courgettes, cut into 5cm long, 2mm thick strips
salt and black pepper
400g linguine, spaghetti, bucatini, pici, fusilli
2 whole eggs, plus 2 extra yolks
70g Parmesan, grated
a few fresh basil leaves

Bring a large pan of water to the boil.

In a large frying pan, warm the olive oil over a medium-low heat, then cook the onion and courgettes gently with a pinch of salt, turning them regularly with a wooden spoon until they are very soft and tender – which will take about 10 minutes. Remove the pan from the heat.

Add salt to the boiling water, stir, then add the linguine, fanning them out, and using a wooden spoon to push them down. Cook until al dente (check the cooking time of the packet and start tasting at least 2 minutes before).

While the pasta is cooking, in a large bowl whisk together the eggs, extra yolks, Parmesan, a pinch of salt and lots of pepper. During the last minutes of pasta cooking time, put the courgette pan back on the heat to thoroughly warm the fat and vegetables and add the ripped basil.

Drain the pasta, reserving some of the cooking water. Add the pasta to the frying pan, stirring so it tangles with the vegetables. Take the pan off the heat, and, working quickly, add the egg mixture and a splash of pasta cooking water, then stir and swirl the pan vigorously until each strand is coated with creamy sauce and the consistency is slithery. Add a little more pasta cooking water if it seems too stiff and stir again.

Pasta c'anciova e muddìca atturrata
Linguine with anchovies, tomato and breadcrumbs
Serves 4

The toasted breadcrumbs, *muddìca atturrata*, mark this as Sicilian, as does the dialect *quagghia*, used to describe the look and tight gurgle when the sauce of tomato and anchovy has thickened to the point of doneness.

100ml extra virgin
  olive oil
red chilli flakes
2 cloves of garlic,
  peeled and with a
  couple of slits
10 anchovies in olive
  oil, roughly
  chopped
2 ripe tomatoes, diced
5 tablespoons chopped
  fresh flat-leaf
  parsley
400g linguine, also
  fettuccine,
  spaghetti, busiate,
  fusilli

**For the muddìca
atturrata**
1 cup of plain
  breadcrumbs
a few drops of extra
  virgin olive oil
salt

In a frying pan, over a medium low heat, warm the oil, red chilli flakes and garlic so the flavours infuse the oil. Add the roughly chopped anchovies and stir with a wooden spoon until they disintegrate.

Add the diced tomatoes (along with their juice and seeds) and half the parsley and let it bubble for a couple of minutes. Add a couple of cups of water, stir, and let it cook on medium-high for about 5 minutes.

While the sauce is bubbling, toast the crumbs by sprinkling them into a small frying pan over a medium heat, adding a few drops of olive oil and a pinch of salt and stirring constantly with a wooden spoon until they are dry gold and smell like toast. Tip on to a plate so they don't continue cooking.

Cook the linguine until al dente, drain, saving a cup of pasta cooking water, then tip straight into the in a large pan of salted boiling water with the anchovy sauce.

Stir for about a minute on a medium heat until the pasta is perfectly coated with the sauce, adding a little of the saved water if it looks too dry. At this point your dish is ready; turn off the heat and add the rest of the parsley.

You can either add the breadcrumbs directly to the pasta in the pan and stir, or you can sprinkle some on top of the plated dish. There are no rules!

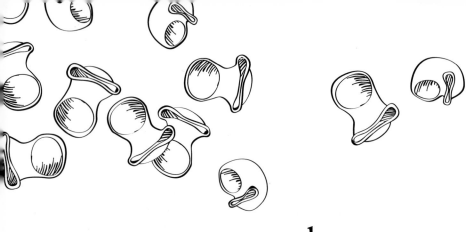

— 1 —

Lumache

Dried pasta is designed to last over time. Our cupboards are testament to this, and of our love of and dependency on it. The packets we have reveal our preferences (5 packets of rigatoni) and fears (of running out), foresight (they were on offer) and extravagance (it is a very rare shape), reflect our good (jar for mixed shapes) or bad management (general stuffing). Then there is the fallback packet.

Lumache, literally snails but actually their shells, are one of many pastas named after animals, or animal parts: mouse tails, chicken gullets, cocks' crests. They have a home-made ancestor formed by pressing and rolling a nugget of dough against a comb, to form a rigid curl. Its geometry means that like its seashell sister, a lumaca doesn't just catch, it holds. The smaller forms broths, medium forms beans, or meat *ragùs*, the largest stuffing. Lumache are also called pipe (pipes) and chiocciole (which is another word for snails).

Planning this section, I made a list of classic regional sauces for lumache – after all, I couldn't dismiss them as my fallback. Until I realized that I must, because it wasn't a dismissal, but a compliment. Ever since I put a packet of lumache, tuna and white beans in a box of essentials to take with us to the family house in Sicily, where they provided us with what felt like a miraculous midnight meal, lumache have been my faithful fallback, as reassuring as an open train ticket or favourite song dancing out of a bar radio. It is also a reminder that as well as rules and traditions, some pairs are consequences, and ours.

Lumache all'insalata
Lumache with tuna, beans, tomato and basil
Serves 4

While it is my fallback, it isn't my combination. White beans, tuna, red onion are a traditional and harmonious trio, and with lumache they find their shape. Rather than *insalata di pasta* (pasta salad) I prefer the name *pasta all'insalata*, which doesn't mean the pasta is a salad, but that the condiment is prepared *like a salad*, so dressed and seasoned, rested, and then mixed with the hot pasta and served at room temperature. Treat the basil as an ingredient, not a garnish. Ideal for lunch on a hot day, Monday lunchtime or, in a pared-down version, the middle of the night.

1 small red onion or
   3 spring onions,
   finely diced
1 x 200g tin of
   oil-packed tuna,
   drained
300g cannellini beans
200g cherry or other
   sweet tomatoes,
   diced
a big handful of fresh
   basil leaves
1 tablespoon capers
olive oil
salt and black pepper
500g lumache,
   conchiglie,
   maccheroni,
   farfalle

Bring a large pan of water to the boil for the pasta.

Taste the onion. If you are happy with it raw leave it just so, but if it is strongly flavoured, soak it in a mixture of half vinegar/half water for 10 minutes, then drain.

In a large bowl, break up the tuna with a fork and then add the beans, tomatoes, onion, ripped basil, capers, and olive oil (6 tablespoons as an estimate), salt and plenty of black pepper, stir and leave to sit while you cook the pasta.

Add salt to the boiling water, stir and add the pasta and cook until al dente, then drain in a colander.

Tip the hot pasta on to the cold condiment and mix thoroughly, then leave to sit for at least 20 minutes before eating.

Lumache con tonno, uova e capperi
Lumache with tuna, egg and capers
Serves 4

If you are familiar with *vitello tonnato*, veal with a tuna, egg and caper sauce, then that will give you some idea of this tuna sauce enriched with egg yolks which clings to the shells, and also shines. The recipe is an adaption of one by Lisa Biondi, a prolific recipe writer and author of numerous stylish and trend-setting books in the 60s and 70s, who turned out to be the entirely fictional creation of a publishing house.

1 large onion
1 stick of celery
6 tablespoons olive oil
salt and black pepper
1 x 200g tin of
   oil-packed tuna,
   drained
2 tablespoons tiny
   capers, rinsed
200ml white wine
1 unwaxed lemon
400g lumache
a sprig of fresh
   flat-leaf parsley,
   finely chopped
2 egg yolks, beaten

Bring a large pan of water to the boil for the pasta.

Peel and dice the onion. Trim the celery to the palest bit, pull away any strings and dice that too. Put the onion and celery into a frying pan with the olive oil and a pinch of salt and then on to a medium-low flame and cook until soft, which will take a while.

Add the flaked tuna and capers, stir a minute, then add the wine and allow to bubble for 10 minutes, adding 3 tablespoons of lemon juice and some zest in the last minutes. It should be saucey – if it is watery, cook a bit longer.

Meanwhile cook the pasta until al dente, drain and tip into a warm serving bowl, tip the sauce on top, add the parsley, toss quickly, then add the yolk, toss again and serve.

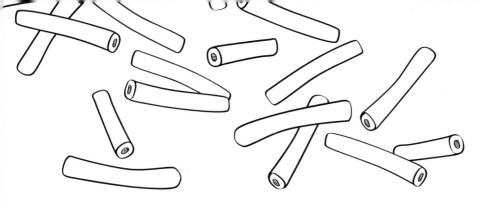

— m —

Maccheroni

Growing up in England at the end of the 1970s I remember four pasta shapes, spaghetti, alphabet, hoops and macaroni. Spaghetti was spaghetti, hoops were hoops, alphabet were letters, and macaroni were short, curved tubes that my mum, like millions of other mums, baked with white sauce and cheese. I grew up and met other pasta shapes, then moved to Italy and met dozens more. Then I became a food writer and bought Oretta Zanini de Vita's marvellous *Encyclopedia of Pasta* and quoted it to anyone who would listen. 'Oretta says there are 500 pasta shapes and 1,300 pasta names,' I told people. 'Maccheroni isn't a shape at all, but the generic name for pasta.'

In Italy, as in England and much of the world, factory-made durum wheat maccheroni are short, slightly curved tubes and extremely popular. *Maccherone* is also the generic name for pasta, a word first mentioned in a document from Campania dated 1041. For centuries it was used, is still used, to describe a huge number of shapes, long, short, tubes and twirls, with those from Sicily and Naples particularly significant, after all they are known as *mangiamaccheroni* – maccheroni eaters. Significant and confusing. Scholars have dedicated their lives to charting the evolution of maccheroni (one describing its path as torturous). Also the etymology of the word, chasing it through punning anecdotes *molto buoni ma . . . caroni* (very nice but expensive) . . . classical texts, a character from ancient theatre called Maccus and the Latin *maccare*, to pound or knead.

Years ago I was given some food writing advice: to recognize when to approach something with my head, and when to approach it with my stomach. Knowing this, the food writer and historian Gillian Riley gave me a slim green book called *Maccheronea*. It is a history of the word, but more importantly it is a book of recipes from antiquity to the present day. The early recipes are a particular delight because it is clear the recipe writers are referring to many shapes, prepared in many ways – but the name is always the same, maccheroni. It is also true, maccheroni is a playful word that rolls out of your mouth. One recipe in particular jumped out from the green book. It is on page 117 and is for *maccheroni al gratin*, which my seven-year-old self sitting at a table in 1979 would recognize well, as macaroni cheese.

Maccheroni al gratin
Macaroni cheese
Serves 4–6

Maccheroni baked with béchamel and cheese. Still my favourite. And if it is yours too, please feel free to adjust, especially when it comes to the sort of cheese. When it comes out of the oven let it rest for at least 10 minutes. I feel slightly naff suggesting a big green salad, but for me a salad with a vinegary dressing (eaten at the same time as MC, an anathema to Vincenzo who is a plate separatist) is as much a part of this as taking a knife to the dish in order to chisel away the crisp bits.

500g maccheroni
80g butter
150g Parmesan, grated
200g mozzarella
extra milk
fine breadcrumbs

For the béchamel
800ml whole milk
80g butter
80g flour
salt, black pepper and grated nutmeg

Make the béchamel (see page 58).

Cook the pasta in well-salted fast-boiling water until very al dente, then drain and toss with 50g of the butter, a handful of Parmesan and a spoonful of béchamel.

Butter an ovenproof dish, put half the pasta in the base, sprinkle with half the remaining Parmesan and the mozzarella and half the remaining béchamel. Cover with the remaining pasta and béchamel, topping with a mix of Parmesan and breadcrumbs. Dot with butter. Bake at 200°C for 20 minutes, allowing it to rest for 10 minutes before serving.

Pasta 'ncasciata
Baked macaroni with meatballs and aubergine
Serves 4–6

Maccheroni 'ncasciati is a generous and rowdy dish of pasta, small meatballs, cheese and fried aubergine. There are a few steps, but once everything is packed in and you have washed up, it is contained satisfaction. My Sicilian partner grew up eating baked pasta dishes such as this, and of course they are the favourite of Commissario Montalbano which makes them even better.

800g tomatoes, ideally fresh but you can use tinned
1 onion, peeled and sliced
2 cloves of garlic, peeled and finely chopped
olive oil
a sprig of fresh basil
salt
300g ground beef
1 slice of crustless bread, soaked in a little milk
1 egg
a sprig of fresh flat-leaf parsley, finely chopped
75g Parmesan, grated
2 aubergines, diced into 2cm cubes
500g maccheroni
200g mozzarella or caciocavallo
butter and breadcrumbs, for dish
2 hard-boiled eggs

If the tomatoes are fresh, peel by plunging them into boiling water for 60 seconds, then into cold water, at which point the skins should split and slip off easily. Chop the tomatoes roughly, separating away most of the seeds. Chop tinned ones with scissors. In a large pan, gently fry the onion and garlic in some olive oil until fragrant, add the tomatoes, basil and a pinch of salt and allow to simmer away for 15 minutes.

Make the *polpette* (meatballs): use your hands to mix the ground beef, bread, egg, parsley and 2 tablespoons of grated Parmesan and mould into walnut-sized *polpette*. Allow them to rest if you can, then fry in a little olive oil until brown and pour in the tomato sauce.

Either deep fry the aubergine or spread on a baking tray, drizzle with olive oil and salt, toss with hands and then bake at 180°C until golden – about 30 minutes.

Boil the pasta in well-salted water until very al dente. Drain and toss gently with the sauce and *polpette* and the mozzarella.

Butter and breadcrumb a large baking dish about 25 x 30cm, 2 litre capacity. Pour in half the pasta/*polpette* mix, make a layer of aubergine and sliced hard-boiled egg, then cover with the rest of the pasta mix. Top with the remaining grated Parmesan and bake at 200°C for 20 minutes.

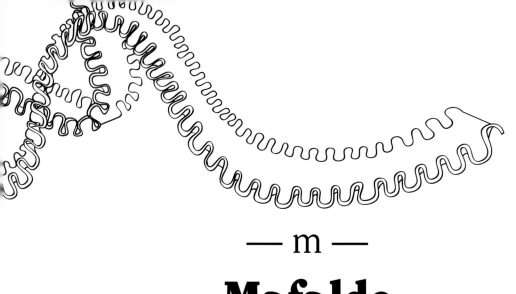

— m —

Mafalde

In 1902 Princess Mafalda of Savoy, the second daughter of King Victor Emmanuel III, was born. This shape is named for her, one of several designed to commemorate the House of Savoy, which was on the Italian throne from Unification in 1861 until the end of the Second World War. Conquest was also given a shape, tripolini, taking their name from the Italian Colony in Libya, while assabesi marked the purchase of the port of Assab in Eritrea, and ridged shells called abissine, the Italo-Abyssinian War.

Mafalde, also known as mafaldine and reginette (little queens), are 2.5cm wide with ruffled edges. They are a popular, playful and excellent shape that holds sauce brilliantly. They also hold a story. Of a princess growing up in a very particular knot of power, politics, war and genocide. In 1944, aged 41, Mafalda was one of the millions killed in concentration camps. You could argue that if you dig deeply enough into the history of any food, you will find painful truths, and really why bring this up before lunch and a recipe for tomato sauce and ricotta? But I think on this occasion remembering is as necessary as the recipe is good.

Mafalde con la mollica alla calabrese
Mafalde with anchovies and tomato paste and breadcrumbs
Serves 4

This Calabrese recipe is a symphony of umami, although it could just as well be Sicilian, for the use of tomato concentrate, anchovy, pine nuts, currants and breadcrumbs, or as my father-in-law likes to remind me, 'Parmesan for the poor'. The chilli is optional, but I think the concentration of flavours needs the heat. Pine nuts and currants are optional too.

4 tablespoons olive oil, plus extra for crumbs
3 cloves of garlic, finely chopped
8 anchovy fillets, minced
2 tablespoons tomato concentrate, dissolved in 300ml warm water
50g pine nuts
50g currants
a small dried red chilli, crumbled, or a pinch of red chilli flakes
400g mafalde, reginette or mafaldine, also spaghetti, linguine, fettuccine, fusilli
100g plain breadcrumbs

Bring a large pan of water to the boil for the pasta.

In a large frying pan, warm the olive oil, garlic and anchovies over a low flame, stirring so the anchovies disintegrate.

Add the concentrate dissolved in water and stir until everything is well mixed. Add the pine nuts, currants and chilli and simmer for 15 minutes, or until the sauce is rich and thick. It should not need salt.

Meanwhile salt the pasta water, stir, add the pasta and cook until al dente.

In a small frying pan, cook the breadcrumbs in a couple of tablespoonfuls of olive oil, stirring all the time until they are golden and smell deliciously toasty.

When the pasta is cooked, drain and add to the sauce, toss and divide between bowls, topping each with crumbs.

Mafalde con sugo di pomodoro e ricotta
Mafalde with tomato sauce and ricotta

Serves 4

Tomato sauce and ricotta is a typically Sicilian combination which swirls into pink, and the ruffled pasta catches it perfectly. It is not traditional to beat the ricotta with Parmesan but I think it works. You could also make a fresh tomato sauce (see page 272).

1 x 800g tin of peeled
    plum tomatoes
6 tablespoons olive oil
1 clove of garlic,
    peeled and crushed
    but still whole
a small dried red
    chilli, crumbled, or
    a pinch of red chilli
    flakes
salt
a sprig of fresh basil
300g ricotta
50g Parmesan, grated
400g mafalde, or
    fusilli, busiate,
    penne, fettuccine

Put a pan of water on for the pasta. Pass the tomatoes through a food mill and into a bowl. If you don't have a mill, chop them in the tin with scissors.

Put the olive oil and garlic into the frying pan, then put it on a low flame so the garlic sizzles very gently for 3 minutes. Watch it doesn't darken or burn.

Add the tomatoes, crumbled chilli, basil and a pinch of salt to the pan and allow it to bubble almost to a boil. If you haven't milled the tomatoes I suggest using a potato masher at this point to break the pieces down. Reduce to a blipping simmer, cover and cook for 20 minutes, uncovering for the last 5.

Meanwhile, in a bowl, beat the ricotta with the Parmesan until it is a soft cream.

In the last 5 minutes of sauce cooking time, add salt to the boiling water, then add the pasta and cook until al dente. Once cooked, lift it into the sauce pan and toss.

Divide between plates and top each with a blob of ricotta, a few chilli flakes and a drizzle of olive oil.

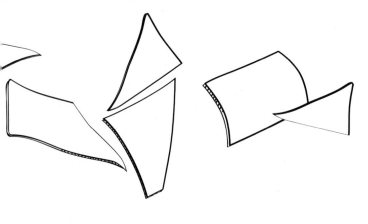

— m —

Maltagliati

As with pastry, paper or fabric, there are almost always remnants after cutting pasta. These corners and trimmings, too-thick-too-thin scraps and irregular bits are united by the fact that they are badly cut, hence the name mal – badly, tagliati – cut. While resourcefulness cannot be owned, the name maltagliati was apparently first used in Emilia-Romagna as a *pasta di recupero*, a way not to waste the odd bits of *sfoglia* (a hand-rolled sheet of pasta) left after making tagliatelle. The day I learned to hand roll and cut tagliatelle with Rina Poletti, she also made maltagliati, cutting the remnants into irregular pieces with her enormous knife. 'These are for minestra,' said Rina, using the side of her hand to sweep the heap off the edge of the board and into a plastic tub, press its lid shut and drum three fingers on the top.

Maltagliati are also made intentionally, both at home and in factories, which makes it a dried pasta shape. The nature of maltagliati is the lack of uniformity, and depending on what it is the remnants of, its proportion can vary. Whether incidental or intentional, maltagliati is the most satisfying shape to eat, especially in thick soups: *pasta e fagioli, pasta e lenticchie, pasta e patate*, chickpea and chestnut. Personally, I am keen on wonky lozenges with a surface area more or less that of a domino, so they'll just about fit on a spoon, but threaten to slither off like sea creatures, that fill your mouth and fold softly.

If you don't have remnants and want to make maltagliati, prepare a batch of flour and egg dough (see page 51) or flour and water dough (see page 83), roll thin and cut badly. If you don't use all the maltagliati straight away, leave in a cool, dry place until completely dried out – at which point they can be stored in a bag or jar. Alternatively freeze them on a tray and then, once hard, tip them into a bag and return to the freezer. They are thin enough to not need defrosting. Simply toss them directly into soup or boiling water and cook until al dente.

Minestra di ceci e castagne
Chickpea and chestnut soup
Serves 4

Chickpeas and chestnuts are both precious for their taste, substance and endurance. They also get on so well, like affectionate old friends, especially in soup. It is important both the chickpeas and chestnuts are really tender so the warm flavours emerge, so don't rush cooking. Another optional addition would be salt cod, a soaked piece added towards the end of cooking, then broken into flakes with the back of a spoon. You decide if you want to blend half the soup.

300g dried chickpeas, or 2 x 400g tins of chickpeas, drained
1 clove of garlic, peeled
1 bay leaf
2 sticks of celery, 1 diced and 1 left whole
salt and black pepper
200g cooked chestnuts
5 tablespoons olive oil
1 small onion, peeled and diced
1 sprig of fresh rosemary
200g maltagliati

If you are using dried chickpeas, cover them with water and leave to soak for at least 12 and up to 24 hours. Drain, cover with fresh water, add a clove of garlic, a bay leaf, the whole stick of celery and a pinch of salt. Bring to the boil and reduce to a simmer for an hour and a half, or until they are tender. If you are using tinned chickpeas, drain them.

The best way to prepare fresh chestnuts is to score them across the curved side and roast for 30–40 minutes, at which point the skins should split open. Wrap them in a tea towel for 10 minutes before peeling, as this loosens the skins. Peeled vacuum-packed chestnuts also work.

In a heavy-based pan, warm the oil over a medium-low flame, then add the diced onion, diced celery, a pinch of salt and the rosemary, and fry until soft and translucent. Add the chestnuts, crumbling them into the pan, then the chickpeas and 1.5 litres of chickpea cooking water, or water, or a mixture of both. Bring to a gentle boil, then reduce to a simmer for 20 minutes. Taste and add salt and pepper.

Raise the heat so the soup bubbles, then add the pasta and cook until al dente, stirring to prevent sticking and adding more water if it seems too thick. Serve with a zigzag of best olive oil and some red chilli flakes if you wish.

Maltagliati con salsa di porri e cozze
Maltagliati with creamed leeks (and mussels if you wish)
Serves 4

Leeks go softly. And even when you trim away much of the green, they retain their savoury grassiness which is welcome when they are softened to an almost purée in butter and olive oil. Cooked this way leeks are a complete sauce, but if you wish you can also add mussels before you toss with the badly cut pasta. I must give thanks to Anna Del Conte for this idea. I am not sure where the idea that you should never mix seafood or shellfish with cheese came from, certainly not Rome, Puglia or Sicily, where they are often combined, most notably *cozze* (mussels) and pecorino.

800g leeks – ideally smallish ones
40g butter
4 tablespoons extra virgin olive oil
salt and black pepper
a generous splash of white wine
1.5kg mussels (optional)
450g fresh egg maltagliati, tagliatelle, pappardelle
grated pecorino or Parmesan (optional)

Prepare the leeks: cut away the root and trim 5–10cm of dark green from the top, depending on freshness, so you are left with just white and light green. Cut the leeks into rounds, then rinse well to get rid of any grit.

Warm the butter and olive oil in a deep frying pan over a low-medium heat, then add the leeks and a pinch of salt and stir until they are glistening. Add the wine. Cover the leeks with a piece of buttered greaseproof paper, then with a lid, and cook for 20–30 minutes, or until the leeks are soft. Pull the pan from the heat. If you are adding the mussels do so now – see below.

Bring a large pan of water to a fast boil, add salt, stir and add the maltagliati, and set the timer for 1 minute less than the time on the packet. Once the pasta is al dente, drain, reserving a little pasta cooking water, then tip into the leek (and mussel) pan and toss well, adding a little pasta cooking water (mussel liquor) if you think it needs it. Serve immediately, with grated pecorino or Parmesan if you like.

For the variation with mussels – which can be done in advance – wash and scrub the mussels, tugging away the beards, knocking off barnacles and discarding any that are damaged or even slightly open. Warm 2 tablespoons of olive oil in a wide pan over a high heat. Add the mussels. Once they start to sizzle, add the white wine, cover the pan and cook for 2–3 minutes. Remove the lid, shake the pan so those on the top (that are slightly open) replace those on the bottom (that are fully open) and put back on the heat until all the mussels are open. Pull from the heat. Use a slotted spoon to lift the mussels from the liquid, pick the flesh from the shells and set aside. Discard the shells. Filter the mussel liquor left in the pan through a fine sieve. Add the mussels to the leek pan, along with a little of the liquor.

Maltagliati con olio e pecorino
Maltagliati with olive oil and pecorino

In Arezzo in Tuscany maltagliati are made with the leftover dough after making ravioli, the remnants gathered into a ball, rolled through (by hand or through a machine) and then cut into wide lozenges, boiled in well-salted water and layered in a bowl with olive oil and freshly grated pecorino. A simple way to appreciate the fullness of fresh egg pasta, extra virgin olive oil and the sheepish nature of pecorino.

— m —

Mezze maniche

What is it about a restaurant trolley? Is it the anticipation of it being wheeled towards you, rattling with good things? Our local *trattoria* La Torricella has three, which like most of the fittings and furniture are children of the late 1970s. One sits near the front door, often home to a cymbal-sized ricotta and cherry crostata. Another is for *antipasti*, which vary, but like the rest of the menu are mostly fish, a salad of flaked bass, lettuce and prawns, a Pyrex bowl containing coral-edged chunks of octopus and celery, possibly some marinated mullet. The third trolley is parked under the glass-fronted fruit cabinet and, more often than not, covered with pasta.

The sort of pasta varies. If it has been made by the owner, Augusto, it is a flour and water shape called fregnacce, which means trifles or bits of gossip, which apparently nods to the way they were traditionally rolled and cut into lozenges, that is quickly and informally, while the makers chatted. If the pasta has arrived from the local fresh pasta shop, it could be a tangle of fresh tonnarelli, ribbons of fettuccine, or mezze maniche, literally short sleeves, so inch-long, ten-pence diameter tubes.

As we have already established, all pasta begins life fresh, that is soft. The question is, is it then left to dry? The mezze maniche delivered to La Torricella are not long out of the extruder, so still pliable and visibly soft. If Augusto were to leave them sitting there they would give moisture to the air and the soft curves would harden. In fact mezze maniche are most commonly a factory-made, dried shape, to my mind one of the best dried shapes; tubes large enough to flatten slightly as they cook so with that lovely mouth-filling quality, but still catchers. They are interchangeable with rigatoni, maccheroni, calamari and paccheri.

The mezze maniche sitting on the trolley at La Torricella never last long enough to dry. Rather they are boiled that same day and served with tiny flying octopus braised in sweet tomato sauce, anchovies and tomato, or courgettes and prawns. At home I do the same, although, sadly, without the trolley.

Mezze maniche con gamberi e zucchine
Mezze maniche with courgettes and prawns
Serves 4

Having two cuts of courgette, some grated, some sliced, is a little thing that makes a difference, creating an almost weave-like texture that catches the prawns. Frozen prawns work well. This is a dish that invites variation. Instead of prawns, try clams, which you need to open in a separate pan and then add both shells and the broth, or white fish such as bream, cut into strips and added in the same way as the prawns.

25–35 small prawns/ shrimps
2 cloves of garlic, crushed but still intact
6 tablespoons olive oil, plus extra to finish
2 large courgettes, sliced into 2mm coins
1 small courgette, grated on the large holes of a box grater
a pinch of red chilli flakes
salt
400g mezze maniche, penne, fusilli, rigatoni

Put a large pan of salted water on for the pasta. Shell the prawns, carefully removing the dark vein with a toothpick or a small knife. An optional step is to put the heads and shells in a bit of muslin or thin cloth, tie the ends together and add to the pasta water as it comes to the boil, removing it before you add the pasta.

In a large, deep frying pan over a medium low heat, fry the garlic gently in the olive oil until fragrant and add both the cut and grated courgette, chilli and a pinch of salt. Stir so the courgette glistens and fry for a minute, then add a little water from the pasta pan and continue cooking, stirring until the courgette is soft, yielding and almost creamy.

Cook the pasta and when it is 3 minutes off being done, put the courgettes back on the heat, add the prawns and raise the heat so they cook through, scooping out another ladle of pasta cooking water and letting everything bubble. Lift the pasta into the pan, add another tablespoon of olive oil and toss, swish, jolt everything vigorously so the starch meets the oil, etc., then serve.

Pasta di mezz'estate
Midsummer pasta
Serves 6

This is my harlequin pasta, another recipe from the Italian food writer Rita Pane that has become a summer favourite, especially if we are a big group. The beauty is that the heat of the pasta and vegetables melts and softens the edges of the mozzarella and Parmesan which unites everything. You can roast the vegetables but frying is best. You could do this in advance, but they will need warming through in the oven before you mix everything together. Use loads of basil – the scent should fill your nose and the room.

olive or vegetable oil, for frying
1 large aubergine, diced into 1cm cubes
1 red pepper, diced into 1cm cubes
2 courgettes, diced into 1cm cubes
salt
2 large ripe tomatoes
1 clove of garlic, peeled and crushed
600g mezze maniche, penne, fusilli, rigatoni
100g Parmesan, grated
200g mozzarella, diced
a big sprig of fresh basil leaves, ripped

Bring a large pan of water to the boil for the pasta.

Pour enough oil into a deep, medium-sized frying pan for it to come 2.5cm up the sides and heat until hot. Working in batches, fry the diced vegetables in the oil until soft and golden, then blot on a kitchen towel, season with salt and keep warm. Tip the oil from the pan.

Plunge the tomatoes into the almost boiling water for a minute, then lift them out with a slotted spoon and refresh under cold water, at which point the skins should slip off. Roughly chop the tomatoes.

Put the frying pan back on the heat with 4 tablespoons of new oil and the garlic. Once the garlic is fragrant, add the chopped tomatoes and a pinch of salt and cook until soft and saucey – about 10 minutes.

Once the water is boiling, add salt, stir, then add the pasta and cook until al dente. Once the pasta is ready, drain, tip into the tomato pan and toss.

Tip the pasta and sauce into a large bowl, add the fried vegetables, Parmesan, mozzarella and ripped basil, toss thoroughly and serve.

— m —

Mista (pasta mista)
Mixed pasta

Ours is squat, with glass as thick as my grandfather's specs and a red screw-on lid, and it sits on the middle shelf of the food cupboard. A jar and home for *la pasta mista*.

While it is surely common anywhere there is pasta and a resourceful cook, pasta mista or mixed pasta is synonymous with Naples and Campania, where they call it *pasta ammiscata, ammescata* or *meschiafrancesco*. As recently as 1970, pasta was sold by weight in grocery stores, shapes scooped from deep wooden drawers with glass fronts. The remains at the bottom of these drawers, the leftovers and fragments, corners and broken bits, were all swept together. These sweepings were called *ammiscata*, given their own drawer and sold cheaply: the Neapolitan equivalent of Woolworths' broken biscuits.

Of course pasta mista was also assembled at home, ends of packets rounded up like unruly children and put in one place. Manufacturers, too, saw profit in a jumble and packaged it. There is pleasure, though, in assembling your own, managing packets stuffed in a cupboard and shepherding them into one place, watching the evolving mix through the glass. While you want to keep an eye on the various shapes you are tipping into the jar, and to be attentive that cooking times are pretty similar, slight differences are part of the beauty. The corkscrew of fusilli firmer than a u-bend of maccheroni, the almost crunchy, ruffled mafaldine rubbing up against an inch of bucatini, all of them at home in a dense *minestra*.

Minestre of all sorts welcome pasta mista, but particularly those with beans and pulses, *pasta e fagioli, pasta e ceci, pasta e lenticchie* and soupy versions of *pasta e broccoli*. An ideal fit, though, is with potatoes for *pasta mista e patate*, essentially potato soup with pasta, which is a beige woolly sock of a dish. An unappealing description I know, but these are soft, comfortable socks and Neapolitan, so rich with olive oil and dense with cheese, Parmesan, scamorza, maybe pancetta or sausage; the rich starchy embodiment of food as comfort. I call on *pasta e patate* often in the winter, and it hasn't failed me yet. Here are two versions for your jar of pasta mista.

Pasta con patate e provola
Pasta with potatoes and smoked provola cheese
Serves 4

Instead of carrot, the colour in the *soffritto* comes from tomato. There are more potatoes in this version, a Parmesan rind, and in addition to Parmesan there is chopped provola cheese (pulled cow or buffalo milk cheese, made in a similar way to mozzarella, so stretched in hot water, then salted, ripened, and occasionally smoked), which melts as it hits the hot soup. All this means the final dish is no soft, brothy *minestra*, but something Neopolitans call *azzeccata*, a rib-sticking and soulful bowlful that confirms they know something about comfort.

1 white onion, peeled and finely diced
1 stick of celery, finely diced
50g pancetta, diced (optional)
5 tablespoons extra virgin olive oil
salt and black pepper
8 cherry tomatoes, roughly chopped
700g potatoes, peeled and diced
a Parmesan rind
300g mixed pasta
50g Parmesan, grated
150g provola, provola affumicata or smoked cheese, diced

In a heavy-based pan, fry the onion, celery and pancetta in the olive oil with a small pinch of salt over a medium-low flame until soft and translucent.

Add the tomatoes and potatoes to the pan, stirring until everything glistens with oil. Add a small pinch of salt, plus 1 litre of water and the Parmesan rind. Bring to the boil, then reduce to a simmer for 20 minutes, or until the potatoes are soft.

Bring the soup back to the boil, add the pasta and cook for 10 minutes or so, or until the pasta is al dente. Add a little more water if the pan looks too dry. Add the grated Parmesan and a little black pepper, taste for salt, stir, then take off the heat. Add the provola, stir and set aside for 5 minutes, then serve.

Variation – squeeze the meat from 2 or 3 large sausages and use instead of the pancetta.

Pasta e patate napoletana
Pasta and potatoes Neapolitan style
Serves 4

A thick potato soup in which you cook pasta, this is greater than the sum of its parts. Let it sit for 10 minutes or thereabouts, so it is *'nè bollente, nè fredda'* (neither hot nor cold), rather somewhere in the middle, which best suits both the flavour and texture: the collapsing potato, various degrees of pasta and fusing cheese, and you.

1 onion, peeled and finely diced
1 carrot, peeled and finely diced
2 sticks of celery
5 tablespoons olive oil
salt
5–6 (1 kg) potatoes, peeled and diced into 1cm cubes
1 bay leaf
250g pasta mista
100g Parmesan, grated
fresh basil

In a large heavy-based pan over a medium-low heat, fry the onion, carrot and celery in the olive oil, with a pinch of salt, until starting to soften.

Add the potatoes to the pan, stir until every cube is glistening with oil, then add the bay leaf and 1.2 litres of water. Bring to the boil, then reduce to a simmer for 12 minutes.

Raise the heat so the soup boils steadily, add the pasta and cook until it is al dente – you may need to add a bit more water. To finish, add the Parmesan and some ripped basil and serve.

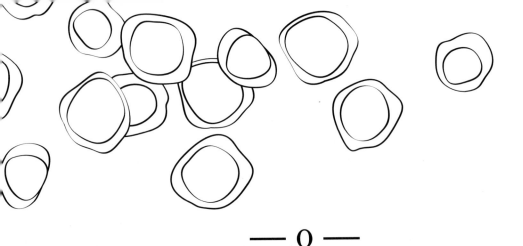

— O —

Orecchiette

Impara l'arte e mettila da parte, learn the art, and store it, is what girls are sometimes told when they are learning to make orecchiette in Puglia. Others tell themselves never to learn and to get as far away as they can, to become a lawyer in another country. I know this person and she gave me her story. The year after her mum died, she decided to teach herself to make orecchiette. So she bought a bag of semolina flour, tipped a pile of it on the table, mixed in some water and kneaded, trying to remember what her mother and grandmother had tried to teach her, that she had so hated. But of course she had never learned, so she couldn't remember. She tried again the next night, and again the night after that, until she said fuck the orecchiette. A few days later when her daughter came over, also a lawyer, she told her what had happened, also more about why, as a child, she refused to learn. In return, the daughter said she understood and that she had taught herself to make orecchiette from YouTube, and she was good at it, that it was as if something good had been stored. Then the daughter offered to teach the mother, who said she didn't need to learn any more, just to eat, so they did.

I like this story, for the person, and also for the idea that cooking traditions are passed on in various often strange ways, that for women cooking traditions often contain a burden that may or may not diminish the pleasure, that choice is a powerful thing. My friend never wants to go back to her home town in Puglia, but when I went she wanted to know about my trip. She was the one who told me to go to Old Bari, and a street called Arco Basso, for the low arch at one end, although everyone calls it *la strada delle orecchiette* because women who make orecchiette work on tables in the street, kneading then rolling dough into ropes, cutting off nuggets which they then drag with knives so they both curl and invert. The women are skilled, and fast, their shapes a symbol of the city.

Orecchiette are also a reminder of the earlier political division of Italy. Puglia, like all of southern Italy, was part of the kingdom of Naples between 1282 and 1861, which for much of this time was under French rule. It has been suggested that the ancestors of orecchiette are the similarly shaped crosets of medieval Provence, brought to Puglia by the Angevins of Provence, another beautiful example of how culinary traditions modify as they come into contact with other traditions, how traditions invent themselves.

Like all the dragged shapes orecchiette require practice to find the movement that works for you as well as the right surface, usually wood. Some recipes recommend tepid water, others hot; I have found warm water works best. The general rule is 2:1 semola : water but because all flour is different, and climatic conditions play a part, you do need to mix the dough a little 'by eye'. The dough needs to be soft but not squishy or sticky. You should be able to knead it and feel elasticity but firmness.

Make a batch of semola and water dough (see page 83). Cut off a piece about 50–60g and return the rest under the bowl. Roll into a rope about 1cm thick. Cut off 1cm nuggets. With the knife held horizontally to the table, line the tip edge of the knife with the edge of the nugget, put a fingertip on top of the blade and drag the tip of the knife across the dough so it spreads into a circle and curls up towards you. Then invert over your thumb so it looks like an ear or little cup.

A note about knives – try different sorts. I can use both a small serrated dinner knife and a rounded butter knife, while others I know like standard (non-serrated) dinner knives, others pointy ones. You can of course buy dried orecchiette.

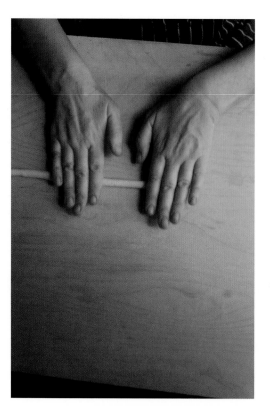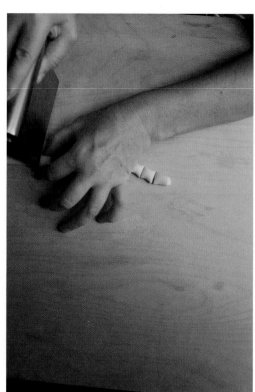

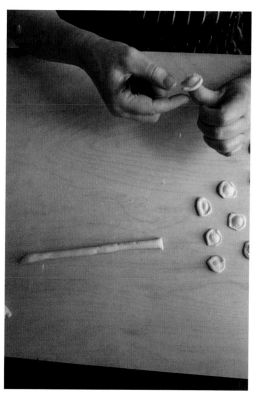

Orecchiette con cime di rapa
Orecchiette with turnip tops, garlic and anchovy
Serves 6

Cime di rapa are turnip tops or rapini in the UK, broccoli rabe in the US, also known as *broccoletti* in Rome, *friarielli* in Naples. I only mention all these names because so much is being imported these days, so many seeds shared. The flavour of cima di rapa (leaves, shoots and stems) is like broccoli leaves, thick and vegetal with mustardy heat and slight bitterness, which is why it needs boiling, so the sweeter sides come out. For this classic Puglian dish cime di rapa is trimmed back, cut small and boiled in with the orecchiette. Both are then tossed with olive oil into which you have melted anchovy, infused garlic and added chilli. It is true that it is hard to recreate dishes so inextricably linked to local ingredients, but it's possible and then – as people have always done – we adapt. It seemed important, though, to have a classic recipe template as a starting point, and this one from the chef Domingo Schingaro is just that.

For the pasta
400g semola
200g warm water
or 400g dried
    orecchiette,
    cavatelli, fusilli

For the cime di rapa
100ml olive oil
2 cloves of garlic,
    peeled, smashed
    and quartered
4 salted anchovies
    (cleaned) or 8
    anchovy fillets
    under oil
red chilli flakes
1.5kg turnip tops
a pinch of salt

Make the orecchiette as instructed on page 195.

Bring a large pan of water to the boil for the pasta. Away from the heat, put the olive oil in a small, cold pan with the garlic and anchovies. Put on the lowest flame and allow to warm slowly so the anchovies dissolve, which will take about 8 minutes. Add a good pinch of red chilli flakes.

Trim the turnip tops, pulling away any big, tough leaves and thick stalks, and pulling away strings as you would with celery – usually you trim away about a third. Cut into 3cm lengths.

When the water for the pasta boils, add salt, stir, wait 30 seconds, then add the cime di rapa (turnip tops), which will stop the water boiling. Once it comes back to the boil, add the orecchiette and boil for 5–6 minutes for fresh, according to the packet for dried. Drain everything, saving some pasta cooking water, then tip into a large warm bowl, add seasoned olive oil and toss, adding a dash of pasta water if it needs it, then serve.

Orecchiette con rucola, patate e pomodorini
Orecchiette with rocket, potatoes and cherry tomatoes
Serves 4

This recipe from my friend Giancarlo, who comes from the town of Foggia, is another in which the vegetables – potato and rocket – are cooked with the pasta. In this way they provide flavour while cooking, collapse enough to wrap around the pasta and, in the case of the potato, provide starchy softness. All three are then mixed with fried garlic and tomatoes, layers of flavour, and the result is just lovely.

1 large potato, approx. 250g, peeled and cut into 1cm cubes
salt
500g fresh orecchiette, 400g dried, cavatelli, fusilli or linguine
150g rocket, tough stems discarded
1 clove of garlic
a pinch of red chilli flakes
8 tablespoons extra virgin olive oil
12–15 cherry tomatoes

Bring a large pan of water to the boil. Once the water boils, add salt, stir, then add the potato. If you are using dried orecchiette add them 2 minutes after the potato. If you are using fresh orecchiette add them 6 minutes after the potato along with the rocket.

Prepare the garlic: peel and crush with the back of the knife for a mild flavour; slice for a stronger one; mince for the most intense flavour. In a frying pan, over a medium-low heat, gently fry the garlic and red chilli in the oil for a couple of minutes, then add the halved tomatoes and cook for a few minutes more, pressing them gently with the back of a wooden spoon so they are saucy at the edges.

Once the pasta is cooked and the potato and rocket tender, drain them all, add to the frying pan, and toss for a minute. Divide between bowls, finishing each one with a little more olive oil.

Orecchiette con pomodori scoppiati e la mollica
Orecchiette with bursting tomatoes and anchovy crumbs
Serves 4

This way of cooking tomatoes, whole with olive oil and covered, so they soften and then split, is often called *'pomodori scoppiati'*, bursting tomatoes. You help them by pressing so the juices split into the oil, making a rich slumping sauce which is ideal with orecchiette. The smaller the better for tomatoes, so they fit with the little ears. Toasted breadcrumbs – again, this time soft crumbs fried in oil and garlic until crisp and golden.

2–3 cloves of garlic, peeled and gently crushed but still intact
8 tablespoons extra virgin olive oil
1kg cherry tomatoes
salt
a generous pinch of dried oregano
a pinch of red chilli flakes
fresh basil, ripped
4–6 anchovy fillets
50g soft breadcrumbs
500g fresh orecchiette, 400g dried, or cavatelli, fusilli, linguine, tagliatelle

Put the garlic and 6 tablespoons of olive oil into a cold pan, then heat gently so the garlic infuses the oil, but doesn't brown. You can pull the cloves out now, if you like.

Add the tomatoes, salt, oregano and red chilli, then stir until each tomato glistens. Cover and cook for 10 minutes, shaking the pan every now and then until all the tomatoes have split/burst. Lift the lid every few minutes and squash the tomatoes with the back of a wooden spoon to help release the juices: by the end you should have lots of thick, oily sauce. Stir in the basil.

Meanwhile in another small frying pan, warm another 2 tablespoons of oil and the anchovies until the anchovies disintegrate and then add the breadcrumbs and raise the heat so they become crisp and golden.

Bring a large pan of water to a fast boil, add salt, stir, then add the pasta, stir again and cook until al dente. Drain, reserving a little cooking water. Tip the pasta into the sauce, stir, adding a little cooking water if it feels at all stiff. Divide and serve, topping each plate with breadcrumbs.

— O —

Orzo

Let's talk about orzo. Which is rarely called orzo in Italy because then it would be confused with orzo, which is pearl barley. It is called rosmarino or rosamarino for its resemblance to a needle of the herb rosemary, or risoni, for its resemblance to rice. I think it looks like a closed eye. It is a durum wheat and water factory-made dried shape and another *pastina*, and I try not to be without a packet or two.

As well as sharing a shape with rice, orzo shares a nature. It is suited to cooking *alla risottata*, so in much the same way as rice for risotto, the liquid and flavours of the other ingredients are absorbed during the cooking process, and helped by your stirring, resulting in a dense, creamy dish. These next two recipes demonstrate this nature well, the first pairing orzo with tomato and basil, the second with peas, Parmesan and lemon zest. There is a sense of completeness about dishes of orzo cooked this way, which comes from the fact that everything is retained and contained. Contained, too, is the chicken in the final recipe, in a deep pan where it pot roasts, on its own to start, then with orzo which swells with flavour. It is an inspired recipe – inspired by Nigella Lawson, the English food writer who I find best expresses her appetite for pasta.

Rosmarino ca' pummarola
Orzo with tomato, basil and Parmesan

Serves 4

A traditional Neapolitan recipe, *ca' pummarola* is dialect for 'with tomatoes'. While you could use tinned ones, waiting for tomatoes that are full of flavour is worthwhile, as is peeling them. You don't need to stir constantly, but don't leave the room. Stay near the pan so you can give it attention every couple of minutes. Be generous with the basil for flavour, and also so the smell fills the room and your sinuses. The final consistency should be soft and wavy *all'onda*.

500g mature tomatoes
80ml olive oil
2 cloves of garlic,
    peeled and sliced
fresh basil, ripped
salt and black pepper
300g rosmarino, orzo
    or risoni
50g Parmesan, grated

Peel the tomatoes by plunging them first into boiling water for a minute, then into cold, at which point the skins should slip away. Chop roughly into a bowl to catch the juices, but discard any tough bits.

In a heavy-based pan starting from cold, warm the olive oil and garlic and cook gently so the garlic sizzles but does not burn. Add the tomatoes, a handful of basil and a pinch of salt and cook for 10 minutes, mashing with the back of the spoon or a potato masher so the tomato breaks into a sauce.

Add 1.2 litres of hot, lightly salted water and allow to bubble a minute. Add the orzo and allow to cook at a lively simmer, stirring often, until it is soft and the consistency of a thick soup. Stir in the rest of the basil, the Parmesan and lots of pepper. Serve immediately.

Orzo con piselli, parmigiano e limone
Orzo with peas, Parmesan and lemon
Serves 4

Peas, Parmesan and lemon are always a harmonious three, even more so in the company of orzo. Again, you don't need to stir constantly, just often.

20g butter
3 tablespoons olive oil
1 small onion, diced
300g peas
300g orzo
1.5 litres salted water
or light stock
zest of 1 unwaxed
lemon
1 heaped teaspoon
finely chopped
fresh flat-leaf
parsley
50g Parmesan, grated

In a large heavy-based frying pan, warm the butter and oil and fry the onion until soft and translucent. Add the peas and stir.

Add the orzo, stir until each grain glistens, then pour over the stock or water and adjust the flame so everything bubbles gently.

Cook, stirring every now and then, until the orzo is tender, which usually takes about 8–10 minutes, and the consistency is that of a thick soup. Add the lemon zest, parsley and Parmesan and serve immediately.

Roast chicken with orzo

Serves 4

Chicken and orzo cooperate well together in this generous and good-tasting recipe from Nigella Lawson. To begin with the chicken cooks alone, half poaching, half baking, and then in the last 20 minutes you add the orzo, which plumps in the stock. I use my oval cast-iron casserole for this – it is just the right size for a 1.5kg chicken. To serve I generally lift the chicken out and cut it into 8 pieces with heavy scissors, then pile the pieces back into the pan so everyone can serve themselves, or pile everything on to a platter, in which case I get to scrape the edges and sticky bottom of the pan.

olive oil
1 x 1.5kg chicken
2 cloves of garlic,
    unpeeled and
    smashed
a pinch of red chilli
    flakes
1 large leek, sliced
2 sticks of celery, cut
    into short batons
a small bunch of fresh
    flat-leaf parsley,
    chopped
salt
250ml white wine
250g orzo
1 unwaxed lemon

Warm some olive oil in a casserole over a medium heat, and starting with the breast down, brown the chicken all over. Remove from the pan.

Put the pan and chicken juices back on the heat and add the garlic and chilli. Let that sizzle for a minute. Then add the leek and celery, half the parsley and a good pinch of salt, and cook, stirring, until they are all coated in oil. Now snuggle the chicken back into the pan so it is packed with vegetables, and pour over the wine and a litre of warm water – the liquid should rise to just below the breast. Bring to the boil, then cover and put into the oven for 1 hour and 10 minutes.

Pull the casserole from the oven, uncover, tip in the orzo and stir it into the broth, re-cover and return to the oven for 20 minutes, by which time the orzo should be plump and cooked.

Remove the casserole from the oven, stir in the rest of the parsley and 2 tablespoons of lemon juice, then leave to sit for 10 minutes.

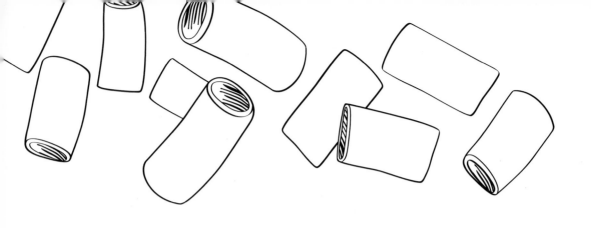

— p —

Paccheri

At the foot of the Monti Lattari mountain range, 30 kilometres south-east of Naples, 15 from Vesuvius and round the cape from Sorrento, is a town called Gragnano. It is part of a staggering landscape, vertiginous, volcanic and productive – lemons, tomatoes, olives, grapes and pasta.

If the story of pasta is a vast jigsaw, Gragnano is a vital piece. To understand it, though, it's a good idea to leave Gragnano. To drive out of the town and to the Valle dei Mulini, the valley of mills. For a few miles the road runs parallel with a creek banked by trees where, every hundred metres or so, is the remains of a water mill, wilderness poking out of the ruined roof but still recognizable and solid. Built in the latter part of the thirteenth century and powered by the creek, natural springs and animals, the numerous mills produced flour (semola) from grain that arrived as cargo at the nearby and important port of Castellammare di Stabia. Fortuitous position, also point in time. It was at this time that home-made pasta was migrating from family kitchens into the workshops of mills where women continued to make the shapes they made for their families, but on a larger scale, initially by hand, then with the help of early machines.

Sergio Cinque explains all this. We are sitting in his office, a glass booth in the middle of the Faella pasta factory in the centre of Gragnano, in the background the steady hum of a machine extruding linguine. He describes the process of making pasta 500 years ago as if it had happened that morning. How semola from the mills, and spring water, became dough in large wooden vats called *madie*, by the trampling of feet, the workers hanging on to ropes as we might grip a strap-hanger on a train. How the dough was rolled and shaped by hand into scrolls of fusilli or worms of vermicelli, before being dried, packed in baskets which were packed on to mules and walked over mountain paths into Naples.

In the middle of the sixteenth century everything changed. *'Ngegni di maccheroni* (remember at this point *maccheroni* was a generic word for many shapes) were the first elemental machines consisting of a wooden cylinder lined with copper, bronze die and a screw piston. In the same way you push air through a bike pump, the piston forced dough into the cylinder and through the die and pierced maccheroni emerged on the other side. The pasta was then hung like a fringe on long sticks, and dried. And this is the other vital thing about Gragnano and its position, in a valley which funnels into the Gulf of Naples; its singular climate.

Standing on the pavement outside the Pastificio Faella on a warm but breezy spring day you understand something of why the streets of Gragnano became a huge open-air drying grid. That isn't to suggest drying was easy, anything but. The head *pastaio* masterminded the operation. Manager and coordinator, he was also a practical soothsayer and human thermometer, forecasting weather and predicting winds so the pasta, hung over sticks, could be set and manoeuvred in such a way that it received the air and atmosphere it needed. Managing the first fast dry outside, then the subsequent slower stages in a series of rooms, was a carefully choreographed process that took just over a week in summer, up to three in winter. Over time work was facilitated by even newer machines, but the process of drying remained similar for centuries. Sergio shuffles copies of pictures held in the town library, of proud men and keen boys standing beside frames holding sticks strung with pasta in the streets of Gragnano.

Out of his glass booth Sergio gives me a tour. It is not my first time in a pasta factory, I know how to put the hairnet on, predict the warm smell. I don't expect the machinery (which reminds me of a green steam train) or the warm steam which makes me feel like I am in a greenhouse. Linguine are being

extruded, they look like strings billowing from a loom, before being portioned and hung over sticks. Everything is mechanized now, and the pasta never sees the street, but it's still a meticulously choreographed process, which (despite what 6-hour-turn-around industrial factories might have you believe) can take anything from 24 hours to 5 days depending on the shape. In a vat near the extruder the bronze dies soak, each one perforated differently. It could be a game. 'Aha, that one makes spaghetti!' 'Look kids, bucatini.' 'Surely that one is for candele.' I have come for them all, but most of all paccheri.

In the eighteenth century there were 22 mills and 97 pasta factories in the Gragnano area. Today there are 23; Sergio is keen that I know which ones are in the Consortium of makers, able to bear the mark Pasta di Gragnano DOC, that Gragnano is the city of pasta. He is even keener we have a good lunch. So we challenge the fanbelt and drive up a sheer road to a restaurant. A high shelf on the back wall is lined with packets from various local pasta makers; we are loyal and order the house *antipasto* and then Faella *paccheri al filetto di pomodoro*.

Paccheri are large, wide tubes made from durum wheat and water. They vary in size according to the maker but are generally about 6cm long, with the diameter of a 50 pence. They take their name from the onomatopoeic *paccarià*, Neapolitan for 'to slap'. Which is exactly what they do when cooked, like soft sacs, they slap and flap when you toss them in the sauce, then again in your mouth. Along with rigatoni, paccheri are my preferred shape, and one of the best ways to understand good quality pasta, its porous surface, substance and bite. *Filetto di pomodoro* turns out to be a sauce of local tomatoes, the pieces still distinct (the fillets) but soft enough to coat the paccheri. We also have *pasta e patate*, because I want to see how they make it, and a salad, just lettuce with olive oil and lemon juice squeezed from one of the pale, oval lemons that hang nonchalantly from trees everywhere you look. Just remembering makes my mouth water. After lunch we pass Faella and fill the boot with shapes, paccheri, rigatoni, spaghetti, linguine, metre-long candele. Also a 3kg bag of archetti, little curved remnants, reminders that before it was cut spaghetti hung over a stick. Everything is good. Everything is the product of a fortuitous position and good choreography.

The way pasta is cooked in Campania and Naples is beautiful choreography. Often, pasta is removed from the boiling water – usually with a spider sieve – before it reaches the desirable point of al dente. This means that the last minutes of pasta cooking are done in with the sauce. In these last minutes, usually in a pan large enough to really jolt and shake so the pasta releases more 'amido', starch, and with the help of a little starchy cooking water, the elements – sauce, shape, starch, fat – meet, bind and thicken. Chefs call this *mantecatura*, home cooks, coming together. If you have ever looked at your plate of pasta in a restaurant and wondered how and why it looks so creamy and united it is most likely because it has been finished like this, and it is a technique (actually I prefer the word 'way') easily picked up and practised at home. Of course better pasta produces better *amido*, which is why it is worth seeking out good brands. Also having a large jolting pan is invaluable, but I have already said that (and will say it again).

Paccheri con crema di melanzane, pomodorini e mozzarella
Paccheri with aubergine, two sorts of tomatoes and mozzarella
Serves 4

Here paccheri are paired with a sauce of roasted aubergine and tomato and topped with roasted cherry tomatoes and cubes of mozzarella. There are a few stages, so it is worth roasting the vegetables beforehand (which is beneficial to flavour), then it is just a case of finishing the sauce, cooking the pasta and assembling. The recipe is an adaptation of one in Luciano Pignataro's *La cucina napoletana*, and the combination of flavours and textures is divine.

2 large aubergines
300g cherry tomatoes, halved
salt
dried oregano
icing sugar
olive oil
1 clove of garlic
300g peeled plum tomatoes, fresh or tinned
ripped fresh basil
400g paccheri, or rigatoni, mezze maniche, penne, fusilli
100g mozzarella

Roast the aubergines whole until they collapse, at 190°C for about 40 minutes, then remove from the oven. Turn the oven down to 130°C.

Put the cherry tomatoes on a baking tray, sprinkle with salt, dried oregano, icing sugar and olive oil, and put them into the oven for 45 minutes or until they wrinkle. Put on one side.

Scoop the flesh from the aubergine.

In a large frying pan, warm some olive oil and the garlic, then add the peeled plum tomatoes, basil and a pinch of salt and allow to bubble for 15 minutes, or until they look saucey. Add the aubergine and stir. The aim is a sauce to coat the pasta, so you can pass it through a food mill (remove the garlic) or simply mash with a potato masher. Pull from the heat.

Cook the pasta until a minute off al dente, turn up the heat on the sauce, and drain or lift the pasta directly into the sauce pan and then swish gently to blend with the sauce and finish the last minute of cooking. Add a bit more water if it looks dry – the consistency should be swishy.

Tip the paccheri on to a large serving dish, and top with the cherry tomatoes, cubed mozzarella and more ripped basil.

Paccheri con patate e cozze
Paccheri with potatoes and mussels
Serves 4

I find myself wanting to describe this dish rather than say the name, fearing it will be misunderstood or won't communicate quite how magical this combination is. If you like mussels, that is! The potatoes contribute to the coming together and along with the starch and oil produce a silky sauce which carries the mussel liquor and coats the paccheri like an expensive pashmina. The hope is that mussels hide inside the tubes.

1kg mussels
a little water or wine
salt and black pepper
300g potatoes, peeled and diced into 1cm cubes
400g paccheri, or mezze maniche, rigatoni, linguine, fettuccine
6 tablespoons olive oil
2 cloves of garlic, unpeeled
a big sprig of fresh flat-leaf parsley, chopped

Rinse the mussels, scrub, pull away the beards and then rinse vigorously again. Put a large frying pan on a lively flame, add the mussels and a little water or wine, cover and shake until you hear them opening. Lift the lid and lift out the open ones using a slotted spoon. Reserve and strain the mussel liquor – taste it, it should be pleasantly salty – if it is too salty, add a little water. Remove most of the mussels from their shells but save a few for show (if you want).

Bring a large pan of water to the boil and add salt. Cook the potatoes in the water until tender – which will take about 6 minutes. Scoop them out and now cook the paccheri.

Back in your large (jolting) pan over a medium-low flame, add the olive oil and garlic (unpeeled and cracked with the heel of your hand or a knife) and allow to sizzle gently, then add 100ml of mussel cooking liquor and let it bubble for 20 seconds. Add the potatoes, mussels and parsley and stir.

When the paccheri is a minute away from being al dente, either drain or, better still, use a spider sieve to lift it into the pan with the potatoes and mussels for the last minute of cooking.

Swish and jolt the pan. You want the starch from the pasta to knock into the starch of the potato and mix with the oil and liquor creation. An opaque sauce. And it should be fluid (although not watery), so add a little more mussel liquor if you think it needs it and swish again.

Paccheri con pesto di fave fresche
Paccheri with broad bean pesto
Serves 4

A vivid green pesto, made with broad beans, either fresh or frozen (both of which need double peeling), mint, cheese and just a little garlic. The pine nuts are not combined in the pesto, rather toasted and added on the top, along with a blob of ricotta: pleasing, contrasting textures.

300g podded broad beans, fresh or frozen
400g paccheri
a handful of fresh mint leaves
3 tablespoons grated Parmesan or Grana Padano
1 small clove of garlic, green shoots removed
3 tablespoons olive oil
salt and black pepper
20g pine nuts
200g ricotta, beaten with 2 tablespoons milk to loosen

Bring a large pan of water to the boil, and add salt. Use it to skin the beans – lower them in for a minute (a sieve is useful), then dip them into cold water, at which point the skins should pop off. Now use the water to cook the pasta.

In a blender, pulse the podded beans with the mint, Parmesan, garlic, olive oil and a good pinch of salt, then scrape into a bowl. Toast the pine nuts in a small pan.

Drain the pasta, add to the bowl and stir, adding a little pasta cooking water if it seems stiff. Serve topped with the pine nuts and ricotta.

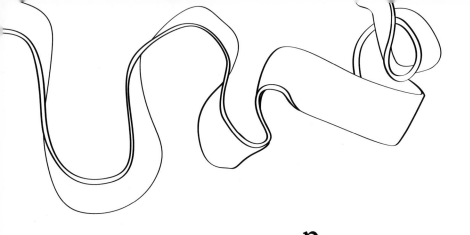

— p —

Pappardelle

It is the way they pleat and fold that makes them so satisfying. First on the plate and then again in your mouth. Pappardelle are typical of all the central and central-northern Italian regions, each one boasting a slightly different width, anything from 2.5 to 6cm. The Tuscans gave it the name; it comes from *pappare*, the colloquial, to eat. Fresh egg pasta cut into wide ribbons, pappardelle goes with many sauces, but the most typical are rich meaty ones, especially game, hare, wild boar, rabbit, also duck. I also love it with onion *ragù*, a deeply flavoured sauce that is ideal for folds and pleats.

Pappardelle, both with and without egg, is also a dried pasta and one that seems to hold its shape particularly well. If you want to make pappardelle, make a standard egg dough, roll, and cut into sheets 18cm wide and 30cm long. Fold the long ends in so they meet in the middle. Now fold the new shorter ends in so they too meet in the middle, producing a sort of envelope. Cut horizontally into strips 3–4cm wide.

Pappardelle al ragù di cipolle
Pappardelle with onion ragù
Serves 4

This is such a good and clever recipe. It is essentially onion, which as we know can cook down its sweetness, but then there is also disappearing carrot and tomato purée which gives real depth and a rich flavour.

6–7 onions, peeled, halved and chopped into slender half-moons
2 cloves of garlic, peeled and finely minced
50ml olive oil
50g butter
salt and black pepper
1 large carrot, peeled and finely grated
3 tablespoons tomato concentrate
½ tablespoon sugar
100ml dry white wine
400g dried pappardelle, 500g fresh pappardelle
grated Parmesan, to serve

Starting from cold, put the onions, garlic, olive oil, butter and a pinch of salt in a heavy-based pan. Cook the onions slowly over a medium-low heat, allowing them to soften and turn translucent – this will take about 12 minutes.

Add the carrot to the pan along with the concentrate and sugar, cook for a minute, then raise the heat and add the wine – which will bubble.

Reduce the heat and cook gently for an hour, stirring every now and then. By the end of cooking the onion should have reduced to a caramel-coloured sauce.

Cook the pasta in plenty of well-salted water, drain, and toss with the sauce, adding a little pasta cooking water in order to loosen everything to a happy consistency. Serve with grated Parmesan.

Pappardelle all'ocio
Pappardelle with duck
Serves 4 generously

This version of duck pappardelle from Osteria Il Canto del Maggio, in Terranuova Bracciolini in Tuscany, takes its name from *ocio*, the local word for a drake. The duck is jointed, browned, then simmered to tenderness in red wine with an abundance of herbs, a *soffritto* of onion, leek and garlic, the zest and juice of an orange and just enough tomato to give it depth of flavour but not so much as to dominate. *Ricco e impegnativo*, rich and demanding, is how they describe this dish. It creates a silky and flavourful sauce, deep in colour, while the meat braises to tenderness. At the Osteria the meat is pulled from the bones and added back into the sauce for a *piatto unico*. Alternatively the duck can be set aside and only the sauce used for the pasta, then served with lentil purée as a second course. Either way it is a celebratory dish that requires plenty of red wine.

1 small duck, approx. 1.5 kg
a bunch of fresh rosemary, sage, thyme and bay
1 large onion
2 sticks of celery
1 small leek
1 clove of garlic
zest and juice of 1 large orange
60ml olive oil
a bottle of Chianti
200ml tomato passata
salt and black pepper
400g dried pappardelle, 500g fresh pappardelle

Clean the duck, reserving the liver if possible, and joint into 8. In a large heavy-based pan brown the pieces slowly and carefully, using tongs to turn.

While the meat browns, first chop the bunch of herbs finely, then chop the vegetables – onion, celery, leek and garlic. When the meat is deep gold on all sides, add the herbs and continue cooking for 30 seconds and stirring so they don't burn. Then add the vegetables, and the orange zest and juice, and continue cooking for a few minutes.

Add the olive oil and wine and raise the heat so the wine bubbles for a few minutes, then lower the heat so the pan simmers gently, half covered, for 2 hours. Add the tomato in the last 30 minutes. If at any point the pan seems too dry or the sauce too reduced, loosen with stock.

Lift the pieces of duck from the pan, allow to cool enough to handle, then pull the meat away from bone and rip into pieces you would like to eat with pasta, and return to the sauce.

Cook the pasta in plenty of well-salted water, drain, then toss with the sauce, adding a little pasta cooking water in order to loosen everything to a happy consistency.

Pappardelle con radicchio, finocchio e parmigiano
Pappardelle with radicchio, fennel, cream and Parmesan
Serves 4

Thinly sliced fennel sautéd in butter and olive oil until as soft and floppy as fabric, a handful of radicchio and a dash of cream with thick ribbons of fresh egg pappardelle and a blizzard of grated Parmesan: this is one of our favourite Saturday night suppers. The important thing is that you only use the white tender heart of the fennel – be ruthless trimming and pulling away the thick outer layers (they can be used for something else) – then slice the fennel so thinly it is almost transparent.

3 bulbs of Florentine fennel
3 shallots or spring onions
1 small bulb of radicchio
50g butter
4 tablespoons olive oil
salt
2–3 tablespoons thick cream or mascarpone (optional)
400g dried pappardelle, 500g fresh pappardelle, tagliatelle, linguine
grated Parmesan, to serve

Cut away any frilly fronds from the fennel, chop them finely and set aside. Trim the fennel rigorously, cutting away the base and stalks and removing the thick outer layer to get to the tenderest white heart. Slice the heart thinly along with the onions or shallots. Pull the leaves from the head of radicchio, then cut into wide ribbons.

Bring a large pan of water to the boil for the pasta. In a large heavy-based frying pan, over a medium-low heat, warm the butter and oil and add the fennel, onion and a pinch of salt. Fry, moving them with a wooden spoon, for about 10 minutes, until they are both translucent and very soft. In the last 2 minutes of cooking, add the radicchio and allow it to wilt, then add the cream or mascarpone if you are using it. Pull to one side and keep warm.

Once the water is boiling, add salt, stir well, add the pasta and cook until al dente, which will take 5 minutes with fresh.

When the pasta is a minute away from being cooked, put the fennel back over a low flame and once the pasta is ready, either lift it directly from the water and into the fennel, using a slotted spoon, or drain it in a colander and tip into the pan. Toss everything together, adding a little pasta cooking water to loosen if necessary. Divide between bowls and top with plenty of freshly grated Parmesan.

— p —

Penne

Writing this book during a global pandemic meant, among other things, an unprecedented opportunity for market research. When people stormed supermarkets and panic-shopped for toilet rolls, plastic gloves, tinned food and pasta, we saw which pasta shapes were the last to go. In Italy the photos of almost empty shelves that circled on social media suggested penne lisce (smooth penne) and farfalle were unloved. In England, too, the last bags were, apparently, penne. Following this revelation a conversation swelled on Twitter, many defending the shape, but many others expressing an almost violent dislike for both smooth and ridged penne.

How can you not like penne? Called for its slanting cut, reminiscent of a feather tip or the metal nib of a quill dip pen. Not liking penne is akin to not liking chips! OK! But, but . . .

Like all shapes, penne has a family tree and ancestors, hand-rolled garganelli and early extruded tubes of maccheroni. But its modern form is a factory-produced, hard wheat and water, dried pasta shape. The slanting cut is thanks to a man from Genoa called Giovanni Battista Capurro, who in 1865 obtained the patent on the manufacture of the diagonal cutting machine, which snipped without flattening the ends, therefore producing perfect quills, quickly. Penne is a doubly good sauce collector, both on its ridges, and – like a dip pen collecting ink – in its slanted tip.

While classic ridged penne are the widely consumed favourites, and Italy's second most sold shape, there are penne variations. Bigger pennoni (my favourite of the family), and in descending order of size siblings, pennette, pennine and pennettine, also mezze penne, half sized, which are ideal with peas, lemon and mascarpone. As with all shapes, the better the brand the better the texture and taste. Regardless of size, all penne share the slanting quill, so need cooking carefully, al dente yes, but at the tamer end of the al dente scale, otherwise the feel of the form can be obstinate, and also get stuck in your mouth. Penne is a jack of many sauces, its pleasing size, proportions, and double sauce-collecting ability making it one of the most recommended dried shapes from the North to the South. If Italian recipe books are to be believed, penne is a shape that quietly ignores many of the 'suggestions' about what should go with what, fitting in almost everywhere, if you pick it from the shelf.

Penne con salsiccia, porcini e porri
Penne with sausage, porcini mushrooms and leeks
Serves 4

Leeks collapse into a silky weave that holds other ingredients together, in this case, crumbled sausage and porcini. It is a recipe from the northern Italian region of Trentino-Alto Adige, so a good moment for a Riesling or Müller-Thurgau.

25g dried porcini
1 leek
1 medium tomato, peeled and roughly chopped, or 1 tinned plum tomato without juice
400g sausage meat
4 tablespoons olive oil
20g butter
salt
grated nutmeg
150ml dry white wine
2–3 tablespoons mascarpone (optional)
400g penne
a handful of fresh flat-leaf parsley, chopped
a handful of grated Parmesan, plus more to serve

Soak the porcini in 100ml of warm water for 20 minutes. Lift the porcini out and chop roughly, then filter the soaking liquid and set it aside. Bring a large pan of water to boil for the pasta. Prepare the leek by pulling away any dry, tough layers, split open lengthways and rinse well, then cut into half-moons. Peel and roughly chop the tomato.

In a large, deep frying pan, fry the leek and crumbled sausage meat in the olive oil and butter, with a pinch of salt, until the leek is soft and the sausage has lost its rawness, then add the porcini, the tomato and a few gratings of nutmeg. Add the wine and a couple of tablespoons of porcini soaking liquid, let it bubble, then cover the pan and leave to simmer for 20 minutes, adding a little more wine if it seems to be dry. By the end of the cooking everything should be soft and united with just a little sauce. Taste for salt.

If you are using it, in a small bowl add a couple of tablespoons of hot water to the mascarpone to loosen it.

In the last 10 minutes of sauce cooking time, salt the pasta water, stir, add the pasta and cook until al dente, then either lift directly into the sauce or drain, keeping back some of the cooking water.

Tip the pasta on to the sauce, along with the parsley, the mascarpone if you are using it, and a handful of cheese, and toss, adding a little pasta cooking water if it seems stiff. Scatter over a few green herbs, if you like, and serve with more grated cheese for those who want it.

Penne all'arrabbiata
Penne with spicy tomato sauce
Serves 4

While the weaving of olive oil, tomatoes, garlic and chilli is common all over southern Italy, the name *all'arrabbiata* signifies Rome. It translates as pasta in an angry style, but in the pan and plate translates as fiery delight. With chilli heat varying so hugely, also personal taste, it is hard to quantify how much chilli you should use, but as a guide I use two 1cm long dried Italian *peperoncini*. Introducing the potato masher as the second most useful tool for tomatoes (the first being a food mill).

2 cloves of garlic
7 tablespoons olive oil
700g plum tomatoes, tinned (without juice) or fresh, peeled and coarsely chopped
small dried chillies, crumbled, or red chilli flakes, to taste
salt
400g penne
1 heaped tablespoon chopped fresh flat-leaf parsley
grated pecorino or Parmesan, to serve

First prepare your garlic, peeled and crushed (so it breaks but remains whole) for a mild flavour, peeled and sliced for a stronger one, peeled and chopped for the strongest flavour. In a frying pan, over a low flame, allow the garlic to fry gently in the olive oil for a few minutes – do not let it burn, or it will be a bitter bully. If you like, at this point you can pull the whole cloves out.

Add the tomatoes to the pan along with the crumbled chilli or flakes (again, this is up to you, but the point of the dish is heat) and a pinch of salt. Allow them to cook, covered, for 10 minutes, then remove the lid (at this point I give it a mash with a potato masher), raise the flame and cook for another 5. By the end of cooking the sauce should be thick, shiny with a slick of oil.

While the sauce is simmering, bring a large pan of water to the boil for the pasta. Add salt, stir, then add the pasta and cook until al dente.

Ideally tip the sauce into a warm bowl, add the drained pasta, parsley and a bit more oil, toss and then divide between bowls. Otherwise mix everything in the pan and serve directly from there, passing round grated pecorino or Parmesan for those who want it.

Penne ai quattro formaggi filanti
Penne with four cheeses
Serves 4

Years ago, on a particularly wet night, my friend Rosalba, inspired by the Roman writer Ada Boni, made me this. Warm in her kitchen, the TV glowing, my shoes drying by the heater, it tasted like heaven. *Filanti* means stringy, the best sort. You melt cheese into a little whole milk to make a rich cheese sauce – any cheese that melts is welcome, but Parmesan, Gorgonzola, fontina, Taleggio, Gruyère, and either mozzarella or provolone for strings work particularly well. Speckle it with black pepper. Don't panic if it seems a little liquid when you first put the pasta in, it will soon thicken into a cream that clings.

400g penne, maccheroni, mezze maniche, fusilli
salt
180ml whole milk
80g Parmesan, grated
80g Taleggio, cubed
80g mozzarella, ripped into little bits
80g Gorgonzola dolce, mashed
black pepper

Bring a large pan of water to the boil for the pasta, add salt, stir, add the pasta and cook until al dente.

Meanwhile, in a deep frying pan, warm the milk gently and after a few minutes add the cheese and keep warming, stirring, until the cheese has melted. Just before it boils, pull from the heat and add pepper.

Once the pasta is al dente, lift it into the melted cheese and toss, pausing to allow it to thicken, then toss again and serve.

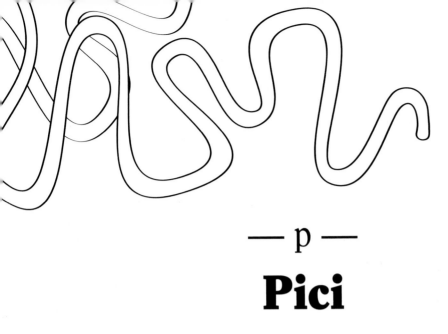

— p —

Pici

Raffaella's movement reminds me of sanding. As she rubs, she is stretching and lengthening the strip of flour and water dough between her palm and the wooden board into a rope, a *picio*. In the corner of the board is a pile of pici, sleeping snakes in yolk-yellow sand.

We are south of Florence, just up from Grosseto in Val d'Orcia in Tuscany, an aorta of good food and even better wine. Raffaella's house sits on top of a hill and her kitchen window looks out over the valley. Through the veil of spring drizzle, the olive groves look like heads of unruly silver hair, while the neat vines are like tramlines on a skinhead. This is land shaped by the fourteenth- and fifteenth-century Tuscan merchants who transformed this part of Tuscany into a model of rural development and beauty, a reason for so much Tuscan pride and fodder for sunburnt novels and, ahem, narrative cookbooks. Much earlier were the Etruscans. Some local historians have tried to trace pici back to the Etruscans, a theory they evidence with the murals on the walls of a tomb in Cerveteri.

In Cerveteri, Umbria and parts of Lazio similar rope-like pasta are called lombrichelli, earthworms, also umbricelli, which makes me think of umbilical cords. In other parts of Tuscany much shorter lengths are called strozzapreti, priest stranglers, gastronomic humour that comes from a time when priests were seen as the greedy and interfering lackeys of the papal state. Raffaella calls them pici. The name surely comes from pinching walnut-sized bits from a ball of dough, which is a common way to make them, as is rolling the dough between your palms as if rubbing a stick into a rock trying to spark fire. Raffaella shows us her way, rolling some of the dough into a circle, cutting that into centimetre-wide strips ready to be rubbed.

Later at a *sagra*, a festival dedicated to the making and consuming of their local shape, a woman tells me that pici are the most primitive of shapes, that there is no right or wrong way, that anyone can do it if they have patience, all the while making pici with such speed and skill, I can barely follow what she is doing. I choose to believe her though, rather than others who would have us believe that there is only one way to do things and that has to be passed on from your mother like an heirloom.

The irregularity is part of the charm of pici, as well as the texture imparted by hands, board and the rough flours traditionally used, a texture which is now achieved by using both soft and hard wheat (semola) flours. The substance and texture of pici means it is satisfying even with very little sauce. Traditionally 'poor folks' food', pici were served with poor sauces (inevitably the best-tasting ones), olive oil and garlic, cubes of crisp pancetta and even crisper breadcrumbs. Richer sauces (for richer folks) were meat, giblets or a mahogany-coloured duck and wine *ragù* known as *nana*.

Raffaella treats us richly like poor folk, making one sauce with olive oil, tomatoes and a gigantic and mild local garlic called *aglione* (or kissing or elephant garlic), then tossing the rest of the pici in the pan with a rubble of salty fried breadcrumbs. We eat and drink, and as we do it rains, and rains, so much so that we are reluctant to leave, so sit back and drink some more.

To make pici

While they are normally made with plain 00 flour, a percentage of semolina flour gives strength to the dough. The general rule is half the quantity of flour in water, so 200g of 00, 200g of semola and 200ml of warm water, but because all flour is different, and climatic conditions play a part, you do need to mix the dough a little 'by eye'. Dough needs to be soft but not squishy or sticky. You should be able to knead it and feel elasticity but firmness. Having rested the dough under a bowl for 30 minutes, cut off a thick slice (and put the rest back under the bowl), use a rolling pin to roll it into a 5mm thick, saucer-sized disc, cut the disc into 1cm strips and then, using the palm of one or both hands, and working on a board, rub into a slender rope.

Pici are also a dried shape, and interchangeable with strozzapreti, also tonnarelli, spaghettoni and spaghetti alla chitarra.

Pici all'aglione
Pici with tomatoes and garlic
Serves 4

This dish is traditionally made with *aglione* (elephant garlic), a large, fragrant and mild variety of garlic grown in Val di Chiana and Val d'Orcia in Tuscany; cooked in oil it is creamy and sweet. If you are using ordinary garlic you have two choices. You could slice 4 cloves very thinly and allow them to cook *very* slowly in oil to bring out the sweetness. Alternatively roast or poach a whole head of garlic in oil and squeeze the flesh out and start cooking from there.

2 cloves of elephant garlic or 6 cloves of ordinary garlic
120ml olive oil
500g ripe tomatoes, or a tin of peeled plum tomatoes
1 small dried red chilli, crumbled or a pinch of red chilli flakes
salt
400g dried pici or 450g fresh, or strozzapreti, tonnarelli, spaghettoni, spaghetti alla chitarra
toasted breadcrumbs or grated Parmesan, to serve

If you are using *aglione* or elephant garlic, peel the garlic, place in a mortar and pound with a little of the olive oil until it forms a cream.

If you are using ordinary garlic, either slice 4 cloves very thin, or squeeze the flesh from 5 roasted cloves.

Peel the tomatoes by plunging them into boiling water for 60 seconds, then into cold water, at which point the skins should split and slip away. Chop the tomatoes roughly, separating away most of the seeds. If you are using tinned tomatoes, lift them from the juice and chop, roughly.

If you have pounded *aglione,* put it into a frying pan with the rest of the olive oil and fry gently on a medium-low heat until the garlic has melted into the oil. If you are using ordinary garlic, warm in oil over the lowest flame for 15 minutes. With roasted garlic, squeeze into oil and warm gently. Add the tomatoes and chilli and allow to almost boil, then reduce the heat and simmer for 20 minutes.

While the sauce simmers, bring a pan of water to the boil, add salt, then the pici and boil until al dente.

Drain the pasta, save some cooking water, or lift out of the pot with a pasta spoon or spider sieve, then tip on to the sauce and mix well. Serve immediately, with toasted breadcrumbs or grated Parmesan.

Umbricelli con zucchine, pancetta e pecorino
Umbricelli with courgettes, pancetta and pecorino
Serves 4

In parts of Umbria, pici are known as umbricelli. This recipe from Alice Adams is not only a favourite, it is a neat illustration of how to use the pasta cooking water to help cook a sauce, softening and all the time adding starch which helps everything come together.

extra virgin olive oil
1 clove of garlic, peeled and squashed
150g pancetta, diced
1 small dried red chilli
salt and black pepper
8 small courgettes, 4 thinly sliced, the other 4 grated
450g fresh pici
100g pecorino, grated

Over a moderate flame, warm a generous pour of olive oil (it should just cover the base of the pan) in a good large high-sided frying pan, with the whole garlic, the diced pancetta and a small broken dried chilli if you like. Let the garlic release its flavour and the pancetta colour a little before adding the courgettes and a pinch of salt.

Bring a large pot of water to the boil. Add a tablespoon of salt and stir, in preparation for the pasta. Gently fry the courgettes, taking care not to let them burn – they will take on a brighter colour and nice glossy sheen. At this point add a couple of ladlefuls of water from the cooking pot to keep the courgettes moist and continue to let them soften and collapse.

Cook the pasta for 3–4 minutes. Continue to cook the sauce, and as the pasta cooks, skim off the cooking water and continue to add to the courgette sauce. Now the gluten from the cooking water will help to thicken up the sauce a little, which should be a good creamy consistency. Don't let the sauce dry out, keep it liquid by adding water from the pasta pot.

Drain the cooked pasta, throw it into the pan with the courgette sauce and toss together well, adding half the grated pecorino. Salt and pepper to taste before serving, finishing with more grated pecorino and a drizzle of olive oil.

— p —

Pizzoccheri

Look at a map of Italy. Run a finger along the northernmost border, the Alpine crown at the top of the boot, stopping in what seems like the middle. Your finger should be on, or near, Valtellina, a broad valley that cuts between the Alps and forms part of the border between Italy and Switzerland. It is a formidable and beautiful place of sheer slopes and capricious pasture and home to a buckwheat flour pasta called pizzoccheri.

Its name is misleading. Buckwheat is not related to wheat. It is a herbaceous plant in the same family as sorrel and rhubarb that adapts easily to difficult terrain, such as Valtellina, where it has been cultivated since the fourteenth century and is known as Grano Saraceno. Its triangular seeds, though, behave like cereal and can be used as whole grains or milled into a speckled flour. Buckwheat flour and water produce a dough that is not unlike the grey granite rock of Valtellina, which then fades as it dries, but retains a distinctive speckled tone, like grey herringbone tweed. The flavour of pizzoccheri is rich, nutty, slightly earthy, and marries blissfully with potatoes and cabbage then layered with lots of melted butter and cheese called Casera.

Whether you make or buy the pizzoccheri, this is a satisfying dish. Also a one-pan dish, and a cooking stagger. Bring a pan of water to the boil, add the diced potato first, after 5 minutes the cabbage, then the pizzoccheri. The stagger means that by the time the pizzoccheri are cooked the potatoes and cabbage are soft and yielding enough to be an almost sauce. The three are then dressed with a very generous amount of butter and cheese. This, and a glass of Rosso di Valtellina, is what I want on a cold night.

~~~~~~

Making your own pizzoccheri

For 4. Make a mountain of 200g of buckwheat flour and 50g of 00 flour, turn it into a volcano, add 125ml of water and work it into the flour to form a consistent and firm dough. You may need more water but work slowly, as the line between dry and slimy is a fine one. Knead gently, briefly. It is unlike normal pasta dough in that it crumbles; the main thing is a firm, neat ball. Rest for 30 minutes. Working carefully, watching the edges and that it doesn't stick, roll it into a circle 1–2mm thick. Cut it into strips 5cm wide and then the strips into 1cm sticks, spreading them out so they don't stick.

Pizzoccheri is also a dried pasta shape, and a wonderful one. Look out for packets labelled Pizzoccheri della Valtellina IGP.

~~~~~~

Pizzoccheri con patate, verza e formaggio
Pizzoccheri with potatoes, cabbage and cheese
Serves 4

The traditional cheese is Valtellina Casera, a cheese made from semi-skimmed cow's milk in the northern Italian province of Sondrio. When young its taste is fresh and bright, but as it ages the flavour deepens, reminiscent of walnuts, intense, piquant and dry with traces of stable. It melts really well. An alternative is a mixture of fontina and Parmesan.

300g cabbage, trimmed and broken into leaves
salt
300g potatoes, peeled and cut into 2cm chunks
500g fresh pizzoccheri (see page 237) or 400g dried pizzocheri
2 cloves of garlic, peeled and sliced
100g butter
100g fontina or Casera
100g Parmesan, grated

Make piles of 3 or 4 cabbage leaves, roll into cigars and then slice into 2cm wide ribbons. Bring a large pan of water to the boil, add salt and stir.

Set the timer for 14 minutes and add the potatoes to the boiling water, then after 5 minutes add the cabbage. If you are using dried pizzoccheri (which take 9 minutes) add that too. If you are using fresh pizzoccheri, wait another 5 minutes, then add.

Meanwhile in another frying pan, over a medium-low flame, gently fry the garlic in the butter until soft and fragrant. Pull the pan from the heat.

When the timer rings, drain everything, reserving some of the cooking water.

Either layer and serve from a large platter, or serve in small individual dishes. For both, put a little of the butter and cheese into the bottom of the dish(es), add half the pasta and vegetables, then half the butter and cheese, then the rest of the pasta, finishing with butter, tossing and serving. It is an optional step to put the layered pizzoccheri under the grill for a couple of minutes (if you do, maybe add a little extra cheese).

— q —
Quadrucci

The name means little squares. While you can buy a factory-made durum wheat and water version, quadrucci are traditionally another *pasta di recupero*, a way to use up scraps. In my adopted home of Rome this means the offcuts of fresh egg pasta after making lasagne, cannelloni, ravioli or fettuccine, which are particularly suited as the ribbons only need cutting into squares. Their 1 x 1cm proportions make them a *pastina* and so served in broth and *minestra*. Larger squares are sometimes called quadrucci too, even though arguably they are a short pasta.

Our local fresh pasta shop, Gatti, has a two-tone metal box on the shelf behind the counter. It looks like a cross between an old-fashioned cash register and a bulbous bread box, but it is actually a quadrucci maker! Inside, a mechanical press forces leftover pasta through a grid, which chops it into 1cm or 5mm squares which then fall into a drawer that can be pulled out so the tiny squares can be scooped into bags and sold by weight. A typical Roman *minestra* is *quadrucci e piselli alla romana* – quadrucci and peas.

You don't need any sort of machine though. Quadrucci are straightforward to make at home. Roll or buy sheets of fresh egg pasta, pile them, and cut first into strips and then squares. If you don't use them all, quadrucci are a particularly neat shape to bag and freeze, next to the peas, and even more conveniently don't need defrosting, simply tossing straight into the boiling broth or soup.

Quadrucci coi spinaci
Quadrucci with spinach, butter and Parmesan
Serves 4

This recipe, like many recipes, is part of a chain. It is my adaptation of Claudia Roden's adaptation of Donatella Pavoncello's adaptation of a family recipe from her book about Jewish family food. It requires larger quadrucci, 3cm squares. I suggest quite thin ones so they wrap themselves around the spinach, which is braised with butter and onion. You could make your own pasta or run a shop-bought pasta through your machine to thin it slightly – then cut it.

400g lasagne or fresh egg pasta (see page 51), cut into 3cm squares
750g spinach
2 medium onions, peeled and finely diced
2 tablespoons olive oil
salt and black pepper
75g butter
red chilli flakes, to serve
100g Parmesan, grated, to serve

If you're using fresh pasta, make the quadrucci by cutting the sheets of egg pasta into 3cm squares.

Wash the spinach and pick over, discarding any very tough stalks or damaged leaves. Drain well and squeeze out excess water.

In a large frying pan over a medium-low heat, fry the onions in the olive oil until soft and translucent, then add the spinach. Cover the pan and leave the spinach to wilt into a crumpled mass in the water clinging to it – lift the lid and stir occasionally.

Meanwhile cook the quadrucci in plenty of well-salted fast-boiling water until al dente. Drain and add to the spinach pan along with the butter, tossing everything together well. Serve with black pepper or red chilli flakes and grated Parmesan.

Quadrucci alla romana
Quadrucci and peas Roman style
Serves 4

A particular favourite of mine for the way it looks, the peas and squares are playful somehow, and its taste, brothy but clouded with cheese, bright and good. We usually have this on a Monday, relief after a weekend cooking. I agree with my mum and my favourite food writer Simon Hopkinson: frozen peas are wonderful, and this is a dish in which they shine. I have suggested light stock, but lightly salted water would work too.

6 tablespoons olive oil
1 onion, peeled and finely chopped
1 stalk of celery, with leaves, finely chopped
a few stems of fresh flat-leaf parsley, finely chopped
salt
300g peas
1.5 litres light vegetable stock
200g fresh egg pasta quadrucci, or 180g dried
grated pecorino and dried red chilli flakes, to serve

Put the oil, onion, celery, parsley and a pinch of salt into a frying pan. Put the pan on a medium-low flame and fry the vegetables, stirring often until they are soft and translucent – about 10 minutes.

Add the peas, stir for a few minutes, then add the stock, bring to a gentle boil, and reduce to a simmer for 10 minutes.

Raise the flame so the soup boils gently, then add the quadrucci and cook until al dente – the consistency should be that of a dense soup but with visible broth.

Serve immediately, encouraging everyone to stir grated pecorino and red chilli flakes into their bowlful.

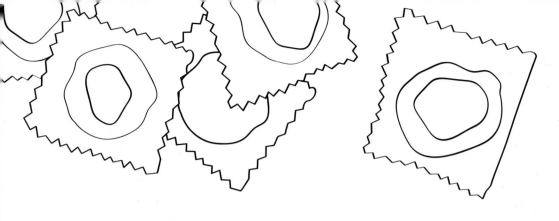

— r —

Ravioli

Having spent many years in London working as a chef, running her own restaurant and leading cookery courses all over Italy, Carla Tomasi came home, near Rome. She toiled and turned a paved yard into a nourished garden, productive vegetable plot and small orchard, rescued a colony of cats, and then, after a few years, began teaching again. Many people are good cooks, but few can teach, even fewer teach well, and Carla is one of them. She is knowledgeable, skilled, warm and wry, and without any bravado, as keen to talk about English puddings and how to puff pitta bread as she is about ravioli. I am fortunate to be one of her many students and in recent years, along with Alice Adams, to have taught alongside her. What we make in lessons varies depending on what time of year it is and what we all want to eat. But there is always pasta, often ravioli, usually spinach and ricotta. Which, far from neat parcels, are asymmetric with frilly edges, and served with butter and sage. This is her recipe, in both our words.

I suggest you sit down with a cup of tea or glass of wine and read through first. It sounds more complicated than it actually is – you are just making parcels – and the passage from page to hands is often awkward. But trust Carla, it is a straightforward and satisfying process.

Fresh egg pasta for ravioli

You can use the standard egg dough here, or try Carla's variation, which is 260g of 00 flour plus 140g of finely ground semolina and produces a more substantial dough with bite. Method as on page 51. I should note that this is our recipe, the pasta rolled thin, the filling spooned in (not piped), cut in easy-going squares with a wide, almost frilly edge. This is not the only way and in time you may decide to roll thicker, make neater edges.

A note about the history of ravioli

Historians suggest the first written source of something like a ravioli was in the *Liber de Coquina*, 'The book of cooking/cookery', maybe the oldest medieval cookbook, dated around 1285–1304. Within its appendix is a study of Arab gastronomy from 1100 noting a *sambusaj*, a triangle of pasta filled with ground meat. This date coincides with the end of the Arab domination in Sicily, a period we know saw the birth of dried pasta. Did the Arabs introduce filled pasta too? Later texts document the adoption of Muslim dishes in Sicilian cuisine, and note that the Latin translation for *sambusaj* is *raviolus*, although there is no note of what shape the *raviolus* actually was. Then in the thirteenth century a Franciscan friar and chronicler, Salimbene da Parma, refers to *raviolis sine crusta de pasta*. After this, the work of historians documents terminological uncertainty, otherwise known as chaos, with nobody clear what was a *gnocco* and what was a *raviolo*, what was covered and what was nude. And remember while all this was going on there were other filled shapes evolving too, their name leaving little doubt as to their form: cappelletti – hats, aneline – rings, tortellini – little *torte* or pies.

What loops this back to Carla is an 1834 recipe manual and a recipe for *ravioli alla romana*, pasta filled with spinach and ricotta, cut in a half-moon. While the confusion didn't end, what is clear is that from the nineteenth century the *raviolo* gained popularity as a form, filled with meat, fish, cheese, vegetables, shaped in half-moons, circles, squares, triangles that echoes that first mention in an Arab text, edges straight or crimped with a fork.

And what can we take from all this as cooks? That the possibilities are endless. That once we get a handle on dough and shaping, what thickness and closure suits, a milky way of ravioli awaits.

Ravioli ricotta e spinaci
Ravioli with ricotta and spinach
Serves 4

250g ricotta, sheep's
   milk or cow's
200g fresh leaf
   spinach
1 egg, beaten
50g Parmesan, grated
salt, black pepper and
   grated nutmeg
1 x 400g flour/4 egg
   batch of egg pasta
   (see page 51),
   rolled into sheets

To serve
150g butter
12 leaves of sage
grated Parmesan

It is important the ricotta is dry, so leave it to drain in a sieve for at least an hour and up to 4 hours in a bowl. Rinse the spinach, then cook in a hot pan, covered, with just the water clinging to the leaves until it has wilted. Sturdier winter spinach could be lightly boiled in salted water. Drain the spinach and once cooled down a bit, squeeze out the water. Chop the spinach finely and mix with the ricotta, beaten egg, Parmesan and nutmeg. Taste and adjust the seasoning accordingly.

Cut the pasta into sheets that are approximately 30cm long by 10cm wide and lay out on a board. Fold the pasta in half to make a crease, then unfold and use the crease as a guide. Use your fingertip to make tiny indents marking 4cm intervals just below the crease.

Place a heaped teaspoon of mixture in every indent and then fold the pasta over. Starting near the fold, press around the heaps of filling to both seal and ease out any air. Run your hand under the strip of pasta to make sure it is not stuck to the worktop, then use a wheel cutter or a sharp knife to cut first along the bottom of the whole strip and then to divide them.

When you are ready to cook, bring a pan of water to the boil. In a frying pan, melt the butter over a low heat and add the whole or chopped sage leaves. Leave to infuse for a little while.

Cook the ravioli in well-salted water at a rolling but not rollicking boil. If the dough is rolled to the thinnest setting on the machine they will take 3–4 minutes, the double-thickness edges firm (but not immovable) and the curve over the filling just starting to turn translucent. Lift out of the pan with a spider sieve, wait a second so the water drips away, then place on a wide platter.

Pour the butter and sage over the cooked ravioli, add a few grindings of black pepper and shower with Parmesan.

Variations. The spinach can be left out and replaced with more Parmesan, also finely chopped marjoram, or lemon and orange zest. Instead of butter and sage, ravioli with ricotta are fabulous served *alla gricia*, so with guanciale and pecorino, or with a simple tomato sauce, or with *pesto alla genovese*, or walnut sauce.

Ravioli con le patate, ricotta, limone e maggiorana
Ravioli with potatoes, ricotta, lemon and marjoram
Serves 6

Of the endless possibilities which to choose? The one I like best is filled with a soft, yielding filling of potato, ricotta, Parmesan and marjoram, and shaped in rounds. This recipe owes much to the Ligurian pansotti, little fat belly pasta, also Sardinian culurgiones.

400g potatoes,
   even-sized
100g ricotta
2 eggs
6 tablespoons grated
   Parmesan
zest of 1 unwaxed
   lemon
1 heaped tablespoon
   finely chopped
   fresh marjoram
salt and black pepper
1 x 400g flour/ 4 egg
   batch of egg pasta
   (see page 45),
   rolled in to sheets

Scrub but don't peel the potatoes, then boil until tender in salted water. Once they are cool enough to handle, peel the potatoes and then mash.

Mix the ricotta, eggs, Parmesan, zest and marjoram with the potato, taste and season with salt and pepper.

Cut the pasta into sheets that are approximately 30cm long by 10cm wide (as a guide this is the right amount for ravioli).

Use your fingertip to make tiny indents marking 4cm intervals just below the fold. Place a heaped teaspoon of mixture in every indent and fold the pasta over. Starting near the fold, press around the heaps of filling to both seal and ease out any air. Use a wheel cutter or sharp knife to cut first along the bottom of the whole strip and then to divide them.

Cook the raviloi in salted water for 3-4 minutes, then drain and serve with butter and sage, *pesto alla genovese,* or simple tomato sauce.

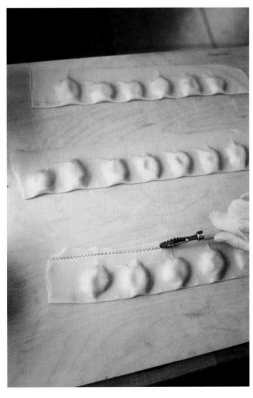

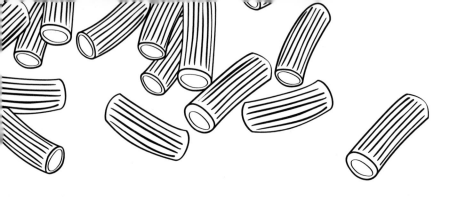

— r —

Rigatoni

Frosted windows are the first thing that comes to mind when I think of Trattoria Perilli. The second is *rigatoni alla carbonara* in a fluted bowl. After that the thoughts pile in, the serving trolleys, starched white cloths that tent the table, speckled terrazzo floor, wood panels, rotary dial telephone on a plinth in the middle of the room (that as far as I know never rings), the waiters' cummerbunds and rural murals.

Like the 14 other *trattorie* in the Testaccio quarter of Rome, and hundreds in the wider city, the menu at Perilli is rigorously *cucina casareccia romana* – Roman home cooking. Their padded and plasticized menu lists three *antipasti*, all pork; four *minestre*; a long and robust selection of *secondi* – lamb, veal, pork and offal; six vegetable sides; eight puddings; two cheeses. It is the dishes listed after the *minestre* and before the *secondi*, though, that bring me through the frosted glass door. Nine pasta dishes giving away the Roman preference for rigatoni, 4cm-long tubes of dried pasta defined by their ridges, especially suited to the deep dark sauce from oxtail stew, or for *carbonara*, which comes in a fluted white bowl.

Some trace *pasta alla carbonara* back to the *carbonari* (charcoal makers) in Abruzzo who in the mists of time filled their plates with flour and water pasta dressed with pancetta, eggs and cheese. This origin story is unpicked by writers like Livio Jannattoni and Luca Cesari, who trace it to the end of the Second World War, American troops stationed in Rome and the testimony of a young

Bolognese chef called Renato Gualandi. Whatever its origins, shepherds, soldiers or both, *carbonara* is a perfect example of culinary alchemy, transforming the pangs of hunger into an occasion of great pleasure. What is certain is that the first recorded recipe for *spaghetti alla carbonara* was published in 1952 in an American restaurant guide, then two years later *La cucina italiana* printed the first recipe in Italy.

Also discussed – at length – are the best ingredients: guanciale, pancetta or bacon, whole eggs or yolks, pecorino, Parmesan or a mix, and how best to bring the ingredients together. *Carbonara* is a pasta dish where the condiment is inseparable from the shape. Helped by starchy pasta cooking water, your tossing and the sides of the bowl, the beaten egg, cheese, cured pork and its fat only become sauce when they meet the surface of the pasta, traditionally long forms, better short ones.

Back in Perilli, the white bowls with high fluted sides aren't just the container for *rigatoni alla carbonara*, they are part of its creation. Having tossed the al dente pasta in the pork fat in a pan in the kitchen, the chef tips both into a bowl containing a mix of egg, grated pecorino and pepper. The bowl is then loaded on to a trolley, rattled across the room and parked beside your table, where the waiter tosses the contents of the bowl with a fork and a spoon, and the canary yellow and silky carbonara is created in the bowl, on the surface of the pasta, before your eyes.

Rigatoni alla carbonara
Rigatoni with egg, guanciale and pecorino
Serves 4

150g guanciale,
    pancetta or bacon
a little olive oil (if you
    are using pancetta
    or bacon)
400g rigatoni, mezze
    maniche, penne,
    spaghetti, bucatini
2 whole eggs, plus
    4 yolks
100g finely grated
    pecorino romano,
    or Parmesan, or a
    mixture of both
salt and freshly
    ground black
    pepper

Bring a large pan of water to a rolling boil for the pasta.

Cut the guanciale into short, thick strips and put into a cold pan. Put the pan on a medium-low heat and cook gently so the fat renders and the pieces turn golden slowly. If you are using pancetta or bacon add a little olive oil too, and again fry gently, encouraging the fat to render and edges to crisp slowly. Remove the pan from the heat.

Salt the boiling water, stir, add the pasta and cook until al dente. While the pasta is cooking, in a large bowl beat together the eggs, yolks, cheese, a pinch of salt and a spoonful of guanciale fat. When the pasta is nearly ready, put the frying pan back on the heat to get the fat hot.

When the pasta is ready, either drain and save some cooking water or, better still, lift it directly into the frying pan and toss thoroughly to coat every tube with fat. **Now you have two options – mixing in a pan, or in a bowl.**

In a bowl
Tip the contents of the frying pan into a warm bowl with the egg mixture. Using two big spoons, toss the pasta with the condiment, lifting from the bottom upwards and swishing so all the elements combine and the sauce is created on the surface of the pasta. It may seem liquid to begin with, but have patience – it will thicken, and continue to thicken as you bring it to the table. Grind over some pepper.

Remaining in the pan
Pull the pan from the heat and add the egg mixture, then stir and swish vigorously until you have a soft golden cream. If it seems too dry or clumpy, add a bit more cooking water and stir vigorously again. Divide between plates, grind over some pepper, and serve immediately.

Rigatoni con sugo di coda
Rigatoni with the sauce of Roman-style oxtail stew
Serves 4–6

Taking the opportunity to include one of my favourite dishes, coda alla vaccinara, oxtail cooked in the style of *i vaccinari*, Rome's historic beef butchers. That is, oxtail braised slowly with wine, celery and tomato, until silky soft and falling from the bone, and surrounded by deep, dark sauce. While the oxtail and enough sauce is saved for a second course, the rest of the deeply flavoured sauce is perfect for pasta, rigatoni or gnocchi. Really Roman, really wonderful.

1.2kg oxtail, cut into sections
1 medium onion, peeled and sliced
4 tablespoons olive oil, for frying
300ml red wine
800g tinned plum tomatoes, chopped
salt and black pepper
200g celery, cut into 5cm batons
30g sultanas
30g pine nuts
dark chocolate or cocoa powder, to taste (optional)
400g rigatoni, also mezze maniche, or potato gnocchi

Wash the oxtail in cold water, drain and pat the pieces dry. In a large heavy-based or enamel pot, that can later contain all the ingredients, brown half the oxtail in the olive oil over a medium heat. Once the oxtail is brown on all sides, transfer to a plate. Brown the remaining meat the same way and transfer to the plate. Add the onions to the pan and fry until golden.

Return all the oxtail to the pan, raise the heat and add the wine. Let it sizzle and partially evaporate. Add the tomatoes, 100ml of water, salt and pepper. Turn the meat, making sure it is covered with sauce. Bring the pot to a steady simmer, then reduce the heat to low. Half cover the pot and cook for 3 hours. Every now and then, turn the meat and add a little more water if the sauce is looking too thick.

Add the celery, sultanas and pine nuts to the pan and stir. Cook for 2 more hours. By then the meat should be incredibly tender and falling from the bone; the sauce, rich and dark. If you don't have time to let the stew rest overnight, spoon away some of the fat that is resting on the surface. If you wish, add grated chocolate or cocoa, taste, and add more salt, if necessary.

Lift the oxtail and just enough sauce on to a warm platter but keep the remaining sauce in the pan. Cook the rigatoni until al dente and then mix with the sauce, also some pasta cooking water if it seems stiff. Serve, passing round grated pecorino for those who want it. Serve the oxtail as a second course with greens and diced, roasted potatoes.

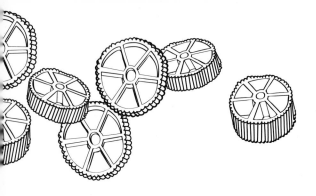

— r —

Ruote

Because of its significance and the enormity of forms, it seems wrong to talk about pasta in terms of fashion. But pasta has always been the height of fashion, and not only that, the height of fashion while maintaining an extensive back catalogue of classic and timeless forms. Whether in the hands of ingenious home cooks, chefs trying to impress their wealthy households, or tenacious early machines, there has always been innovation, invention and evolution.

It was the advent of the industrialized pasta industry in the nineteenth century that meant an explosion of shapes. The increased capacity of machines and die forms and growing demand meant that the shapes and sizes offered went from dozens to hundreds. Between 1887 and 1935 seven of what are still the largest *pastifici* in Italy were established – Barilla, De Cecco, Buitoni, Antonio Amato, Fratelli di Rugantino, Di Martino and Garofolo, not to mention the hundreds of smaller makers, all with different standards and scope of production, but all innovating.

Who better to mirror the changing shape of a country and society than a newly industrialized industry that made shapes. I'd love to travel back in time and eavesdrop on the conversation about which shape best honoured a newborn princess or a victory abroad, how best to extrude a car radiator, wheel, aeroplane propeller or flying saucer. The pasta industry also mirrored changing habits and working lives. I've passed far too much time watching 1960s footage of the Italian singer Mina advertising Barilla pasta, her lyrical promise of everyday elegance while she strokes boxes of traditionally fresh shapes now dried and ready for the pan. There has always been innovation with fresh and filled pasta too, now more than ever, as young chefs move easily between tradition and innovation, thank goodness.

And it continues, as pasta makers invest in 3D printers which allow them to sculpt forms that could never be made by hand or mechanical extrusion. Every year the pasta maker Barilla holds a competition to design a new shape and receives hundreds of entries, especially from children. Barilla also holds the pasta world championships, inviting 14 young chefs from all over the world to compete for the title Barilla Master of Pasta. The winner in 2019 was Keita Yuge for his *penne Gorgonzola* with a Japanese 'perfume' of sake, sansho and yuzu.

And so to the shape, ruote, wheels, if possible made by the *antico pastificio* Benedetto Cavalieri, an exceptional pasta maker in a town called Maglie in Puglia, who didn't invent the wheel, but makes them extremely well.

I have paired ruote with ricotta, Gorgonzola and mascarpone. That's three dishes of white wheels I know, but I wanted them grouped together, also because they share a method. That is – mix or melt the cheese and whatever else, loosen with pasta cooking water, add pasta and finish with nuts for texture. These are basic recipes that invite innovation and invention.

Ruote con Gorgonzola, salvia e noci
Ruote with Gorgonzola, sage and walnuts
Serves 2

There are two sorts of Gorgonzola. Gorgonzola piccante, which as its name suggests is feisty and piquant; the prominent veins in this firmer, at times crumbly, cheese have a musty tang and bite, even a slightly metallic note. *Dolce* means sweet, and, although it is not actually sweet, Gorgonzola dolce is certainly sweeter in nature, the veins lighter both in look and taste, and pleasantly tangy next to the creamy cheese.

I think dolce is better here. Its sweet sharp nature is a good match for sage, with its inherent musty bitterness. Toasted walnuts, milky but with slight nicotine-like bitterness, add a rubble of texture to the rich sauce.

200g ruote, or farfalle, penne, fettuccine or tagliolini
salt
150g Gorgonzola
50ml cream
10 sage leaves
10 walnuts, broken into pieces

Bring a large pan of water to the boil for the pasta, and once it boils, add salt, stir, then add the pasta and cook until al dente.

In another frying pan, over a low flame gently warm the Gorgonzola, cream, sage leaves and walnuts until they have become a smooth sauce.

Once the pasta is al dente, lift out of the water and into the sauce, toss and divide between plates.

Ruote con mascarpone e noci
Ruote with mascarpone and walnuts
Serves 2

Mascarpone is cream cheese, that is, thick cream coagulated with acid, but gently so it has no sourness, just depth and richness. It originated in the northern Italian region of Lombardy but is now diffused and is often added to pasta dishes. Here it is the star, enriched further with egg yolk and Parmesan and black pepper. Again the pasta cooking water helps loosen it so it is silky rather than clingy.

200g ruote, or farfalle, penne, fettuccine or tagliolini
100g mascarpone
1 egg yolk
20g Parmesan, grated
black pepper
30g walnuts

Bring a large pan of water to the boil for the pasta. Once it boils add salt, stir, then add the pasta and cook until al dente.

Meanwhile, in a large bowl, mix the mascarpone, egg yolk, Parmesan and grinds of black pepper, loosening slightly with a little water from the pasta pan. In a small pan toast the walnuts over a low flame until golden.

Once the pasta is al dente, lift it out of the water and into the sauce, toss carefully and divide between plates, topping each with a few toasted walnuts.

Ruote con ricotta e pinoli
Ruote with ricotta and pine nuts
Serves 2

Ricotta. The name means recooked or cooked again, which is exactly what has happened. Leftover whey from cheese making is cooked again with a bit of extra milk and curdles into a soft whey cheese. Wherever there is cheese making in Italy, there is ricotta. There is a particularly strong culture of sheep's (*pecora*) milk ricotta in Lazio and Sicily. Ricotta made from sheep's milk is creamy and ever so slightly gamy, cow's milk ricotta is one-dimensional in comparison, goat's milk ricotta is distinctive for its tang, and buffalo milk ricotta is the creamiest of them all. All work for this recipe.

200g ruote, or farfalle, penne, fettuccine or tagliolini
salt
150g ricotta
40g Parmesan, grated
zest of 1 small unwaxed lemon
black pepper
30g pine nuts

Bring a large pan of water to the boil for the pasta, and once it boils, add salt, stir, then add the pasta and cook until al dente.

Meanwhile in a large bowl, mix the ricotta, Parmesan, zest and a few grinds of black pepper, loosening slightly with a little water from the pasta pan. In a small pan toast the pine nuts over a low flame until golden.

Once the pasta is al dente, lift out of the water and into the sauce, toss and divide between plates, topping each with a few pine nuts.

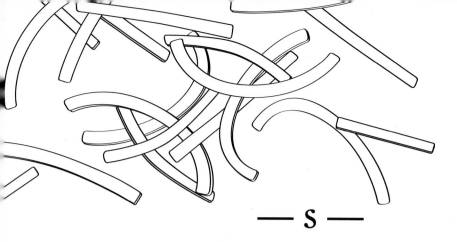

— S —

Scialatielli

I'm so used to Roman *trattorie* serving Roman food that when I see something beyond the defined parameters, as I did at Da Salvo, I become my Grandma during her first holiday to Greece, a succession of raised-eyebrow oooh's filled with *Carry On* delight. Not only did the blackboard offer caponata and fried fish, but sea bass and lemon with a pasta shape I'd never heard of, scialatielli. Which turned out to be fresh egg pasta about half the length and width of tagliatelle, but with a dishevelled aspect which I – with my head of frizzy hair – identified with. In fact many say the name derives from *sciglià* which is Neapolitan dialect for *scompigliare,* to mess or ruffle.

It turns out Da Salvo is run by Salvatore, who is Sicilian and likes to cook Campanian food. From our table a glass panel provided a view into the kitchen, so we could see him, his head low for the most part but every now and then lifted as he raised the pan for the pan-jolt-wave that promises your pasta will have the opaque sheen that means everything has come together. I suppose anyone who puts a glass panel at pan-jolt level must be proud of their pan-jolt! Everything had come together, dishevelled pasta, the pieces of sea bass and opaque lemon sauces, as had Vincenzo's triangles of ravioli with ricotta and thyme. Taste memories are like any other memories, their staying with you depends on how they are set. If they are surrounded by a cluster of other memorable things, however banal – an unexpected interior and lunch we can't afford, a pan flick through a glass panel and new dishevelled shape – they work themselves into your consciousness with a jolt.

To make scialatielli

Make a dough of 200g of semola, 200g of 00 flour, 40g of grated Parmesan, a tablespoon of finely chopped fresh flat-leaf parsley, 150ml of water and 1 egg. Rest for 30 minutes. Then roll, by hand or using a machine, into a sheet 3mm thick, leave for 10 minutes then roll into a log, and then cut into strips 5–6mm wide and 12cm long. You can roll them around a rod to get the ruffled/twisted shape, alternatively you can just lift and mess them with your fingers.

Scialatielli all'amalfitana
Scialatielli Amalfi style with shellfish, squid and tomatoes and breadcrumbs
Serves 4

It is rare that a shape has an inventor beyond a legendary one, but scialatielli does: Enrico Cosentino, a chef from the Amalfi coast who invented the shape for a competition in 1978, drawing inspiration from the home-made, twisted fusilli of his childhood and from tagliatelle. The recipe on page 263 is his recipe for scialatielli, here served with clams, squid and finished with crisp breadcrumbs.

300g clams
200g mussels
150g prawns, shelled
250g squid
olive oil
2 cloves of garlic
200g sweet cherry
  tomatoes,
  quartered
20g capers (optional)
20g green olives
  (optional)
400g dried or 600g
  fresh scialatielli
  (see page 263)
75g soft white
  breadcrumbs
salt
chopped fresh flat-leaf
  parsley

Prepare the fish. Rinse the clams, and rinse and scrub the mussels, pulling away the beard. Peel the prawns and cut the squid into short strips. Put a large pan of water on for the pasta.

In a large frying pan, warm the oil and garlic, bashed for a gentle flavour, sliced for a stronger flavour, diced for the strongest. Regardless of cut, cook gently and do not let it burn. Add all the fish, stir and cook for a few minutes, then add the tomatoes, capers and olives if you are adding them and cook for 5 more minutes.

While the sauce simmers, drop the pasta into salted boiling water. In a small frying pan, fry/toast the breadcrumbs in some olive oil with a pinch of salt until crisp, then tip on to kitchen paper to blot.

When the pasta is al dente, drain or, better still, lift directly into the frying pan, along with the parsley and a ladle of cooking water, and complete the last minute of cooking, swishing the pan so everything comes together. Divide between plates, topping each one with toasted crumbs.

Scialatielli con spigola e limone
Scialatielli with sea bass and lemon
Serves 4

The idea is simple: you scent olive oil with lemon and orange zest and garlic, then add the cooked pasta, swish, and then use the heat of the pasta and the pan, and the help of add-on pasta cooking water, to cook the fish. Again, the big jolting pan is useful because everything has space to swish. The simplicity is disconcerting, the result so good.

1 unwaxed orange
1 unwaxed lemon
1 clove of garlic
salt and black pepper
a small dried red
   chilli, crumbled, or
   a pinch of dried red
   chilli flakes
6 tablespoons olive oil
400g dried or 450g
   fresh scialatielli,
   tagliolini, linguine
250g sea bass fillets,
   cut into 2cm cubes
1 heaped tablespoon
   finely chopped
   fresh flat-leaf
   parsley

Bring a large pan of water to the boil for the pasta.

Using the fine side of a box grater or microplane, grate the zest from the orange and lemon. Squeeze half the lemon and set aside the juice. Peel the garlic, then crush it gently with the back of a knife, so it breaks but remains whole.

In a large, deep frying pan, unite the zest, garlic and a pinch of salt and chilli with the olive oil. Place the pan on a really low flame – you want the flavours to infuse the oil gently.

Meanwhile add salt to the boiling water, stir, add the pasta and set the timer for 3 minutes less than the recommended cooking time.

When the timer rings, lift out a cupful of pasta cooking water and set aside, then, using a spider sieve or tongs, lift the pasta on to the oil.

Working fast, raise the heat and swish and stir the pasta for 30 seconds. Add the sea bass, lemon juice, parsley and some of the pasta cooking water, then stir and swish vigorously for another minute with the aim of cooking the fish and creating a creamy sauce as the citrus oil meets the lemon meets the starchy pasta cooking water. Serve immediately.

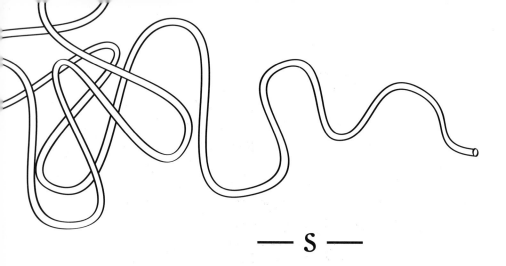

Spaghetti

The ideal simmer. A gentle rumble with an occasional rising bubble that bursts and sends a red splatter across the stove or up the wall, a reminder the sauce may be calm, but won't be contained. Spaghetti is like that too, not contained in one letter, rather splattered all over the alphabet. Back in B – Busiate and the origins of pasta we met its ancestor *tria*, those first strings of pasta made by the Arabs in Sicily. We meet strings again in M – Maccheroni, for centuries the generic name for pasta, including forms we would now call spaghetti. While V – Vermicelli is where we understand that for hundreds of years vermicelli was a name for strings of pasta until, in the mid-nineteenth century, spaghetti entered the Italian language, collective consciousness and – it seems – DNA.

Long, string-shaped durum wheat pasta, which according to the writer and author Giuseppe Prezzolini 'has the same right or more to belong to the Italian civilization as Dante'. If Italians had to give shape to the idea that pasta is not just a food but a symbol, flag, culture and way of life, it could well be a string. In my experience the gravitational pull of passion and opinion around pasta is at its most intense around spaghetti. It is also the shape the food historian Massimo Montanari uses to illustrate his thoughts about identity and how traditions evolve when they meet other traditions, how dried pasta from the Arabs and tomatoes from America (which arrived with the Conquistadors in the 1500s but only in the eighteenth century, when suspicion gave way to acceptance, were widely grown) converged in Italy, forming a new identity.

My partner's grandfather knew this. Orazio D'Aleo was a tomato farmer in a town called Gela in Sicily, his deep-rooted produce turned into gallons and gallons of tomato sauce, *salsa*, each August, a process which was masterminded by Vincenzo's grandmother, demanded the whole family and took over the whole street. Vincenzo and his cousins remember the process, the rest of the year being sent to the cellar for bottles of *salsa* which were tossed with pasta, often spaghetti. Their grandparents are long gone. But the house and family are still there, and when we go back each summer we bottle some *salsa*, a fraction of what once was, but it feels like continuation. As does making sauce from tinned tomatoes, every pan evoking the past, in the extraordinary and ordinary way only food can, splattering our white stove, coating our spaghetti. In tribute, here is a week or so of *spaghetti al pomodoro*, spaghetti with tomatoes, recipes and thoughts to be splattered as you wish.

— Monday —
Spaghetti with simple tomato and basil sauce

— Tuesday —
Spaghetti with simple fresh tomato sauce

— Wednesday –
Spaghetti with rich tomato *ragù*

— Thursday —
Pasta al forno

— Friday —
Roasted tomato sauce

— Saturday —
Two raw summer sauces for spaghetti

— Saturday night —
Spaghetti with garlic olive oil and chilli

— Sunday —
Spaghetti alla Norma

— Monday —
Frittata di spaghetti

— Monday —

Spaghetti al sugo
Spaghetti with simple tomato and basil sauce

Serves 4

The week begins with the simplest tomato sauce, or *sugo di pomodoro*, the one we eat more than all the others put together. I am diligent and exacting about this sauce, because I know how good it can be, and also because in an inconsistent world, tinned tomatoes provide certainty, and this sauce is an everyday bliss.

1 x 800g tin of peeled plum tomatoes
6 tablespoons olive oil
1 clove of garlic
a small dried red chilli, crumbled
12 leaves of fresh basil
salt
400g spaghetti
50g Parmesan or pecorino, grated

After years of trying different brands, and feeling frustrated, I am happily wed to a Sardinian brand of whole peeled plum tomatoes called Antonella. I pass the entire contents of the tin through a food mill, a piece of equipment so useful for making tomato sauce, I wish we could give one away with this book. An alternative to the mill is a potato masher. Having learned the hard way, I begin away from the heat, putting 6 tablespoons of olive oil (no less), and a peeled and split clove of garlic into my deep sauté pan. Then the pan goes on a medium-low flame so the oil warms gently and the garlic does the gentlest shimmy for about 3 minutes, and it smells sweet. Now the milled tomatoes, chilli and at least 12 leaves of basil. I let the sauce almost, but not quite boil, then reduce to a simmer, covered, for 20 minutes, the last 5 uncovered with me stirring so it thickens and takes on that slightly grainy aspect and the oil is visible at the edges. I lift the spaghetti out of the boiling water when it is a minute off the al dente, so I can finish cooking it with the sauce, add a handful of grated Parmesan, swishing so the starch is released, the cheese melts and everything comes together. Mixing can also be done in a bowl.

A note about spaghetti
Historically spaghetti was much longer, and for some makers this is still the case, a few selling it as dried hanging over a rod, so with a u-bend. Modern dimensions, though, are generally 25–30cm long with 1.5–2mm diameter, depending on the maker. Some makers produce a range of spaghetti, different dimensions classified by different numbers. Dimensions are also defined by suffixes, -ini the diminutive, spaghettini, -oni the augmentative, spaghettoni. As always, the better quality the pasta the better the texture, therefore ability to hold sauce, and taste.

— Tuesday —

Spaghetti with simple fresh tomato sauce
Serves 4

While tins provide consistency and ease, fresh tomatoes (in regard to pasta) demand thought, even in summer, even in Sicily. Not very demanding thoughts, simply what is best here? Sweet cherry or datterini are good, blistered until they burst in lots of oil (see orecchiette, page 201). Both firm and well flavoured and incredibly fleshy tomatoes can be used for raw sauce, while an abundance of ripe tomatoes can be milled into passata or roasted. There is also fresh tomato sauce, which demands 600g of ripe, fleshy tomatoes, which could be a mix. The tomatoes need peeling, by plunging them into boiling water for a minute, then cold, at which point the skins should slip away, then cutting into strips, free of seeds and tough bits. In a pan warm 6 tablespoons of olive oil and a peeled sliced clove of garlic very gently to start, increasing to a sizzle, then add the tomatoes and handful of basil leaves. While you boil 400g of spaghetti, the tomato should simmer, the flesh collapsing into a soft, fleshy, oil-rich sauce. Once the pasta is cooked, lift it into the sauce pan, add a dash more oil, swish and serve. Its simplicity, and the fact it is dependent on the weather, makes this my absolute favourite.

A note about tinned tomatoes

Look for whole, plum tomatoes in juice. San Marzano are a well-known variety and a protected one, protection which extends to the fruit pickers who are mostly immigrants. But there are lots of wonderful brands, using different varieties. Taste different brands to see which suits you – they should be deep red and fleshy with a rounded taste, both savoury and sweet, and the juice should be just as palatable, with no bitter or metallic aftershock.

— Wednesday —

Spaghetti con ragù di pomodoro
Spaghetti with rich tomato ragù

Makes enough for two meals for 4

Still using tinned tomatoes, but a slightly stouter sauce here. Sauces are like buildings. It is all about the foundations, cooking the vegetables in lots of oil with a pinch of salt until they are soft and mellow. Then it is about time, letting the sauce blip gently until it is rich red. Half for spaghetti, half for baked pasta on Thursday.

While this ragu misses nothing, sausages - unsurprisingly - make a wonderful addition. Add the crumbled meat of 4 pork sausages after frying the *soffritto* and before adding the tomatoes.

8 tablespoons extra
    virgin olive oil
1 medium onion,
    peeled and finely
    chopped
1 carrot, peeled and
    finely chopped
1 stick of celery, finely
    chopped
a few fresh flat-leaf
    parsley stalks,
    finely chopped
1–2 cloves of garlic,
    crushed or peeled
1 bay leaf
salt
3 x 800g tins/jars of
    whole plum
    tomatoes
1 small dried or fresh
    chilli, minced
a splash of red wine

In a large heavy-based pan warm the olive oil, chopped onion, carrot, celery, parsley stalks, garlic, bay leaf and a pinch of salt, allowing the vegetables to soften, go translucent and not brown but mellow – it will take at least 10 minutes.

Use scissors to chop the tomatoes in the tin, then add to the pan along with the chilli, wine if you are adding it and another pinch of salt. Raise the heat to bring the tomatoes to almost boiling, then reduce to a very gentle simmer, pressing the tomatoes against the edge of the pan with a wooden spoon or even a potato masher. Simmer at a blip blip for an hour or so, or until the sauce is reduced and shiny. Divide in two.

To serve with pasta, either 400g of spaghetti, spaghettoni, or spaghetti alla chitarra, penne, rigatoni, fusilli. Bring a large pan of water to a fast boil over a high heat, add salt, let the water come back to the boil, add the pasta, stir and cook until al dente, then drain. Tip on to the sauce, stir and divide between warm bowls, passing round grated pecorino or Parmesan.

— Thursday —

Pasta al forno

Serves 4

One day tipping into the next and working with the remaining *ragù*, all the better for a rest. Cook 400g of short pasta – penne, maccheroni, mezze maniche, rigatoni – in well-salted boiling water, draining while it is still al dente (I would say 2 minutes off the usual cooking time, but no more). Drain, mix with enough *ragù* to generously coat, 2 handfuls of grated Parmesan and some ripped mozzarella. Tip into a buttered ovenproof dish, top with more grated cheese, maybe breadcrumbs, and bake for 20 minutes at 200°C, or until the top is golden and the sides bubbling.

— Friday —

Roasted tomato sauce

Serves 8

There are no two ways about it. You need a food mill for this sauce! Also if you don't already have one, and have got this far in the book without buying one, I have in one respect failed and really should send you one. Roasting concentrates flavour, colour, consistency and juices which mix with the olive oil and mill into a rich, soft orange-red sauce.

Take 2kg of ripe tomatoes, of all sorts and sizes. Wash and cut larger ones into 8, medium ones into 4 and small ones in half. Get your largest baking tray and put all the tomatoes into it, pour over at least 10 tablespoons of olive oil, sprinkle with salt, throw in as many cloves of garlic as you want, toss everything together, then bake at 180°C for an hour, by which time the tomatoes have collapsed into a slump, and the edges are bubbling. Let it cool slightly, then pass the whole lot through the food mill, making sure you scrape everything from the bottom of the tin. There will be enough sauce for 8 portions, so save half and mix the rest with 400g of al dente spaghetti.

— Saturday —

Two raw summer sauces

Like granita and cold showers, spaghetti with raw tomato sauces only really makes sense in high summer, because of their cool, fresh nature, also because it is when tomatoes are plentiful and tasty. The first version is Sicilian, the second Roman. They both work best with spaghettini, which tangles more densely, creating a sort of weave that catches the bits of tomato and flecks of herbs. In both cases the cold sauce needs to sit for a while to macerate, for juices to form and herbs to infuse, all of which are then awakened by the hot pasta.

Spaghettini a picchi pacchi
Spaghettini with raw tomato sauce and oregano
Serves 4

For this Sicilian version, the tomatoes need to be riper, and peeled, meaning the sauce is softer. It also needs to be stirred for longer so the flavours deepen even more.

1kg ripe tomatoes
3 cloves of garlic
2.5cm piece of red chilli, crumbled
a generous pinch of dried oregano
salt
100ml olive oil
400g spaghettini

Peel the tomatoes – plunge them into boiling water for a minute, then scoop them out and plunge into cold, at which point the skins should slip off. Cut the tomatoes in half, scoop out their seeds, then roughly but finely chop, catching the juices. Finely slice the garlic and crumble the red chilli and add to the bowl with generous pinches of oregano and salt and 100ml of olive oil. Mix everything well, cover the bowl and leave to sit for 3 hours. Bring a large pan of water to the boil, add salt, stir, add the spaghettini and cook until al dente, then drain. Tip the spaghettini on to the sauce.

Spaghettini alla checca
Spaghettini with raw tomato sauce and lots of herbs
Serves 4

Spaghettini, diced tomato, masses of herbs and oil – this Roman dish is apparently named *alla checca* for its maker, Francesca. Dice small, rest and toss vigorously. Some people also add diced mozzarella.

400g firm and tasty
tomatoes
1 clove of garlic
60g green, fleshy
olives, chopped
1 heaped tablespoon
capers
1 heaped tablespoon
chopped fresh
flat-leaf parsley
a handful of fresh
basil, ripped
1 heaped tablespoon
chopped marjoram
a pinch of fennel seeds
6 tablespoons best
olive oil
salt and black pepper
400g spaghettini

Quarter the tomatoes, scoop out the seeds and then dice. Peel and finely chop the garlic. In a large bowl mix the tomatoes with the garlic, olives, capers and herbs, fennel seeds, olive oil, salt and pepper, and leave to sit for 30 minutes. Bring a large pan of water to the boil for the pasta, add salt, stir, then add the pasta and cook until al dente. Tip the drained pasta on to the tomatoes, toss really well and serve.

A note about passata
Italian recipes often call for simple tomato sauce or *passata di pomodoro*, which literally means passed tomatoes. That is, passed through a food mill – an invaluable tool which both pulps, sieves and presses all the goodness and flavour from the skins and seeds. You can buy passata but I am rarely a fan (both in Italy and the UK) of the consistency or taste, so I make my own. With tinned tomatoes this just means milling them juice and all. With fresh I cut them in two, put them in a pan over a medium heat and cook them down until collapsed (they don't need extra water, just a squash to create juices to get things going), then mill them. In both cases if the passata is watery it can be reduced by simmering over a medium-low flame.

— Saturday night —

Spaghetti aglio, olio e peperoncino – gli spaghetti di mezzanotte
Spaghetti with garlic, olive oil and chilli – midnight spaghetti

Serves 4

No tomato here. They call this *ajo ojo* in Rome – it is not only a meal, it is a solution, an answer, an urge, especially at midnight. The key to this version is cooking the garlic gently, which brings out its sweet side, then finishing the cooking of the spaghetti in with the oil and garlic, that familiar jolt. I have not specified what type, or amounts of chilli as there are too many variables – you decide how hot you would like it to be.

400g spaghetti
130ml olive oil
dried red chilli,
    crumbled, a fresh
    red chilli, chopped,
    or dried chilli
    flakes
2–4 cloves of garlic,
    peeled and sliced
    very thinly
salt
a handful of fresh
    flat-leaf parsley,
    chopped

Bring a large pan of water to the boil for the spaghetti, add salt and stir. Add the spaghetti, stir, and set the timer for 2 minutes before the end of the recommended cooking time.

In a large frying pan, warm the oil, chilli and sliced garlic, allowing the garlic to sizzle very gently: you do not want it to colour at all – just to release its scent and become soft and sweet. Add a pinch of salt and stir.

When the timer rings, put a ladleful of spaghetti cooking water into the garlicky oil and swish it around. Then, using a slotted spoon, or tongs, lift the spaghetti into the oil, sprinkle over the parsley, and toss and swirl everything for the final minute of the spaghetti cooking time. Divide between bowls.

— Sunday —

Spaghetti alla Norma or Spaghetti con la coppola
Spaghetti with tomato, aubergine and salted ricotta
Serves 4

While Norma is the most famous name for this dish (supposedly a tribute to the Bellini opera), I have always known it as *spaghetti con la coppola*, spaghetti with a cap, of fried aubergine, which as the partner of a Sicilian who is rarely outside without a flat cap, I love.

500g aubergine, in 5mm slices
150ml olive oil
a portion of simple tomato sauce (see Monday)
a handful of fresh basil
salt
400g spaghetti
150g salted ricotta, grated

Bring a large pan of water to the boil for the pasta.

Pat the aubergine slices dry with a kitchen towel, pressing the towel firmly. Warm the olive oil in a frying pan and fry the slices of aubergine until deep gold on both sides. Drain on kitchen paper and sprinkle with salt.

Heat the tomato sauce with half the basil, then taste for salt.

Add salt to the boiling water, stir, then add the spaghetti and cook until al dente. Drain, tip into the sauce pan and toss with the tomato.

Either tip on to a large, warm platter and top with the aubergine slices, torn basil and grated ricotta, or divide between individual bowls.

Postscript – **Monday lunchtime, or why you should always make too much spaghetti and tomato sauce, otherwise known as** *frittata di spaghetti*

Luciano Pignataro dedicates an entire chapter to *frittate di pasta* in his book on Neapolitan food, also an ode to leftover pasta by Bruno Macrì which includes the sort of detail that only an etymologist who loves fried pasta could write, the smells and flavours of a Neapolitan kitchen spluttering off the page like hot oil out of a pan. Macrì also explains how: you simply take your leftover spaghetti and tomato and put it into a non-stick pan in which you have heated a little oil, press it down and fry until '*arrustacata, ben rosolata e croccante, bruciacchiata*' – 'well browned and crunchy, scorched'.

— S —

Spaghetti alla chitarra

This is where my theory that every pasta shape can be made with things you find around the house falls apart. To make spaghetti alla chitarra you need a *chitarra*, a guitar. The culinary sort, a wooden frame strung with 16 wires or more, on to which you press a sheet of pasta so firmly the strings cut the dough into thick, square spaghetti. It is a shape typical of Abruzzo, Lazio and upper Molise and was traditionally – like so many shapes – called maccheroni alla chitarra. If you're lucky enough to know someone who has a *chitarra*, the process is incredibly satisfying to watch, for the know-how of the maker and the unavoidable sense of cheerleader go go go as the pasta falls through the strings and on to the table. More alphabet jumping; when spaghetti alla chitarra migrated to Rome, it became known as tonnarelli and established itself as a canonical shape often paired with *cacio e pepe*, pecorino and pepper.

These days both spaghetti alla chitarra and tonnarelli are dried shapes as well as fresh. Fresh or dried though, spaghetti alla chitarra and its Roman counterpart are thick, so need sauces that cling and help the strings to act as a sort of weave that catches, for example, tiny meatballs.

If you want to try making spaghetti alla chitarra at home, the dough is the basic flour and water on page 83, but then you need to find yourself a *chitarra*, or, hang on, do you have a harp?

Spaghetti alla chitarra teramana
Spaghetti alla chitarra in the style of Teramo
Serves 4

Teramo is the capital of the province of Teramo in Abruzzo, situated between the highest mountains and the resplendent Adriatic coast. This sauce of tiny meatballs in tomato sauce is their typical sauce for spaghetti alla chitarra. When I asked the woman who gave me this recipe how big the meatballs or *pallottine* should be she said '*piccine*', little, and when I asked how little that was, she pointed to the nail of her index finger.

125g ground beef
125 ground pork
salt
grated nutmeg
butter
simple tomato sauce
 (page 270)
fresh basil or other
 herbs
450g fresh spaghetti
 alla chitarra or
 tonnarelli, 400g
 dried spaghetti alla
 chitarra, spaghetti,
 tagliatelle, pici,
 mafalde
a handful of finely
 grated pecorino, to
 serve

In a bowl mix the meat, salt and nutmeg and then, using your hands, form tiny balls, more or less the size of the nail of your index finger. Fry the meatballs in butter until sealed and lightly golden.

Meanwhile make the sauce, scenting it with chilli or more basil or other herbs, and drop the meatballs in.

Cook the pasta until al dente, drain, tip into a large bowl, add a handful of finely grated pecorino, then tip on the balls and sauce, toss and serve.

Spaghetti alla chitarra con pallottine di pollo in bianco
Spaghetti alla chitarra with tiny chicken meatballs and white wine
Serve 4

More tiny meatballs, this time made with chicken, and without tomato, which is how so many dishes once were. The beauty here is how the loose breadcrumbs from the chicken *escape* into the juices and wine, in turn thickening them, producing a sauce that clings to the pasta.

For the pallottine
220g ground chicken
   (ideally thighs)
75g fine dried
   breadcrumbs, plus
   more for rolling
30g Parmesan, grated
1 small egg
grated nutmeg
salt and black pepper

For the sauce
1 small carrot
1 onion
1 small stick of celery
olive oil
3 bay leaves
4 tablespoons olive oil
white wine or lightly
   salted water
450g fresh spaghetti
   alla chitarra or
   tonnarelli, 400g
   dried spaghetti alla
   chitarra, spaghetti,
   tagliatelle, pici,
   mafalde
a handful of finely
   grated pecorino,
   to serve

Make the meatballs by mixing the chicken, breadcrumbs, Parmesan, egg, nutmeg, salt (go easy, the Parmesan is salty) and lots of black pepper until you have a consistent mass. Break off small hazelnut-sized lumps and roll into balls – I find wet hands make this easier. Once you have shaped all the balls, roll them in dry breadcrumbs.

Peel and small dice the carrot, onion and celery and tip into a frying pan, along with the oil and the bay leaves. Fry over a medium heat until the vegetables are soft and translucent. Add the meatballs and using a wooden spoon move them around the pan so they seal. Raise the heat and add enough wine to three-quarters cover the meatballs, let everything bubble wildly, then reduce to a gentle simmer for 20 minutes. Turn the balls from time to time. Remember that you want plenty of sauce, so add a little more wine if it seems dry.

Meanwhile cook the pasta until al dente, drain, tip into a large bowl, add a handful of finely grated pecorino, then tip on the balls and sauce, toss and serve.

Cacio e pepe
Spaghetti alla chitarra or tonnarelli
with pecorino cheese and black pepper
Serves 4

Cacio is the Roman word for cheese, and *cacio* in Rome means pecorino Romano, the creamy but also piquant sheep's milk cheese that is so integral to so many classic dishes. *Pepe* is black pepper. Like Parmesan and butter, or olive oil, garlic and chilli, *cacio e pepe* have been tossed with pasta for centuries, providing the answer to the question, what shall we eat? Quick fix or plate of midnight spaghetti. My landlady describes it best: pasta in a bowl, cheese and lots of pepper on top, jig jig jig. Exactly when it turned from a homely jig jig jig to more of a smooth condiment is not certain, but according to friends the creamy *cacio e pepe* that we see now were not served 20 years ago. Jig jig jig has evolved into a technique for many chefs and home cooks. Which is how it should be, dishes evolving with time. I like this modern approach, and have Andrea Passi from the bakery Passi in Testaccio to thank for teaching me to make a creamy and wavy *tonnarelli cacio e pepe* that curls around the fork, makes my heart skip.

Cold water is the key to this version of this dish. It keeps the temperature down, as too much heat will give you clumps. Also mixing away from the heat, in a wide bowl. You want to mix just enough water with the cheese to make a really thick paste – so add the water slowly, tablespoon by tablespoon. When you have drained the pasta, ideally by lifting with a spider sieve or tongs, pause and count to 8, then drop the pasta into the bowl and swish. Toasting whole peppercorns and crushing them yourself is unbeatable, for texture, heat, flavour – your nose should twitch.

150g pecorino Romano

black pepper, either 10 grinds from a mill, or 1 tablespoon whole peppercorns

400g spaghetti alla chitarra, or 450g fresh tonnarelli

Put a large pan of water on for the pasta.

Grate the cheese, ideally on the star side of a box grater rather than the microplane. If you are using peppercorns, toast them in a dry pan for a minute, or until the smell comes up and out of the pan. Crush them in a mortar with a pestle, or wrap in cloth and bash with a rolling pin.

Put the cheese and either half a dozen grinds of pepper or a great pinch of those you have crushed into a large bowl. Add – **really cautiously** – enough cold water to create a thick paste (the consistency of toothpaste) and use the back of a spoon to swirl it on the base of the bowl.

Salt the water, stir and add the pasta, and cook to al dente. Drain in a colander or, better still, lift the pasta from the pan, count to 8, hover, then tip into the cheese bowl and stir so the cream coats the pasta, adding a little more cold water if you think it needs loosening.

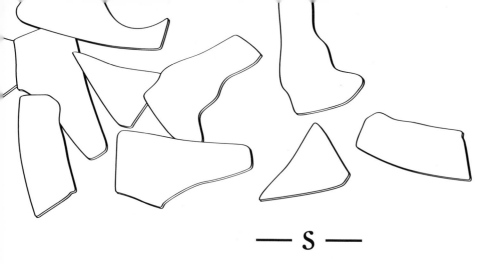

— S —

Stracci

With pasta, as with everything, there are times when you must let rip. It was the cook and teacher Carla Tomasi who introduced me to this shape. We had rolled flour and egg dough for ravioli, but had leftover sheets, which is not uncommon, and I'm used to seeing Carla cut remnants into maltagliati one of us can take home. However, on this occasion she picked up a sheet and ripped it up. It recalled the day, years before, when my needlework teacher started to cut a piece of fabric with scissors but then continued the rip with her hands, an act so unexpected, sudden and – in that moment – so wild, a room of 13-year-olds gasped as if she had ripped her shirt off.

The word *stracci* means rags and derives from the verb *strappare*, to rip, as does *straccio*, dishcloth. Stracci (di pasta) are also known as pasta strappata, stracce, pasta straccia, sagne strasciate, and are typical of the cummerbund of central Italian regions, Lazio, Molise, Abruzzo, Le Marche, Tuscany. Home-made using white flour, but also whole wheat or fine bran and with egg or water, stracci are one of the so-called poor pasta shapes, for their resourcefulness and the hands that made them, often (paradoxically) for feast days. Having learned to recognize them thanks to Carla, we met them again in Bagnaia, part of the city of Viterbo, 80 kilometres north of Rome and in the heart of Tuscia. They were served with onion and tomato sauce, with gasps of chilli and finished with lots of local pecorino. I have also included Carla's recipe for stracci (or as she calls it pasta strappata) with guanciale and peas, a brothy dish.

To make stracci, make the egg and flour dough on page 51 or the flour and water on page 83. I have seen people ripping stracci directly into the broth or pan of boiling water, which requires some speed in order that they cook evenly. I rip mine into a cloth so I can lift the end up and tip them in quickly. Cooking times depend on how thick you have rolled the dough, also if they contain egg, which cooks more quickly than plain flour and water stracci. Shape-wise they interchange with maltagliati and fregnacce, all of which share the ability to curl and fold in sauce or soup.

Stracci con la vignarola
Stracci with Roman spring stew of artichokes, peas and broad beans
Serves 4

Here stracci, ideally soft flour and egg, are paired with *vignarola*, a glorious Roman spring stew of onions, artichokes, broad beans and peas braised in olive oil and their own sweet juices. A bottle of frascati, for after grilled lamb chops and some potatoes roasted Roman style (so diced, tossed in olive oil with salt and lots of roughly chopped rosemary) and a slice of chocolate and almond cake and you have a scrumptious spring lunch. Alternative shapes are maltagliati or lagane. You could also make a less brothy version and pair it with tagliatelle or tagliolini.

1 unwaxed lemon, to acidulate the water
2 large artichokes
200g shelled broad beans
200g shelled peas
6 tablespoons olive oil
1 large white onion or 8 spring onions, peeled and sliced
150ml water
salt
a sprig of fresh mint
400g stracci
a handful of grated pecorino

Cut the lemon in two, squeeze the juice into a big bowl of water, then rub your hands with the empty halves. Prepare the artichokes by first pulling away the darker tougher leaves, pulling them down the artichoke and snapping them off just before the base. Then, using a sharp knife, pare away the tough green flesh from the base of the artichoke and the stem, rubbing cut surfaces with the lemon halves as you go. Cut away the top third of the artichoke. Detach the trimmed stem and slice it into 4 lengthways, then cut the trimmed artichoke globes into 8 wedges, pulling away any very hairy choke. Immediately, drop the wedges and stems of artichoke into the acidulated water.

If the broad beans are large and have a tough outer coat, remove it by plunging the broad beans into first hot water, then cold, and squeezing/pinching off the opaque coat.

Warm the olive oil in a heavy-based frying pan. Fry the sliced onion over a medium-low heat until it is soft and translucent. Add the artichoke wedges and stems, then stir, so each piece is glistening with oil. Add the water and a pinch of salt, stir again, then cover the pan and cook for 10–15 minutes, stirring and jigging the pan from time to time.

Add the peas and broad beans and cook for another 5 minutes, adding the torn mint in the last minute. Taste, season with salt and taste again. The *vignarola* is ready when the vegetables are tender and come together into a soft, tumbling stew.

Cook the strappati in plenty of salted boiling water until al dente –
which won't take long, and also depends on how thinly you rolled
the dough. Drain or lift the pasta directly into the *vignarola* pan,
add a handful of grated pecorino, and toss everything together.

Stracci con piselli, guanciale e pecorino di Carla
Stracci with peas, spring onion, guanciale and pecorino Carla style

Serves 4

For this recipe flour and egg stracci are cooked in with the other, brothy ingredients. The beauty of this dish is the way the stracci absorb the other flavours and then fold in the spoon.

6 spring onions
4 tablespoons olive oil
150g guanciale, cut
　　into 2mm cubes,
　　or pancetta
salt and pepper
400g peas, ideally
　　fresh
100ml white wine
100ml light vegetable
　　broth or water
400g flour and egg
　　stracci
a handful of fresh
　　mint

Trim the root end off the spring onions and the top couple of centimetres of the green, then slice into thin rings.

Put the oil and guanciale into a large frying pan, then the pan on a medium flame and fry gently until the fat of the guanciale is translucent and starts to render. Add the spring onions and a pinch of salt and cook until the onion is soft.

Add the peas, stir, then add the white wine and the water or broth, let it bubble, then reduce the heat, cover the pan and let everything simmer for 10 minutes.

Now uncover. Check the level of liquid – there should still be a good couple of centimetres (if not, add more lightly salted water, or veg broth). Raise the flame, then add the pasta, which will cook in about 3 minutes. Keep stirring and an eye, you want the pasta to be done and in just a little soupy sauce. Stir in the chopped mint and season with black pepper.

Serve immediately, making sure everyone gets pasta, peas and onion, just a little soupy sauce. Sprinkle with grated cheese. Serve in bowl, with a spoon.

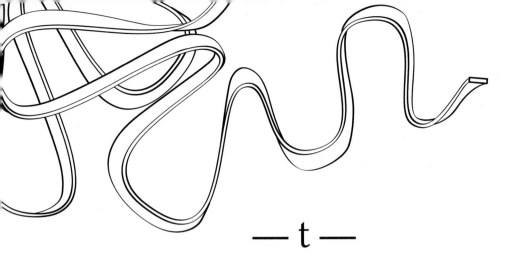

— t —
Tagliatelle

Rina's apron is yolk yellow. Also printed with the words 'Accademia della Sfoglia' and an illustration of a clock with rolling-pin hands. The Academy is her bright, modern kitchen in her house on the fringes of Piolino, a town almost exactly in the middle of a triangle formed by Bologna, Modena and Ferrara. The *sfoglia* is the ever-increasing circle of pasta dough she is extending with her metre-long rolling pin, *il matterello*, a dexterous movement that seems somewhere between breaststroke and a rippling spin.

Hand rolling has a history as long and diffused as pasta itself. It is in Emilia, (half of the now united Emilia-Romagna region) where the everyday act of hand rolling has been elevated into an everyday art with its own set of expectations and language. Rina Poletti is a *sfoglina*, a term from Emilia that describes a woman who is particularly skilled at rolling pasta, strictly by hand, using a rolling pin. The result is a near perfect circle of pasta called *la sfoglia*, which is used to make tagliatelle, tortellini, tortelloni and lasagna.

Tagliatelle is the reason I caught the 5:08 train from Rome to Bologna to stand in Rina's kitchen. Why I have watched her work 5 eggs and 500g of *grano tenero* (soft wheat flour) into a ball, knead it, rest it and then roll it out while wondering if a day is enough for me to do anything like the same (it isn't). The clock on Rina's apron is an appropriate symbol. Not only for time taken, but also the clockwise rotation of the ever-increasing circle as it is rolled and extended methodically and evenly. *Un, due, tre, quattro, cinque. Un, due, tre, quattro, cinque. Un, due, tre quattro, cinque.* Rina counts three sets of five strokes, with each stroke pushing the pin forward firmly but also freely so it spins under her hands, her movements as much a part of her as her breathing. At the same time as telling a story, of which Rina has an endless stream, she talks me through the turning, wrapping the *sfoglia* around the pin like a flag round a pole, in order to turn it 45 degrees (or fifteen minutes) then opening it out again. As the *sfoglia* gets bigger, half of it hangs off the edge of the board like a tablecloth, gravity playing its part. By the end of rolling *la sfoglia* is 1mm thick, the size of a bicycle wheel and a perfect circle, the test of which is to fold it in half so the bottom edge meets the top and they 'kiss'.

As much as the mesmerizing rippling spin, it is the texture of *la sfoglia* that strikes you. Working on a wooden board, the wooden *matterello* creates a cross-hatching of strokes and texture that's as much fabric as pasta. Hand rolling also gives structure and energy. *La sfoglia* may be flat, but rolled into readiness for cutting it seems to have a life of its own. It is the action of cutting, *tagliare*, which gives the name, tagliatelle.

It is evident that tagliatelle, like all shapes cut from a sheet, is related to early forms of sheet pasta. There is also a legend, a court cook who invented tagliatelle as a tribute to Lucrezia Borgia when she visited the king in 1501, the egg-rich ribbons echoing her golden hair. What is certain is that in 1972 Bolognese members of the Accademia Italiana della Cucina, along with the city's mayor, registered the dimensions of an authentic ribbon, *la tagliatella bolognese*, precisely 8mm or it loses its 'inimitable character'. *La cucina bolognese* by Molinari Pradelli engages me more by not using the word authentic and suggesting 6–8 mm.

The only dimensions Rina seems bound by are her own. The knife she uses is almost a sword. Once she has cut the whole length, she slides the knife under the cut dough like an arm under a back and lifts so the tagliatelle hangs either side of the blade like streamers. She shakes them out before dropping them into a pile. They are golden, also *'in piedi'*, standing up, she notes. It is a perfect description. Unlike the floppy ribbons of flour-dusted tagliatelle I am used to, Rina's arch and lift, like elbows and knees, so much so that I wonder if they might leap unassisted into the pan of water which is coming to the boil. Next to the water is a pan of *ragù bolognese*, the colour of bricks, seemingly muttering away to itself, its burrowing smell making the room feel smaller. I wonder how often Rina has a pan of *ragù* cooking, or just cooked, or about to be cooked, and not just because she is a teacher.

Like the tagliatelle it goes with, there are a lot of precise opinions about *ragù bolognese*, how it should and shouldn't be, colour, proportions of wine, tomato and milk, cooking time. I now realize that strong opinions about *ragù*, or any dish for that matter, are expressions of nostalgia. That repeating them is almost as comforting as eating the dish because it's another way of saying this is the way I know this is and how I hope it will stay.

The expression *la morte sua* in relation to food is common in Italy. It means 'its death', and is the highest praise, two things so perfectly matched that they are the death of each other. Rina knows this as she mixes the *ragù* with the golden tagliatelle and serves me at the kitchen island. She is a woman at the height of her powers.

La sfoglia, hand-rolled fresh egg pasta

The following is my attempt at communicating the method of hand rolling *la sfoglia*, as taught to me by Rina. It is a precise technique that requires patience and practice, also a certain amount of speed as it dries out. I am told it is also fun, eventually.

You will need a large wooden board and a long rolling pin, 400g of 00 flour and 4 medium eggs.

A wooden surface is ideal. Make a mountain of flour, then use your fist to swirl in a crater so the flour resembles a broad volcano with a wide crater for the eggs. Break in the eggs, then use a fork to whisk them and knock the flour inwards – being careful not to break the protective crater that is keeping them in. Once the flour and eggs are sticky enough to stay firm, use a dough scraper and the side of your other hand to mix, lifting and turning the egg and flour mixture repeatedly until it resembles an almost dry scrambled egg. Under the scramble, though, is softness and the dough comes together into a rough ball relatively easily.

Knead. Use the heel of your hand to bring the bottom half of the dough up and over, then rotate the dough and repeat until the ball is soft and smooth. Pat the dough into a slightly flattened patty, then wrap in cling film or cover with an upturned bowl and leave to sit for at least 1 hour, ideally 2. The rest is even more important with hand rolling, as the dough needs to relax – you will see it widen – in order to be rolled.

To roll, place the round of dough in the middle of the board and flatten it slightly with the flat of your hand. Place the pin in the bottom third of the dough and roll forward to just before the edge and back; do this a few times. Then turn the dough 45 degrees and repeat the rolls, then another 45 degrees and so on until you have a cymbal-sized round.

Move the round towards the bottom of the board so half hangs off the edge and gravity can play its part. Imagine it is a clock, and work in three sets of five rolls, all the time remembering you are extending the dough. The first five are towards 12, then hold the pin at an angle and roll towards 10 five times, angle again and roll towards 2 five times. Now lay the pin at the top of the dough, bring the dough up, and roll the pin down so the dough wraps round it like a flag, stretching as it does. Turn the circle 45 degrees and spread in the same way as before, half hanging off. And repeat, three sets of five, wrap and turn. The idea being that the dough gets bigger and bigger and as it does, you are possessed by the spirit of Rina as the rolling pin spins through your fingers. You should end up with a perfect, almost translucent circle of dough, just 1mm thick. You may also end up with a pear or amoeba, which I assure you make perfectly lovely tagliatelle, if you roll them into a log, and cut at 8mm intervals.

~~~~~~~~~~~~~~~~~~~~~~~~~~~~~~~~~~~~~

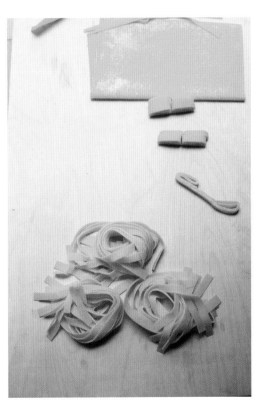

Tagliatelle con ragù bolognese
Tagliatelle with ragù
Serves 4–6

This is the same recipe as that used as part of a *lasagne alla bolognese*, and inspired by Rina. The key is a long, slow simmer, covered except for when you lift the lid to add the milk, bit by bit. One batch is enough for 500g of fresh, or 400g dried tagliatelle. I always make a double quantity.

30g butter
3 tablespoons olive oil
1 onion, peeled and finely diced
1 stick of celery, finely diced
1 carrot, peeled and finely diced
150g pancetta or bacon, finely diced
300g ground beef
150g ground pork
100g chicken livers, cleaned and chopped (optional)
salt, black pepper and nutmeg to taste
120ml white wine
300g passata di pomodoro (see page 277)
200–300ml milk
450g fresh tagliatelle, or 400g dried tagliatelle, fettuccine, pappardelle
grated Parmesan, to serve

Some say terracotta is best for *ragù bolognese* but any heavy-based sauté pan or enamelled cast-iron casserole works well.

Put the butter, olive oil, onion, celery, carrot and pancetta into the pan and cook, stirring, over a medium heat until they start to soften and turn translucent.

Add the meat (and the chicken livers if you are using them), crumbling it as you drop it into the pan, and a pinch of salt and cook, breaking up lumps in the mince with a wooden spoon, until all the pink has gone.

Add the wine and allow it to bubble for a few minutes, then add the passata. Let everything bubble for 2 minutes before turning the heat down so the *ragù* cooks at the laziest simmer, with just the odd blip burp bursting to the surface, for no less than 2 hours. During cooking, lift the lid every now and then and add the milk bit by bit. By the end of cooking the *ragù* should be rich and thick.

Bring a pan of water to the boil, add salt, stir, then drop in the tagliatelle and cook until al dente.

Meanwhile put half the hot *ragù* into a large, wide, warm bowl. When the pasta is al dente, drain and tip into the bowl, add a handful of grated Parmesan and the rest of the *ragù* and toss well. Serve, passing round extra cheese for those who want it.

Bomba di tagliatelle
Baked tagliatelle with ragù
Serves 4–6

Prepare a 25cm ring mould or cake tin by rubbing it thickly with butter. Cook 400g tagliatelle, drain, and mix with 2 ladles of *ragù*. Put half in the tin, spoon over another 2 ladles of *ragù*, sprinkle with grated Parmesan and dot with butter, then cover with the second half of the *ragù*. Bake at 180°C for 20 minutes. Allow to cool for 5 minutes, then invert on to a plate. You could of course make a smaller version with leftovers.

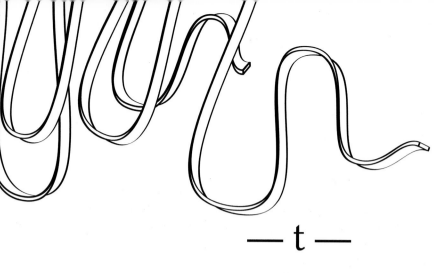

— t —

Tagliolini

What a difference 5mm makes! Compared to 8mm tagliatelle, 3mm tagliolini are different creatures, tangling in a completely different way, collecting sauce not just on the surface but between strands like a fisherman's net.

To make tagliolini, take a batch of egg dough, roll into sheets, fold and cut into 3mm ribbons. It is also a dried shape.

Tagliolini al limone e basilico
Tagliolini with lemon, Parmesan and basil
Serves 4

I have the same thought every time I make this recipe: I could add some cream or mascarpone. And sometimes I do, and enjoy it. But never quite as much as this version where the lemon is queen, sharp and bright and supported by the cheese but not smothered. It is mostly oil, but with the addition of a little butter round the edges. The way the heat awakens the scent of the basil is delightful.

2 medium unwaxed
  lemons
20g butter
100ml olive oil
100g Parmesan,
  grated
12 leaves of fresh basil
450g fresh tagliolini
  or 400g dried, also
  tagliatelle,
  fettuccine, linguine

Zest the lemons into a large bowl and then squeeze the juice into another bowl or a measuring jug (the amount of juice varies massively, so this is a way to note it). Add 8 tablespoons of the lemon juice to the zest bowl, add the butter and oil, and balance the bowl over a pan of water coming to the boil for the pasta so they warm.

Move the bowl (but keep it near the heat to stay warm), add the Parmesan and basil and mix.

Cook the pasta, which will take just 2 minutes, drain, then lift into the big bowl and swish swish so everything comes together.

Tagliolini con galletti e datterini
Tagliolini with chanterelles and datterini tomatoes
Serves 4

In Italy chanterelles, the orange-yellow mushrooms with soft gills that look like a wind-inverted umbrella, are called *galletti*. One of my favourite dishes this year was eaten at Taverna Mari in Grottaferrata, tagliolini with *galletti* (which cook into almost velvet softness) and sweet datterini tomatoes flecked with chilli. I had a moment of mourning when I ate the last forkful. The mushroom and tomatoes are cooked separately, an extra step, but a worthwhile one as it means two layers of juices and flavour.

200g galletti
olive oil
20g butter
2 cloves of garlic
300g sweetest cherry tomatoes, quartered
salt
450g fresh tagliolini or 400g dried, also tagliatelle, fettuccine, linguine, busiate, fusilli
fresh flat-leaf parsley, finely chopped

Clean the *galletti*, brushing away dry dirt with a brush or soft cloth, rubbing any stubborn bits with a bit of damp kitchen paper. Try to avoid submerging them in water. Thumbnail ones can be left whole, cut medium ones in half or quarters, large ones in strips. Put the water on for the pasta.

In a frying pan, warm 2 tablespoons of olive oil, the butter and sliced garlic, allow to infuse and sizzle gently, then add the *galletti* and cook until they have wilted down; they will give off liquid, good – bubble until it reduces. Tip on to a plate.

Back in the same pan, warm more oil, add the tomatoes and a pinch of salt and cook in a lively way for about 8 minutes, pressing with the back of the spoon so they split their juices and collapse. You can continue working in the pan, or tip both tomatoes and mushrooms and all the juices into your large jolting pan.

Meanwhile cook the tagliolini – it will only take a couple of minutes – put the tomatoes and mushrooms on the heat, lift the pasta out of the water directly into the pan, add parsley, toss rigorously and serve.

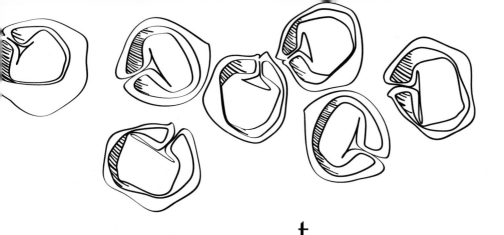

— t —

Tortellini

As inspiring as my day making pasta with Rina Poletti was, and as intoxicating the idea that one day I too would hand roll a circle so perfect it kissed at the edges, I admit scepticism. This feeling grew on the train, aggravated by the fact I had an Ikea bag filled with paper trays of tagliatelle, tortellini, tortelli, caramelle and a tub of maltagliati. As we all know, Ikea bags are conmen, they pretend to be spacious, but then you pick them up and they squash everything into a funnel, further funnelled by crowds on a train. I could see the carefully crafted results of our lesson suffering. How dare I dream to be a *sfoglina* if I couldn't even get Rina's shapes home safely.

Fortunately I wasn't going home, but travelling 30 kilometres from Rina's town to Bologna Centrale where I was scooped up by my friend Francesca. She drove me to her house, told me to have a shower and took the Ikea bag. Twenty minutes later I went up to the kitchen with a towel on my head and she had separated the conjoined tortelli and tortellini, put the tagliatelle back on its feet and the maltagliati in a bigger box. She had rescued both me and my shapes, which in that moment seemed acts of such kindness I wanted to cry.

The next day she showed me how she rolls. Like Rina, Francesca hand rolls pasta until it looks like fabric. Only she isn't a *sfoglina*, she doesn't have a vast working table, rather an ordinary pasta board on her small kitchen table, and while she does work with a long pin, she doesn't have a mesmerizing technique. That isn't to say she isn't lovely to watch, she is, and skilled. Only it doesn't feel like a 'technique', rather a 'way', rolling the dough, turning, rolling, turning, rolling. In the end her *sfoglia* was an oval that almost filled the board, the edges soft, and reassuring.

Her parents live in the same building and joined us to shape the tortellini. As I am a friend who is also a food writer, this both was and wasn't a display for me, in that it is something they do together every week, sometimes more. The family work side by side, Francesca cutting the dough, her mum dotting, or rather smudging, the filling on to the neat squares. They all shape. Francesca's father Anacleto is particularly adept. As a boy his slender fingers were singled out as good for tortellini and thousands have been wrapped around his index fingertip. There is a pink cloth on the table, which makes the yellow of the belly button tortellini pop.

Tortellini are – along with lasagne and tagliatelle – the pride of Bolognese gastronomy. Apparently origins are disputed, legends cited, recipes and size debated, and – such is the gravitational pull of pride and passion around tortellini – notarial acts have been passed. Warm in Francesca's kitchen, though, the only thing pulling us was a bowl of tortellini bobbing hopefully in broth. I have never doubted that *tortellini in brodo* is an ambrosial dish, like plump buttons, delicate, strong, their filling tender, the essence of Bologna, but here was more proof anyway. It also gave me confidence that I too might make tortellini the size of chickpeas. I also had a new bag to take my galaxy of stuffed shapes home in.

Tortellini in brodo
Tortellini, filled with pork, prosciutto, mortadella, served in broth
Serves 4 (with extra tortellini for the freezer)

In Bologna pasta, *la sfoglia*, is hand-rolled. As we have already established, this requires some skill, especially for tortellini when the dough has to be almost transparent. Until I can do this (which may be never) I use a machine, rolling a half quantity of standard egg dough to the thinnest setting. This quantity of filling and dough will make roughly 250 tortellini, enough for 6 servings, so many hands are useful. Tortellini will keep covered for 2 days and freeze brilliantly, as does any leftover filling.

30g butter or bone marrow
100g ground pork
100g prosciutto
100g mortadella
1 egg yolk
150g Parmesan, grated
salt and black pepper
grated nutmeg
a ½ batch of fresh egg pasta (see page 51)
1.5 litres broth (see page 13)

To make the filling – ideally the day before
In a heavy-based pan, melt the butter or bone marrow and add the pork, crumbling it into the pan, breaking it up with a wooden spoon and stirring, until lightly golden. Remove from the pan and allow to cool.

Mince the prosciutto and mortadella very finely; use a mincer or a food processor, or a very sharp knife, mincing until you have almost a paste.

Add the paste to the fried pork along with the egg yolk, Parmesan, salt, pepper and lots of nutmeg. Use your hands to knead it into a consistent and uniform paste and leave to rest, ideally overnight.

To shape the tortellini
Roll the dough into thin sheets. Using a knife or a pastry cutter/wheel, cut the dough into 3cm squares. Working a few at a time (and covering the rest with plastic wrap so they don't dry out), put a pea-sized dot of filling on the middle of the batch of squares. Pick the square up, fold in half diagonally, and then use both thumbs to press and flatten the edges to seal, folding the corners down. Now, with the point to the sky, close the triangle into a ring around the tip of your left index finger so it makes a pointy signet ring, pinching hard to to make sure it seals.

To serve
Bring the broth to a steady boil, add the tortellini and boil for 5–6 minutes, or until tender, then serve immediately.

Tortellini con crema di parmigiana
Tortellini with Parmesan cream
Serves 2

Just before I left Francesca asked if I would like a snack. I said yes. She brought me a teacup filled with something she was given as a child, the tortellini we had made coated with cream and Parmesan.

150g single cream
50g Parmesan, grated
200g tortellini

Warm the cream in a frying pan. Just before it boils, when the edges of the cream are fringed by bubbles, turn the heat to low. Add the Parmesan and stir until the cream thickens. Pull from the heat.

Meanwhile boil the tortellini in a light broth, toss in the cream and serve immediately.

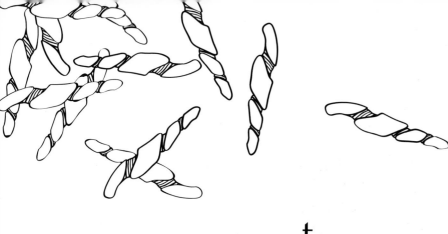

— t —

Trofie
(but first the pesto)

We smell them before we see them. Eight bunches of Genovese basil lifted from a heavy-duty shopping bag and lined up on the kitchen counter. Genovesi are proud of their basil, particularly that grown on the fringes of the city in a quarter called Pra'. Its pale green leaves are small and tender enough to smudge between two fingers if you press hard enough, their scent like cinnamon, grass and sweet green tea, but without the head-girl mintyness that comes with ruffled leaves of Neapolitan or lettuce basil. Every bunch is wrapped in paper with plastic wrapped around the base, a man bun for roots.

The day has already been green, an impromptu basil tasting in a supermarket and a plate of trofie with *pesto alla genovese* at a restaurant near the station. It is May 1st, Genoa is green, also long and narrow. Set in the steep curve of coastline, the whole densely populated city slopes upwards. I navigate the *creuze*, narrow footpaths that criss-cross the city, threading up and down, in and out, making you feel like you are in an Escher lithograph. Halfway up I look down on a swathe of green and blinking glass, which I am later told is the Serre di San Nicola, greenhouses of Saint Nicola, also orchards, vegetable and herb gardens, communal after being saved from a car park fate.

Back in the kitchen Maria Paola, a chemical engineer, Lalli, a teacher and I wash basil in the sink then pat it dry with a kitchen towel. While we pull the leaves from the stems we talk about Maria Paola's time in London with our mutual friend Kath, politics and pesto, and the fact that Genovese do eat it all the time. Both women, though, refuse to be dragged into any sentimental nostalgia or fanaticism about ingredients or technique. I have noticed a huge marble pestle and mortar hiding under the counter and wonder if it will be pulled out, giving me a story for this book, a chance to tick boxes of tradition and the right way, also that pesto comes from the word *pestare*, to pound. It isn't and Lalli makes the pesto in a small 80s food processor, pulsing first the pine nuts, garlic and salt then adding the basil and pulsing until it is the greenest green I have ever seen, and smells like pure chlorophyll. She carefully stirs in the cheese. I am just about to ask about the mortar and pestle, when the rest of the family arrive home and the water is put on. Then friends arrive and adding the extension section to the table is more important. Another friend arrives and cooks the artichokes I have brought from Rome, others arrive with savoury tarts and wine. The incredible thing about *pesto alla genovese* is how insistent the smell is, burrowing, how it roars once again when it is mixed with the hot pasta, on this occasion bavette. The greatest greenest smell, Lalli says as she lifts the greenest pasta on to 10 plates that are passed person to person around the table. We all agree. Why is pesto so insistently good? How was your journey from Rome and day in Genoa? asked Maria Paola's husband. Did you get the pesto story for your book? Yes, I replied, and it is green, and just right.

Pesto alla genovese
Basil pesto

Serves 4 – enough to dress 450g fresh or 400g dried pasta

It is all in the name, which comes from the action, *pestare*, to pound, with a *pestello* (pestle) *e mortaio* (mortar), which in Liguria are made of wood and marble respectively. Tradition honours the action (which does release the fragrance better and create a unique consistency) and the local ingredients, especially tender, small-leaved Ligurian basil, which does pound more easily. In fact it is quite hard to pound the larger leaves of more sturdy basil, while a food processor will blend them easily. I feel fortunate to be surrounded by cooks and teachers for whom there is more than one way to do things, that you can hold tradition in one hand, variations in the other. Here are the methods for making pesto by hand and with a food processor. And of course the basic proportions of pesto are a wonderful template for endless herb and nut pounded sauce variations, which can be used in countless ways.

1 clove of garlic
15g pine nuts
a pinch of salt
50g fresh basil leaves
30g Parmesan, grated
15g pecorino, grated
80ml olive oil

In a pestle and mortar

Put the garlic, pine nuts and a few grains of coarse salt in the mortar and pound with the pestle, until they are reduced to a rough paste. Add half the basil and pound until it is crushed, then add the rest and pound again – either a firm push and twist or a wider rotating movement, until the basil is a paste. Add the cheese and mix, then add the oil and mix again.

In the food processor

Pulse the garlic, pine nuts and a few grains of salt into a rough paste. Add the basil and a little oil and pulse again, and then the rest of the oil. Scrape into a bowl and stir the cheese in with a spoon.

Pradelli pesto

Serves 4

Pesto according to Alessandro Molinari Pradelli, translated from his books about the food of Genoa and Liguria.

45 leaves of fresh Genovese basil, 2 cloves of garlic, a pinch of coarse salt, olive oil, a fistful of pine nuts, a tablespoon and a half of grated Parmesan, a tablespoon and a half of grated pecorino.

To make pesto, place the basil and garlic in a marble mortar with the salt and pound with a pestle, adding a little oil. Add the pine nuts, continue to pound turning it into an emulsion with oil, then add the cheese. The consistency should be that of an ointment, the amount of oil depending on the absorbing ability of the other ingredients.

Crema di noci
Cream of walnut sauce

Serves 4

Acerbic and creamy, walnuts pounded with bread and oil make a singularly good (or blitzed) sauce, for trofie, also linguine. It is not traditional but I also like this with green beans and potatoes – proceed as above, but with this sauce.

200g shelled walnuts
30g soft white
   breadcrumbs
50ml whole milk
1 clove of garlic
a pinch of fresh
   marjoram
salt
30g Parmesan, grated
125ml olive oil

Bring a pan of water to the boil, add the walnuts and boil for 5 minutes. With the help of a cloth and a sharp knife, rub and lift the skin from the walnuts. Soak the breadcrumbs in the milk for 10 minutes.

In a pestle and mortar or a small blender, pound the walnuts with the garlic, marjoram and a pinch of salt. Add the soaked breadcrumbs and pound/blend again, then stir in the cheese.

Add the oil – if you are working with a mortar, stir in with the pestle, if you have used a blender, stir in with a spoon. Taste for salt.

And now the trofie

Twist, tadpole, spindle, piglet tail, the piece of paper you had been rolling between your fingers all through double maths – just some of the things that come up when you ask people to describe trofie, children being more imaginative than adults. Spindle is probably the most common descriptor of trofie, the one that best helps us picture the short, twisted, flour and water shape with tapered ends.

Typical of Liguria, the region that snakes up the coast from Tuscany to the border of France and Provence, and Liguria's capital Genoa, trofie descend from the medieval gnocco. It is another shape born of necessity and made from whatever was available: poor flours, bran, chestnut flour, bread soaked in water, or cooked potatoes kneaded into a dough. The origin of the name is unclear – some scholars remark it is from the Greek for nourishment, others that it comes from the verb strufuggiâ, 'to rub', which in turn comes from the Greek, to spin. Trofie with a proportion of potato can be dated to the 1800s, when the starchy migrant from the new world rooted itself in the soil and edible culture of Liguria. By the twentieth century trofie was a codified shape made fresh at home, sometimes including potato, bread or chestnuts, also factory-made, so with hard wheat and water, which as we know can be equal to fresh, only different.

I had every intention of T – Trofie referring only to the dried pasta shape. Then, convinced by Alessandro Venturi, I decided to try making fresh. My first attempts were as predicted, poor. I made slugs and squashed things, wisps and drags. I might have sworn at the dough. Then I spun a spindle, then another. Like every other pasta shape the key to trofie is practice. Make a dough of 300g of 00 flour and 150ml of hot water, work into a ball, knead and rest. Then take a handful of dough, and with the other hand pinch off a pea-sized lump and use the hollow of your palm to roll it back and forth against the board, until it resembles a 2cm slug. Now roll your palm up and over it again, then pause and roll your palm back down at a slant, therefore dragging and hopefully twisting the dough under the edge of your hand so as to form a spindle. Trofie are also available dried.

Trofie con pesto alla genovese
Trofie with pesto alla genovese, potatoes and green beans
Serves 4

The addition of potatoes and green beans is traditional and wonderful. Some recipes suggest cooking things separately. I prefer a cooking stagger, so adding the potatoes to the boiling water first as they take 15 minutes, adding the beans after 2 minutes as they take 12, then adding the trofie 3 minutes later as they take 10 minutes. The idea being that everything is cooked at the same time (if the potato is a bit soft, all the better). I then toss all three with the pesto and a little extra cooking water if it needs loosening. The potato acts as a starchy binder. A glorious dish, also one to remember for a crowd.

200g potatoes, peeled and diced
200g green beans, trimmed and cut in 3
400g fresh trofie or 350g dried trofie, linguine, bavette, fusilli
a portion of pesto (see recipe on page 318, which makes enough for 4)

Bring a large pan of water to the boil, add salt, and stir. Add the potatoes first, then after 2 minutes the beans and then, in accordance with cooking time, the pasta.

Meanwhile scrape the pesto into a large, warm bowl and loosen with a spoonful of cooking water. When the pasta, potatoes and beans are cooked, drain and save the water or lift directly into the pesto bowl and toss, adding a little more cooking water if it seems stiff. Serve immediately.

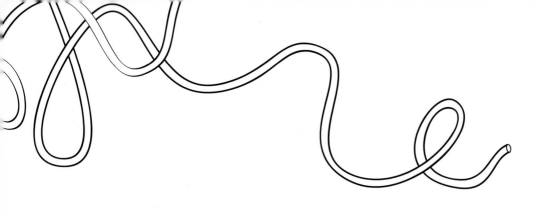

— v —

Vermicelli

For a while my son was (reluctantly) part of a school choir that rehearsed at another school in the nearby quarter of Trastevere. He would run up the steps without looking back and then I had an hour. Not long enough to go home, so I walked, one week through the green door of a church where I was met by blue and gold, and pasta makers.

I now know more about the church and its significance, the particulars of the exquisite decoration, but that first visit was a bolt of golden festoons and symbolism. Also a stained glass M, which when I moved closer turned out to be composed of fruit. Once you've seen the fruit M, it's like noticing a grey hair, you see them everywhere; another fruit window, fruit mosaics on the floor, and the words *I fruttaroli*, the fruit sellers. Next a plaque for the salami makers, and then the chapel of the *pollaroli* – chicken sellers, by which point your appetite is leading and you can't stop looking for what you are going to eat next, *molinari* – millers, *vignaioli* – winemakers, *ortolani e pizzicaroli* – grocers, and, near the door, *vermicellari*, the pasta makers.

The church of Santa Maria dell'Orto was built between 1489 and 1567 as the dedicated church for the 13 guilds involved in the food supply to Rome. This is a book about pasta, and the pasta makers *I vermicellari* are significant, also reminding us just how significant the word vermicelli is. Also how much of its history has, rightly, been assimilated into that of spaghetti, a word that came much later. Let's return briefly to Sicily between the ninth and twelfth centuries, when Arab culture dominated, and the dried pasta 'strings' known as *itryya*, which were transported all over the Mediterranean by Genovese merchant ships. *Itryya* became known – broadly speaking – as fidelini in some places and vermicelli, little worms, in others. Four centuries later in Naples, once a city of *mangia foglie* (leaf eaters) turned *mangia maccheroni* (pasta eaters), the other well-documented shape at that time was vermicelli.

A description in Maestro Martino's landmark fifteenth-century recipe collection *Libro de Arte Coquinaria (The Art of Cooking)* gives us instructions: 'Moisten the dough, and spread it out into a thin sheet. Use your hands to break it into little pieces that look more or less like little worms and leave them in the sun to dry.' By 1559 the production of dried pasta was so significant in Naples that the guild of *vermicellari* broke away from the guild of bakers. Then in Rome in 1602, in response to the great demand and by order of the Vatican, the confraternity *dei vermicellari* was founded. Soon after, the guild of *vermicellari* were given a chapel in Santa Maria dell'Orto.

When did the word spaghetti supplant the word vermicelli? According to Giuseppe Prezzolini in his book *Maccheroni &C.*, the word spaghetti first appears in a Neapolitan dictionary in 1849, having been mentioned twenty-five years earlier in a poem by the Neapolitan poet Antonio Viviani. It wasn't until the early twentieth century, however, that the word spaghetti entered popular use. Once the word spaghetti displaced vermicelli, makers differentiated by making vermicelli of differing proportions to establish an independent shape. De Vita and Prezzolini, though, are categorical that vermicelli is the old word for spaghetti.

Some southern recipe books still preference the name vermicelli, with clams, roasted tomato, the inimitable puttanesca, so I have too.

Vermicelli alle vongole in bianco
Vermicelli with clams
Serves 4

The winking shells under running water, the clatter into the pan, the unzipping tinkle as the shells open and release their liquor, the distillation of the clam and sea. I enjoy making *vermicelli (linguine* or *spaghetti) alle vongole* as much as I enjoy eating it. This is another recipe where tossing and jolting of the pan is vital, knocking the starch from the pasta which meets the oil and the clam liquor, resulting in an almost creamy aspect to the tangle of vermicelli, which then catches the clams for the second time. Fried anchovies to start, this and a bottle of wine, is a favourite meal.

1kg clams (vongole veraci, carpet, Venus or palourde)
6 tablespoons extra virgin olive oil
2 cloves of garlic, peeled and crushed
a small glass of white wine or dry vermouth (about 125ml)
400g vermicelli or spaghetti
salt
a pinch of red chilli flakes
a handful of fresh flat-leaf parsley

Rinse the clams in cold water. In a large, deep frying pan, deep enough to accommodate the pasta later, warm 2 tablespoons of olive oil with one of the cloves of garlic, peeled and crushed. Add the clams and the wine, shake, then cover. After a minute shake again, then lift the lid and, using a slotted spoon, lift the clams into a bowl as they open. Discard any that don't open.

Strain the clam broth through a fine sieve and set aside. Remove the flesh from half the clams. Leave the rest of the clams in their shells.

Meanwhile, cook the pasta in boiling salted water until al dente.

Put the frying pan back over a low heat, add 4 tablespoons of olive oil, the rest of the garlic and the chilli. Once the garlic is fragrant, add the clam broth and let it bubble until it is reduced by about half – it should be slightly thickened. If the pasta is not ready, pull the clam pan from the heat.

Put the clam pan back on the heat, drain the pasta, reserve a cup of pasta cooking water or lift the pasta directly into the pan. Add the clam flesh and the clams in shells and the parsley, then toss and jolt the pan rigorously, adding more pasta cooking water and a little more oil to create an emulsion. Divide between plates.

Vermicelli alla puttanesca
Vermicelli with tomatoes, anchovies, garlic, capers, olives and parsley
Serves 4

Of all the many legends about the origin of this Campanian dish, I like the play on words best. That someone asked someone else *'Facci una puttanata qualsiasi'*, make us any bloody bullshit, that is to say, make-me-something-good-to-eat-with-what-you-have. Because it best captures the spirit of the dish for us cooks and eaters, using what we have – anchovies, capers, olives, tomatoes, parsley, pasta to make a highly tasty plate of food. With this in mind, to suggest a right way would contradict its nature, which is anarchic, how else could it be with such demanding flavours? All that said, a template is useful, so here it is. Abuse it.

100ml olive oil
1–3 cloves of garlic
a pinch of red chilli flakes
4–8 anchovy fillets
2 tablespoons capers
2 tablespoons black olives
12 sweet cherry tomatoes, quartered or crushed
a pinch of dried oregano
400g vermicelli or spaghetti
a handful of fresh flat-leaf parsley, finely chopped

Bring a large pan of water to the boil.

In a frying pan large enough to mix the pasta later, warm the olive oil, garlic, crushed (but still whole for a gentle flavour, sliced for a stronger one) and red chilli, then – still low – add the anchovies and cook until they dissolve. Add the capers and olives.

Add the tomatoes and oregano and cook over a lively flame, pressing them so they get saucey, for about 8 minutes. Meanwhile cook the vermicelli until al dente.

Either drain the pasta or use tongs or a spider sieve to lift it directly into the sauce – residual water will be helpful. Add the parsley and swish and stir. Serve immediately.

Vermicelli con vongole, zucchine, mandorle e mollica
Vermicelli with clams, courgettes, almonds and breadcrumbs

Serves 4

An unmistakably Sicilian combination, and a good one, the courgettes and clams well matched, the toasted crumble of almonds and breadcrumbs adding texture, lemon and mint expansive scent. Like so many of my Sicilian recipes, this is inspired by the journalist and recipe writer Ada Parisi.

1kg clams
olive oil
2 cloves of garlic, peeled and crushed
a small glass of white wine
40g dried breadcrumbs
30g toasted almonds, roughly chopped
salt
4 courgettes
6–8 leaves of fresh mint
400g vermicelli, spaghetti, linguine
zest of 1 unwaxed lemon

Bring a large pan of water to the boil for the pasta.

Rinse the clams under cold water (don't soak). Warm a couple of tablespoons of olive oil and a clove of garlic in a large pan and let the garlic sizzle gently for a couple of minutes. Raise the heat, add the clams and wine, cover, then reduce the heat and cook, shaking the pan for a couple of minutes. As soon as you hear the clams opening, lift the lid and start scooping them into a bowl – at this point I pull half the clams from the shell for easier eating later. Pull the pan from the heat and filter the liquor. In another frying pan over a medium heat, toast the breadcrumbs in a little olive oil with the almonds and a pinch of salt.

Wash the courgettes, cut them in half lengthways and then into 2mm thick half-moons. Put the pan back on the heat, add 4 tablespoons of olive oil and the second clove of garlic and let it sizzle gently, then add the courgettes, raise the heat and cook and stir until lightly gold. Add the mint and the drained clam liquor and bubble for a few minutes, then add the clams. Pull the pan from the heat.

Cook the pasta until al dente, then lift the pasta into the frying pan and toss or jolt the pan rigorously, adding more pasta cooking water and a little more oil to create an emulsion.

Serve, topping each plate with a little of the toasted breadcrumbs, more fresh mint and lemon zest.

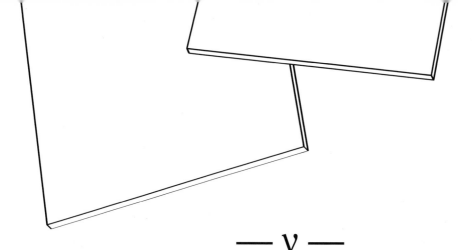

— v —

Vincisgrassi

Baroque lasagna is how some describe this monument of Gastronomia Marchigiana. It is certainly an exuberant dish, layers of pasta, enriched with butter and sweet wine, *ragù* maybe enriched with offal and porcini, and folds of béchamel, the name of which is sometimes credited to an Austrian general stationed in Ancona in the late 1700s, other times to a rich truffle sauce.

As always with important dishes, opinions about how best to make vincisgrassi are forthright and there are many variations. I have enjoyed making what I understand to be a traditional version by Alessandro Molinari Pradelli in his book of *La cucina delle Marche,* which includes sweetbread, liver and brain in the *ragù*. Also a version from a friend which includes lots of fresh porcini and truffles. My favourite, though, is inspired by Ann and Franco Taruschio, and their version made and served at their restaurant The Walnut Tree, a magical coming together of Le Marche and Wales, which feels just right for this book. And it is a glorious meeting of pasta enticed with eggs and sweet wine, mushrooms, prosciutto and béchamel. Like lasagna, vincisgrassi are a project that will take over the kitchen, but the result is divine. Be generous with the final layer of grated Parmesan on top, and irregular with the edges – golden corners are good.

Vincisgrassi

Serves 6

For the pasta
300g 00 flour
100g semola
3 eggs
50g soft butter
2 tablespoons vin
santo or Marsala

For the rest
50g dried porcini
300g field
mushrooms, or
fresh porcini, sliced
150g butter
60g flour
800ml whole milk
60ml extra virgin olive
oil
200ml single cream
3 sprigs of fresh
flat-leaf parsley,
finely chopped
14 slices of prosciutto,
cut into strips
roughly 1cm wide
and 5cm long
salt and black pepper
150g Parmesan,
grated

Soak the dried porcini in plenty of warm water for 30 minutes.

Working on a board or in a bowl, make a mountain of flour, use your fist to swirl a crater and into it break the eggs, butter and vin santo. Use a fork to start and then your hands, to make a rough dough. Knead until firm and smooth, then cover with an upturned bowl and leave to rest.

Roll out by hand or with a machine and cut into 20cm squares. Bring a pan of salted water to the boil and blanch the sheets in batches for 1 minute, plunge them into cold water, then spread them out on clean cloths.

Drain the porcini, keeping the liquid. Slice the mushrooms.

For the béchamel, melt 50g of butter, add the flour and cook until golden and toasty. Add the warm milk and 400ml of porcini soaking liquid, a little at a time, beating well with a balloon whisk and then simmering until as thick as double cream.

In a frying pan, melt 20g of butter and the olive oil and fry the mushrooms until soft and collapsed, then add the soaked porcini. Add to the béchamel along with the cream and parsley, season, stir for a minute longer and then pull from the heat.

To assemble the vincisgrassi, butter a 2 litre ovenproof gratin dish and cover the bottom with a layer of pasta. Lay on some of the prosciutto, then spread over a layer of the béchamel, dot with butter and sprinkle with some Parmesan. Continue the process, making layer after layer, finishing with the seventh layer of pasta with defiant extruding corners, and top with the last of the béchamel and a final sprinkling of Parmesan.

Bake in the oven at 220°C for 20 minutes, then put under the grill for 3 minutes to toast the top.

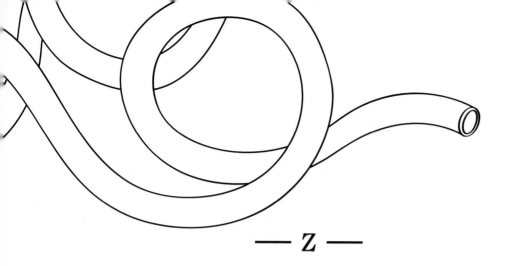

— Z —

Ziti / Zite

And so the last shape. Which is the longest, 60cm to a metre depending on the maker. We bought ours from Faella in Gragnano and the packet has been sitting in the oversized section, on top of the cupboard, ever since.

Originating in Sicily, ziti or zite are part of the long, pierced dried pasta tribe that began with busiate, but whose piercing is so extreme it is actually a tube. They are the shape that takes longest to dry, 6 days if in the hands of makers who care enough, after which they seem like exquisite hollow sculptures, or – if you are 9 – the claws of Wolverine. The name derives from *maccheroni della zita*, a dish traditionally prepared by the *Zita* (bride in Neopolitan) and served as part of a lavish and abounding wedding feast. They are a wonderful shape, cooked and wound into a *timballo* with peppers and smoked cheese, or spezzati, snapped into short lengths and served with a rich beef and onion sauce called *Genovese*.

Ziti con la genovese
Ziti with onion and beef sauce
Serves 7

There are various stories about the origin of *La Genovese*, the classic Neapolitan sauce of onion and beef – sailors from Genoa being the most familiar (and obvious). I was taught to make it by Benedetta Gargano, scriptwriter of – among other things – the Italian soap *Un posto al sole*. In fact the day we made it, as the onion and beef cooked until they collapsed into a silky almost-cream, their colour *marrone-ambra*, we discussed the early plot lines of *EastEnders*. Of all the recipes in this book, I hope you make this – it is a disconcertedly simple bit of stovetop alchemy, the final sauce soft, and deeply, richly savoury. Ziti or candele, snapped into short lengths, are traditional, but penne, fusilli and ruote work too. Crostini and fried courgette flowers to start and cheese and salad for after, *Genovese is* Sunday lunch.

1kg onions, peeled, halved and thinly sliced
500g piece of beef chuck or rump, cut into 2cm chunks
200ml olive oil
salt and black pepper
white wine
600g ziti or candele
a handful of grated Parmesan

Starting from cold, put both the onions and the beef into a pan, pour on the olive oil, add a good pinch of salt and set over a medium flame. Allow the onion and beef to fry gently with you stirring, then reduce the flame and cook for an hour. Then remove the lid (the onions will have collapsed, making it brothy) and cook, stirring every now and then, for another hour, in which time the sauce will reduce so you need to keep it topped up and gently saucey with white wine. By the end everything should have cooked into an almost-cream.

Break the ziti into 5cm lengths and cook in well-salted boiling water, then drain and mix with the sauce and a handful of Parmesan in a large warm bowl.

Timballo di ziti
Baked ziti with roasted peppers, provola and Parmesan
Serves 6

Depending on the occasion you can arrange the ziti in neat concentric whorls, or simply see how they fall when you tip and press them into the tin. Either way, the effect is a bit like a swirling lolly. Like all Sicilian *timballi* this one can be enriched with more cheese, the tomato sauce replaced with meat sauce. If you can't find ziti, penne or rigatoni work too, though they won't give you the same swirling effect, and make it more baked pasta than *timballo*. A great dish for a celebration, the cross-section of tubes, fiery velvet of roasted red pepper held together – as so many of us are – by cheese, is joyful.

olive oil
1 clove of garlic,
    peeled and crushed
    but still whole
1kg peeled plum
    tomatoes
a handful of fresh basil
salt
5 red peppers
350g ziti, alternatively
    candele
1 egg, beaten
150g Parmesan,
    grated
butter and
    breadcrumbs for
    the tin
300g smoked provola
    or scamorza

Make a tomato sauce. In a large frying pan or terracotta pot, warm 6 tablespoons of olive oil and allow the garlic to fry very gently until fragrant. Add the tomatoes, a sprig of basil and a pinch of salt, using the back of a wooden spoon to crush the tomatoes, then cover the pan and cook until the sauce is visibly thickened and shiny.

Roast the whole red peppers in a hot oven (200°C) until blackened and collapsed, which takes about 40 minutes. Put in a bowl, cover with cling film and leave for 20 minutes. Peel and deseed the peppers and rip into strips.

Cook the ziti in plenty of well-salted water until 3 minutes off the recommended cooking time, drain and refresh in cold water. Mix them with the tomato sauce, beaten egg and half the Parmesan.

Butter and breadcrumb a 25cm cake tin or ring. Arrange a layer of ziti, as neatly as you like, then press some of the pepper strips, basil leaves and diced provola into the gaps and cover with a layer of Parmesan. Repeat the layers until all the ingredients are used up, ending with a layer of breadcrumbs dotted with butter.

Bake in a preheated oven at 200°C for 25 minutes, and allow to cool for 10 minutes before inverting.

While ziti is the last shape in this alphabet, it is not the last in this most marvellous, compelling, edible universe. There are square zizziridd, or gullet ticklers from Basilicata, wide strips of flour and water pasta called zugolotti from Umbria, and zumari, a sort of tagliatelle from Puglia. And the pasta universe isn't fixed, shapes are always being invented. There may be more Zs. But for now, this is where we end. By bundling the last 150g of ziti up and squashing the packet in the cupboard, thinking that the pasta shelf could really do with a tidy, that we need to eat some fusilli, stock up with rigatoni and put the clothes peg back on that precarious open packet of alfabeto! A is for Alfabeto.

Index

A

abissine 172
Abruzzo 34, 43, 138, 250, 282, 283, 288
Accademia della Sfoglia 294–6
Adams, Alice 234, 244
agnolotti 67
ajo ojo 278
Al-Idrisi 44
alfabeto 12–15
  alfabeto in brodo 13
  chicken broth 14, *15*
  golden vegetable broth 13
all'amatriciana 34–5, 36, *37*
all'arrabbiata 228
alla carbonara 250–51, 252, *253*
alla gricia 34–5, 38, 247
alla Norma 279
alla puttanesca 330
alla romagnola 126
almonds
  busiate with basil, tomato and almond pesto (*pesto trapanese*) 48, *49*
  cavatelli with sage and almond pesto and salted ricotta 88
  vermicelli with clams, courgettes, almonds and breadcrumbs 331
Amalfi 264
Amatrice 36, 138
amatriciana see all'amatriciana
Anacleto (author's friend) 311
anchovies 27
  bigoli with onion and anchovy 28, *29*
  bucatini with cauliflower, saffron and anchovies 40
  fettuccine with butter and anchovy 112
  fusilli with tinned sardines, fennel, lemon and anchovy crumbs 123
  linguine with anchovies, tomato and breadcrumbs 160
  mafalde with anchovies and tomato paste and breadcrumbs 173
  minestrone soup from Genoa 32, *33*
  orecchiette with bursting tomatoes and anchovy crumbs 201
  orecchiette with turnip tops, garlic and anchovy 198, *199*
  pasta and chickpeas 144
  vermicelli with tomatoes, anchovies, garlic, capers, olives and parsley 330
Anna Tasca Lanza cooking school 46, 88

anelli 16–23
  anelli baked with tomato, aubergine and cheese *20*, 21–2
  anelli in mushroom and potato broth 23
anolini 67
Antonio Amato 256
Arabs 44–6, 245, 326–7
Arezzo 181
arrabbiata see all'arrabbiata
arselle 115
  fregula with clams or arselle 116, *117*
artichokes *291*
  minestrone 31
  stracci with Roman spring stew of artichokes, peas and broad beans 290–91
Artusi, Pellegrino 131
assabesi 172
aubergines *280*
  anelli baked with tomato, aubergine and cheese *20*, 21–2
  baked macaroni with meatballs and aubergine 170
  midsummer pasta 186, *187*
  paccheri with aubergine, two sorts of tomatoes and mozzarella 214, *215*
  spaghetti with tomato, aubergine and salted ricotta 279
  white ragù with pork, aubergine and fennel 47
Augusto (restaurateur) 182

B

bacon *see* pancetta
Bagnaia 288
Barberis, Corrado 44
Barilla 256–7
basil
  busiate with basil, tomato and almond pesto (*pesto trapanese*) 48, *49*
  lumache with tuna, beans, tomato and basil 163
  minestrone soup from Genoa 32, *33*
  orzo with tomato, basil and Parmesan 203
  pesto alla genovese 316–18, *319*
  Pradelli pesto 320
  spaghetti with simple tomato and basil sauce 270, *271*
  spaghettini with raw tomato sauce and lots of herbs 277

spinach and potato gnocchi with cream, Parmesan and basil *134*, *135*, 136, *137*
  tagliolini with lemon, Parmesan and basil 307
  trofie with pesto alla genovese, potatoes and green beans 324, *325*
Basilicata 82, 140, 340
beans
  borlotti 91, *91*
  lumache with tuna, beans, tomato and basil 163
  minestrone 31
  minestrone soup from Genoa 32, *33*
  minestrone with tomato, and two kinds of beans 102
  paccheri with broad bean pesto 217
  pasta and beans 92, *93*
  stracci with Roman spring stew of artichokes, peas and broad beans 290–91
  trofie with pesto alla genovese, potatoes and green beans 324, *325*
  using dried 92
béchamel sauce 54, 58, 95, 126, 148–9, 150, 168, 332, 334
beef
  baked macaroni with meatballs and aubergine 170
  baked tagliatelle with ragù 304
  cannelloni in the Lazio style 58–9
  fettuccine with chicken livers and sage 110
  lasagna Bolognese style with ragù, béchamel and Parmesan 148–9, *151*
  Romagna-style ragù 126
  spaghetti alla chitarra in the style of Teramo 283
  tagliatelle with ragù 302, *303*
  ziti with onion and beef sauce 337
bigoli 24–9
  bigoli with onion and anchovy 28, *29*
  bigoli with tuna and peas 28
Biondi, Lisa 164
Boccaccio, Giovanni 130
Bologna 125, 146, 294, 311, 312
bolognese 148–9, *151*, 296, 302, *303*
Boni, Ada 53, 131, 229
Borgia, Lucrezia 295
Braudel, Fernand 42–3
breadcrumbs
  anelli baked with tomato, aubergine and cheese *20*, 21–2

breadcrumbs *continued*
  baked macaroni with meatballs and
    aubergine 170
  baked ziti with roasted peppers,
    provola and Parmesan 338
  bucatini with cauliflower, saffron
    and anchovies 40
  casarecce with broccoli 78, *79*
  cream of walnut sauce 321
  fusilli with tinned sardines, fennel,
    lemon and anchovy crumbs 123
  linguine with anchovies, tomato
    and breadcrumbs 160
  macaroni cheese 168, *169*
  mafalde with anchovies and tomato
    paste and breadcrumbs 173
  orecchiette with bursting tomatoes
    and anchovy crumbs 201
  scialatielli Amalfi style with
    shellfish, squid and tomatoes
    and breadcrumbs 264
  spaghetti alla chitarra with tiny
    chicken meatballs and white
    wine 284, *285*
  vermicelli with clams, courgettes,
    almonds and breadcrumbs 331
brichetti 30–33
  minestrone 31
  minestrone soup from Genoa
    32, *33*
broccoli
  casarecce with broccoli 78, *79*
brodi 12–15
  alfabeto in brodo 13
  anelli in mushroom and potato
    broth 23
  capelli d'angelo in fish broth 65
  chicken broth 14, *15*
  golden vegetable broth 13
  tortellini, filled with pork,
    prosciutto, mortadella, served in
    broth 312, *313*
bucatini 34–41, *41*
  bucatini with cauliflower, saffron
    and anchovies 40
  bucatini with guanciale and
    pecorino Romano 38
  bucatini with tomato, guanciale
    and pecorino Romano 36, *37*
buckwheat 236
Buitoni 256
busiate 42–9
  busiate with basil, tomato and
    almond pesto (*pesto trapanese*)
    48, *49*
  white ragù with pork, aubergine
    and fennel 47
butter
  chestnut, pumpkin and potato
    gnocchi with butter and sage
    133
  fettuccine, butter and Parmesan
    111
  fettuccine with butter and anchovy
    112

fettuccine with chicken livers and
  sage 110
fettuccine with porcini
  mushrooms, butter and garlic
  113
mafalde with tomato sauce and
  ricotta 174, *175*
pizzoccheri with potatoes, cabbage
  and cheese 238, *239*
pumpkin cappellacci 72, *73*
quadrucci with spinach, butter and
  Parmesan 241
ravioli with ricotta and spinach
  246–7, *247*

C

cabbage
  minestrone 31
  minestrone soup from Genoa 32,
    33
  pizzoccheri with potatoes, cabbage
    and cheese 238, *239*
cacio e pepe 77, 286–7
caciocavallo
  anelli baked with tomato,
    aubergine and cheese *20*, 21–2
Calabria 65, 82, 102
Campania 96, 118, 188, 213, 330
Campofilone 62
cannelloni 50–59
  cannelloni in the Lazio style 58–9
  cannelloni in the Sorrento style
    55, *56, 57*
  cannelloni with pork, spinach and
    Parmesan 54
capelli d'angelo 60–65
  capelli d'angelo in fish broth 65
  capelli d'angelo with leeks, cream
    and saffron 64
  fresh capelli d'angelo with prawns
    and lemon 62, *63*
capers
  fusilli with tomato and tuna ragù
    122
  linguine with swordfish Messina
    style 157
  lumache with tuna, beans, tomato
    and basil 163
  lumache with tuna, egg and capers
    164, *165*
  scialatielli Amalfi style with
    shellfish, squid and tomatoes
    and breadcrumbs 264
  spaghettini with raw tomato sauce
    and lots of herbs 277
  vermicelli with tomatoes,
    anchovies, garlic, capers, olives
    and parsley 330
cappellacci 66–73, *69–71*
  pumpkin cappellacci 72, *73*
cappelletti 68
Capurro, Giovanni Battista 224

carbonara see *alla carbonara*
carrots 13, 14, 31, 58, 65, 98, 120,
  126, 148, 192, 273, 284, 302
  pappardelle with onion ragù 219
casarecce 74–81
  casarecce with broccoli 78, *79*
  casarecce with peperonata 80
Casera
  pizzoccheri with potatoes, cabbage
    and cheese 238, *239*
casonei 67
cauliflower
  bucatini with cauliflower, saffron
    and anchovies 40
Cavalieri, Benedetto 257
cavatelli 82–9, *85, 89*
  cavatelli with sage and almond
    pesto and salted ricotta 88
  cavatelli with sausage, mint and
    tomato 86, *87*
celery
  quadrucci and peas Roman style
    242, *243*
  rigatoni with the sauce of
    Roman-style oxtail stew
    254, *255*
  roast chicken with orzo 206, *207*
Cerveteri 230
Cesari, Luca 250–51
cheese
  anelli baked with tomato,
    aubergine and cheese *20*, 21–2
  baked macaroni with meatballs and
    aubergine 170
  baked ziti with roasted peppers,
    provola and Parmesan 338
  bucatini with guanciale and
    pecorino Romano 38
  bucatini with tomato, guanciale
    and pecorino Romano 36, *37*
  cannelloni in the Lazio style 58–9
  cannelloni in the Sorrento style
    55, *56, 57*
  cannelloni with pork, spinach and
    Parmesan 54
  cavatelli with sage and almond
    pesto and salted ricotta 88
  conchiglie with peas, bacon and
    ricotta 94
  conchiglioni stuffed with spinach
    and ricotta 95
  cream of walnut sauce 321
  ditali and pumpkin 97
  fettuccine, butter and Parmesan
    111
  fettuccine with chicken livers and
    sage 110
  fregula with sausage and saffron
    115
  garganelli with spring vegetables,
    crisp pancetta and Parmesan
    128
  grating 35

lasagna Bolognese style with ragù, béchamel and Parmesan 148–9, *151*

linguine with courgettes, egg and Parmesan 158, *159*

macaroni cheese 168, *169*

mafalde with tomato sauce and ricotta 174, *175*

maltagliati with olive oil and pecorino 181

midsummer pasta 186, *187*

minestrone 31

minestrone soup from Genoa 32, *33*

minestrone with tomato, and two kinds of beans 102

orzo with peas, Parmesan and lemon 204

orzo with tomato, basil and Parmesan 203

paccheri with aubergine, two sorts of tomatoes and mozzarella 214, *215*

paccheri with broad bean pesto 217

pappardelle with radicchio, fennel, cream and Parmesan 222

pasta al forno 274

pasta and potatoes Neapolitan style 192, *193*

pasta with potatoes and smoked provola cheese 190

pecorino 35

penne with four cheeses 229

pesto alla genovese 316–18, *319*

pizzoccheri with potatoes, cabbage and cheese 238, *239*

Pradelli pesto 320

pumpkin cappellacci 72, *73*

quadrucci with spinach, butter and Parmesan 241

ravioli with potatoes, ricotta, lemon and marjoram 248, *249*

ravioli with ricotta and spinach 246–7, *247*

rigatoni with egg, guanciale and pecorino 252, *253*

ruote with Gorgonzola, sage and walnuts 258

spaghetti alla chitarra or tonnarelli with pecorino cheese and black pepper 286–7

spaghetti alla chitarra with tiny chicken meatballs and white wine 284, *285*

spaghetti with simple tomato and basil sauce 270, *271*

spaghetti with tomato, aubergine and salted ricotta 279

spinach and potato gnocchi with cream, Parmesan and basil 134, *135*, 136, *137*

stracci with peas, spring onion, guanciale and pecorino Carla style 292, *293*

stracci with Roman spring stew of artichokes, peas and broad beans 290–91

tagliolini with lemon, Parmesan and basil 307

tortellini, filled with pork, prosciutto, mortadella, served in broth 312, *313*

tortellini with Parmesan cream 314

trofie with pesto alla genovese, potatoes and green beans 324, *325*

umbricelli with courgettes, pancetta and pecorino 234, *235*

vincisgrassi *333*, 334, *335*

ziti with onion and beef sauce 337

chestnuts

chestnut, pumpkin and potato gnocchi with butter and sage 133

chickpea and chestnut soup 178, *179*

Chiaravalle Abbey 35

chicken

chicken broth 14, *15*

roast chicken with orzo 206, *207*

spaghetti alla chitarra with tiny chicken meatballs and white wine 284, *285*

chicken livers

baked tagliatelle with ragù 304

fettuccine with chicken livers and sage 110

Romagna-style ragù 126

tagliatelle with ragù 302, *303*

chickpeas

chickpea and chestnut soup 178, *179*

chickpeas, pasta and fried pasta 145

pasta and chickpea soup with tinned chickpeas 142, *143*

pasta and chickpeas 144

chillies 65

penne with spicy tomato sauce 228

spaghetti with garlic, olive oil and chilli – midnight spaghetti 278

chiocciole *see* lumache

ciceri e tria 145

Cinque, Sergio, 208–12

Civitanova

Chalet Galileo 62

clams *265*

fregula with clams or arselle 116, *117*

mezze maniche with courgettes and prawns 184

scialatielli Amalfi style with shellfish, squid and tomatoes and breadcrumbs 264

vermicelli with clams 328, *329*

vermicelli with clams, courgettes, almonds and breadcrumbs 331

cod, salt

chickpea and chestnut soup 178, *179*

conchiglie 90–95

conchiglie with peas, bacon and ricotta 94

conchiglioni stuffed with spinach and ricotta 95

pasta and beans 92, *93*

Cosentino, Enrico 264

courgettes *185*

garganelli with spring vegetables, crisp pancetta and Parmesan 128

linguine with courgettes, egg and Parmesan 158, *159*

mezze maniche with courgettes and prawns 184

midsummer pasta 186, *187*

minestrone soup from Genoa 32, *33*

umbricelli with courgettes, pancetta and pecorino 234, *235*

vermicelli with clams, courgettes, almonds and breadcrumbs 331

cream

capelli d'angelo with leeks, cream and saffron 64

pappardelle with radicchio, fennel, cream and Parmesan 222

ruote with Gorgonzola, sage and walnuts 258

spinach and potato gnocchi with cream, Parmesan and basil 134, *135*, 136, *137*

tagliolini with lemon, Parmesan and basil 307

tortellini with Parmesan cream 314

vincisgrassi *333*, 334, *335*

culurgiones 67

currants 40

bucatini with cauliflower, saffron and anchovies 40

mafalde with anchovies and tomato paste and breadcrumbs 173

D

D'Aleo, Orazio 269

De Cecco 256

Del Conte, Anna 180

Di Martino 256

ditali 96–9

ditali and pumpkin 97

ditalini and lentils 98, *99*

Dolomites 146

dough

fresh or dried 16–17

gnocchi dough 138–9

hand rolling fresh egg dough 294–8, 310–11

ingredients 17–18

dough *continued*
  making flour and water dough
    83–4
  making fresh egg dough 51–3,
    69, 70
duck
  pappardelle with duck 220, *221*

E

eggs
  baked macaroni with meatballs and
    aubergine 170
  linguine with courgettes, egg and
    Parmesan 158, *159*
  lumache with tuna, egg and capers
    164, *165*
  rigatoni with egg, guanciale and
    pecorino 252, *253*
  ruote with mascarpone and
    walnuts 259
equipment 124, 274, 277, 282, 318
Etruscans 43, 230

F

farfalle 100–105, *103*
  farfalle with salmon and
    mascarpone 104, *105*
  minestrone with tomato, and two
    kinds of beans 102
fennel
  fusilli with tinned sardines, fennel,
    lemon and anchovy crumbs 123
  minestrone 31
  pappardelle with radicchio, fennel,
    cream and Parmesan 222
  white ragù with pork, aubergine
    and fennel 47
fennel seeds
  spaghettini with raw tomato sauce
    and lots of herbs 277
Ferrara 68, 72, 294
fettuccine 106–13, *108, 109*
  fettuccine Alfredo 111
  fettuccine, butter and Parmesan
    111
  fettuccine with butter and anchovy
    112
  fettuccine with chicken livers and
    sage 110
  fettuccine with porcini
    mushrooms, butter and garlic
    113
fish
  capelli d'angelo in fish broth 65
  chickpea and chestnut soup 178,
    179
  fusilli with tinned sardines, fennel,
    lemon and anchovy crumbs 123
  linguine with swordfish Messina
    style 157

scialatielli with sea bass and lemon
    266, *267*
  see also anchovies; clams; mussels;
    prawns; tuna
Foggia 200
fontina
  pizzoccheri with potatoes, cabbage
    and cheese 238, *239*
food mills 142, 174, 214, 270, 274,
    275, 277
Francesca (author's friend) 125, 277,
    310–11, 314
Fratelli di Rugantino 256
fregnacce 182
fregula 114–17
  fregula with clams or arselle 116,
    117
  fregula with sausage and saffron
    115
frittata di pasta 281
fusilli 118–23, *119*
  fusilli with tinned sardines, fennel,
    lemon and anchovy crumbs 123
  fusilli with tomato and tuna ragù
    122
  lamb ragù with lots of herbs
    120, *121*

G

Garafalo 256
garganelli 124–9, *127, 129*
  garganelli with spring vegetables,
    crisp pancetta and Parmesan
    128
  Romagna-style ragù 126
Gargano, Benedetta 337
garlic 86
  fettuccine with porcini
    mushrooms, butter and garlic
    113
  orecchiette with turnip tops, garlic
    and anchovy 198, *199*
  pesto alla genovese 316–18, *319*
  pici with tomatoes and garlic 233
  Pradelli pesto 320
  spaghetti with garlic, olive oil and
    chilli – midnight spaghetti 278
  trofie with pesto alla genovese,
    potatoes and green beans
    324, *325*
  vermicelli with tomatoes,
    anchovies, garlic, capers, olives
    and parsley 330
gasse see farfalle
Gela 34, 269
Genoa 30, 32, 46, 316–20, 322
La Genovese 337
Giada (restaurateur) 157
Giancarlo (author's friend) 200
gnocchi 19, 130–39, *134, 135*
  chestnut, pumpkin and potato
    gnocchi with butter and sage
    133

curly gnocchi 138–9, *139*
potato gnocchi 132
spinach and potato gnocchi with
    cream, Parmesan and basil *134*,
    135, 136, *137*
Gorgonzola
  penne with four cheeses 229
  ruote with Gorgonzola, sage and
    walnuts 258
  types 258
Gragnano 208
  Faella pasta factory 208–12,
    210, 211
Grana Padano 35
  paccheri with broad bean pesto
    217
Greeks, ancient 43–4
gricia see alla gricia
Grottaferrata
  Taverna Mari 308
Gualandi, Renato 250–51
guanciale 38, *39*
  bucatini with guanciale and
    pecorino Romano 38
  bucatini with tomato, guanciale
    and pecorino Romano 36, *37*
  ravioli with ricotta and spinach
    246–7, *247*
  rigatoni with egg, guanciale and
    pecorino 252, *253*
  stracci with peas, spring onion,
    guanciale and pecorino Carla
    style 292, *293*

H

ham
  cannelloni with pork, spinach and
    Parmesan 54
Hopkinson, Simon 242
Horace 44, 140

I

itryya 44, 326–7

J

Jannattoni, Livio 58, 250–51
Jews 44, 72

L

lagana 44
lagane 140–45
  chickpeas, pasta and fried pasta
    145

pasta and chickpea soup with
tinned chickpeas 142, *143*
pasta and chickpeas 144
Lalli (author's friend) 316–17
lamb
lamb ragù with lots of herbs
120, *121*
Lanza, Anna Tasca 46, 88
lasagne 146–51
lasagna Bolognese style with ragù,
béchamel and Parmesan
148–9, *151*
variations and tips 150
Lawson, Nigella 202, 206
Lazio 58, 107, 230, 260, 282, 288
leeks
capelli d'angelo with leeks, cream
and saffron 64
maltagliati with creamed leeks (and
mussels if you wish) 180–81
minestrone 31
pappardelle with duck 220, *221*
penne with sausage, porcini
mushrooms and leeks 226, *227*
roast chicken with orzo 206, *207*
Leigh, Rowley 123
lemons *205*
farfalle with salmon and
mascarpone 104, *105*
fresh capelli d'angelo with prawns
and lemon 62, *63*
fusilli with tinned sardines, fennel,
lemon and anchovy crumbs 123
orzo with peas, Parmesan and
lemon 204
ravioli with potatoes, ricotta, lemon
and marjoram 248, *249*
ravioli with ricotta and spinach
246–7, *247*
roast chicken with orzo 206, *207*
ruote with ricotta and pine nuts
260
scialatielli with sea bass and lemon
266, *267*
tagliolini with lemon, Parmesan
and basil 307
vermicelli with clams, courgettes,
almonds and breadcrumbs 331
lentils
ditalini and lentils 98, *99*
lettuce
garganelli with spring vegetables,
crisp pancetta and Parmesan
128
Liber de Coquina 245
Libro de Arte Coquinaria 327
Liguria 318, 320, 322
linguine 152–61, *154, 155, 161*
linguine with anchovies, tomato
and breadcrumbs 160
linguine with courgettes, egg and
Parmesan 158, *159*
linguine with swordfish Messina
style 157
lombrichelli *see* pici

lumache 162–5
lumache with tuna, beans, tomato
and basil 163
lumache with tuna, egg and capers
164, *165*

M

maccheroni 166–71
baked macaroni with meatballs and
aubergine 170
macaroni cheese 168, *169*
Macrí, Bruno 281
Mafalda, Princess 172
mafalde 172–5
mafalde with anchovies and tomato
paste and breadcrumbs 173
mafalde with tomato sauce and
ricotta 174, *175*
Maglie 257
maltagliati 176–81
chickpea and chestnut soup
178, *179*
maltagliati with creamed leeks (and
mussels if you wish) 180–81
maltagliati with olive oil and
pecorino 181
Mancini pasta factory 152–6, *154, 155*
Manuela (author's friend) 114
Le Marche 67, 124–5, 146, 152, 288,
332
Maria Paola (author's friend) 316–17
marjoram
cream of walnut sauce 321
lamb ragù with lots of herbs
120, *121*
ravioli with potatoes, ricotta, lemon
and marjoram 248, *249*
ravioli with ricotta and spinach
246–7, *247*
spaghettini with raw tomato sauce
and lots of herbs 277
Martino, Maestro 327
marubini 67
mascarpone 259
farfalle with salmon and
mascarpone 104, *105*
pappardelle with radicchio, fennel,
cream and Parmesan 222
penne with sausage, porcini
mushrooms and leeks 226, *227*
ruote with mascarpone and walnuts
259
tagliolini with lemon, Parmesan
and basil 307
Maurizio, Adam 43
meatballs
baked macaroni with meatballs and
aubergine 170
spaghetti alla chitarra in the style
of Teramo 283
spaghetti alla chitarra with tiny
chicken meatballs and white

wine 284, *285*
Messedaglia, Luigi 130
messinese 157
Messisbugo, Cristoforo di 66
mezze maniche 182–7
mezze maniche with courgettes
and prawns 184
midsummer pasta 186, *187*
midnight spaghetti 278
midsummer pasta 186, *187*
Mina 256–7
minestra di ceci e castagne 178, *179*
minestre 90–91
minestrone 30, 31
minestrone soup from Genoa
32, *33*
minestrone with tomato, and two
kinds of beans 102
mint
cavatelli with sausage, mint and
tomato 86, *87*
paccheri with broad bean pesto
217
stracci with peas, spring onion,
guanciale and pecorino Carla
style 292, *293*
stracci with Roman spring stew of
artichokes, peas and broad beans
290–91
vermicelli with clams, courgettes,
almonds and breadcrumbs 331
mista (mixed pasta) 188–93, *191*
pasta and potatoes Neapolitan style
192, *193*
pasta with potatoes and smoked
provola cheese 190
Molise 82, 282, 288
Montanari, Massimo 42, 268
mortadella
tortellini, filled with pork,
prosciutto, mortadella, served in
broth 312, *313*
mozzarella
anelli baked with tomato,
aubergine and cheese *20*, 21–2
baked macaroni with meatballs and
aubergine 170
cannelloni in the Sorrento style
55, *56, 57*
macaroni cheese 168, *169*
midsummer pasta 186, *187*
paccheri with aubergine, two sorts
of tomatoes and mozzarella
214, *215*
pasta al forno 274
penne with four cheeses 229
mushrooms
anelli in mushroom and potato
broth 23
cannelloni in the Lazio style 58–9
chestnut, pumpkin and potato
gnocchi with butter and sage
133

mushrooms *continued*
    fettuccine with porcini
        mushrooms, butter and garlic
        113
    penne with sausage, porcini
mushrooms and leeks 226, *227*
    tagliolini with chanterelles and
        datterini tomatoes 308, *309*
    vincisgrassi *333*, 334, *335*
mussels
    fregula with clams or arselle
        116, *117*
    maltagliati with creamed leeks (and
        mussels if you wish) 180–81
    paccheri with potatoes and mussels
        216
    scialatielli Amalfi style with
        shellfish, squid and tomatoes
        and breadcrumbs 264

N

Naples
    recipes and food traditions 146,
        166, 188, 190, 192, 203, 281, 337
    and spaghetti's evolution 327
Norma see alla Norma
nuts *see* pine nuts; walnuts

O

Old Bari 194–5
olive oil 31
    cream of walnut sauce 321
    maltagliati with olive oil and
        pecorino 181
    pesto alla genovese 316–18, *319*
    Pradelli pesto 320
    spaghetti with garlic, olive oil and
        chilli – midnight spaghetti 278
    trofie with pesto alla genovese,
        potatoes and green beans
        324, *325*
olives
    fusilli with tomato and tuna ragù
        122
    linguine with swordfish Messina
        style 157
    scialatielli Amalfi style with
        shellfish, squid and tomatoes
        and breadcrumbs 264
    spaghettini with raw tomato sauce
        and lots of herbs 277
    vermicelli with tomatoes,
        anchovies, garlic, capers, olives
        and parsley 330
onions
    bigoli with onion and anchovy 28,
        29
    casarecce with peperonata 80
    lumache with tuna, beans, tomato
        and basil 163

    pappardelle with onion ragù 219
    quadrucci with spinach, butter and
        Parmesan 241
    stracci with peas, spring onion,
        guanciale and pecorino Carla
        style 292, *293*
    stracci with Roman spring stew of
        artichokes, peas and broad beans
        290–1
    ziti with onion and beef sauce 337
oranges
    ravioli with ricotta and spinach
        246–7, *247*
    scialatielli with sea bass and lemon
        266, *267*
orecchiette 194–201, *196*, *197*
    orecchiette with bursting tomatoes
        and anchovy crumbs 201
    orecchiette with rocket, potatoes
        and cherry tomatoes 200
    orecchiette with turnip tops, garlic
        and anchovy 198, *199*
oregano
    spaghettini with raw tomato sauce
        and oregano 276
    vermicelli with tomatoes,
        anchovies, garlic, capers, olives
        and parsley 330
orzo 202–7
    orzo with peas, Parmesan and
        lemon 204
    orzo with tomato, basil and
        Parmesan 203
    roast chicken with orzo 206, *207*
oxtail
    rigatoni with the sauce of
        Roman-style oxtail stew 254,
        255

P

paccheri 208–17
    paccheri with aubergine, two sorts
        of tomatoes and mozzarella
        214, *215*
    paccheri with broad bean pesto
        217
    paccheri with potatoes and mussels
        216
pancetta 38
    baked tagliatelle with ragù 304
    conchiglie with peas, bacon and
        ricotta 94
    fettuccine with chicken livers and
        sage 110
    garganelli with spring vegetables,
        crisp pancetta and Parmesan
        128
    lasagna Bolognese style with ragù,
        béchamel and Parmesan 148–9,
        151
    pasta with potatoes and smoked
        provola cheese 190

    Romagna-style ragù 126
    tagliatelle with ragù 302, *303*
    umbricelli with courgettes,
        pancetta and pecorino 234, *235*
    see also guanciale
Pane, Rita 136, 186
pansotti 67, 248
Paola (author's friend) 50
pappardelle 218–23
    pappardelle with duck 220, *221*
    pappardelle with onion ragù 219
    pappardelle with radicchio, fennel,
        cream and Parmesan 222
Parisi, Ada 331
Parmesan 35
    anelli baked with tomato,
        aubergine and cheese *20*, 21–2
    baked macaroni with meatballs and
        aubergine 170
    baked ziti with roasted peppers,
        provola and Parmesan 338
    cannelloni in the Lazio style 58–9
    cannelloni in the Sorrento style
        55, *56*, *57*
    cannelloni with pork, spinach and
        Parmesan 54
    conchiglie with peas, bacon and
        ricotta 94
    cream of walnut sauce 321
    fettuccine, butter and Parmesan
        111
    fettuccine with chicken livers and
        sage 110
    garganelli with spring vegetables,
        crisp pancetta and Parmesan
        128
    lasagna Bolognese style with ragù,
        béchamel and Parmesan 148–9,
        151
    linguine with courgettes, egg and
        Parmesan 158, *159*
    macaroni cheese 168, *169*
    mafalde with tomato sauce and
        ricotta 174, *175*
    midsummer pasta 186, *187*
    minestrone 31
    minestrone soup from Genoa 32,
        33
    minestrone with tomato, and two
        kinds of beans 102
    orzo with peas, Parmesan and
        lemon 204
    orzo with tomato, basil and
        Parmesan 203
    paccheri with broad bean pesto
        217
    pappardelle with radicchio, fennel,
        cream and Parmesan 222
    pasta al forno 274
    pasta and potatoes Neapolitan style
        192, *193*
    pasta with potatoes and smoked
        provola cheese 190
    penne with four cheeses 229
    pesto alla genovese 316–18, *319*

pizzoccheri with potatoes, cabbage and cheese 238, *239*
Pradelli pesto 320
pumpkin cappellacci 72, *73*
quadrucci with spinach, butter and Parmesan 241
ravioli with ricotta and spinach 246–7, *247*
ruote with mascarpone and walnuts 259
ruote with ricotta and pine nuts 260
spaghetti alla chitarra with tiny chicken meatballs and white wine 284, *285*
spaghetti with simple tomato and basil sauce 270, *271*
spinach and potato gnocchi with cream, Parmesan and basil *134*, *135*, 136, *137*
tagliolini with lemon, Parmesan and basil 307
tortellini, filled with pork, prosciutto, mortadella, served in broth 312, *313*
tortellini with Parmesan cream 314
trofie with pesto alla genovese, potatoes and green beans 324, *325*
vincisgrassi *333*, 334, *335*
ziti with onion and beef sauce 337
parsley, flat-leaf
lamb ragù with lots of herbs 120, *121*
spaghettini with raw tomato sauce and lots of herbs 277
vermicelli with tomatoes, anchovies, garlic, capers, olives and parsley 330
Passi, Andrea 286
pasta
basic shapes 18–19
competitions for new shapes 257
cooking 24–6, 58, 213
etymology 7, 17
largest industrial producers 256–7
making flour and water dough 83–4
making fresh egg dough 51–3, *69*, *70*, 294–8, 310–11
matching shapes and textures with sauces 74–7
origins and history 42–4, 326–7
see also dough
pasta al forno 274
pasta asciutta 90
pasta corta 18
pasta di mezz'estate 186, *187*
pasta e fagioli 90–91, 92, *93*
pasta lunga 19
pasta minestra 90
pasta mista *see* mista
pasta 'ncasciata 170
pasta ripiena 19, 66–8
see also cannelloni; cappellacci;

ravioli; tortellini
pasta strappata *see* stracci
pastina 12, 18
Pavoncello, Donatella 241
peas
bigoli with tuna and peas 28
conchiglie with peas, bacon and ricotta 94
garganelli with spring vegetables, crisp pancetta and Parmesan 128
minestrone 31
orzo with peas, Parmesan and lemon 204
quadrucci and peas Roman style 242, *243*
stracci with peas, spring onion, guanciale and pecorino Carla style 292, *293*
stracci with Roman spring stew of artichokes, peas and broad beans 290–91
pecorino 35
bucatini with guanciale and pecorino Romano 38
bucatini with tomato, guanciale and pecorino Romano 36, *37*
fettuccine with chicken livers and sage 110
fregula with sausage and saffron 115
maltagliati with olive oil and pecorino 181
minestrone soup from Genoa 32, *33*
pesto alla genovese 316–18, *319*
Pradelli pesto 320
ravioli with ricotta and spinach 246–7, *247*
rigatoni with egg, guanciale and pecorino 252, *253*
spaghetti alla chitarra or tonnarelli with pecorino cheese and black pepper 286–7
stracci with peas, spring onion, guanciale and pecorino Carla style 292, *293*
stracci with Roman spring stew of artichokes, peas and broad beans 290–91
trofie with pesto alla genovese, potatoes and green beans 324, *325*
umbricelli with courgettes, pancetta and pecorino 234, *235*
penne 224–9
penne with four cheeses 229
penne with sausage, porcini mushrooms and leeks 226, *227*
penne with spicy tomato sauce 228
pepper
spaghetti alla chitarra or tonnarelli with pecorino cheese and black pepper 286–7
peppers *81*

baked ziti with roasted peppers, provola and Parmesan 338
casarecce with peperonata 80
midsummer pasta 186, *187*
pestle and mortar 318
pesto 48
busiate with basil, tomato and almond pesto (*pesto trapanese*) 48, *49*
cavatelli with sage and almond pesto and salted ricotta 88
minestrone soup from Genoa 32, *33*
paccheri with broad bean pesto 217
pesto alla genovese 316–18, *319*
Pradelli pesto 320
trofie with pesto alla genovese, potatoes and green beans 324, *325*
pici 230–35
pici with tomatoes and garlic 233
umbricelli with courgettes, pancetta and pecorino 234, *235*
see also spaghetti alla chitarra
Pignataro, Luciano 214, 281
pine nuts
bucatini with cauliflower, saffron and anchovies 40
mafalde with anchovies and tomato paste and breadcrumbs 173
minestrone soup from Genoa 32, *33*
paccheri with broad bean pesto 217
pesto alla genovese 316–18, *319*
Pradelli pesto 320
rigatoni with the sauce of Roman-style oxtail stew 254, *255*
ruote with ricotta and pine nuts 260
trofie with pesto alla genovese, potatoes and green beans 324, *325*
Piolino 294
pipe *see* lumache
pizzoccheri 236–9
pizzoccheri with potatoes, cabbage and cheese 238, *239*
Poletti, Rina 148, 178, 294–6, 302, 310
pork
baked tagliatelle with ragù 304
cannelloni with pork, spinach and Parmesan 54
lasagna Bolognese style with ragù, béchamel and Parmesan 148–9, *151*
spaghetti alla chitarra in the style of Teramo 283
tagliatelle with ragù 302, *303*
tortellini, filled with pork, prosciutto, mortadella, served in broth 312, *313*

pork *continued*
  white ragù with pork, aubergine
    and fennel 47
  see also guanciale; ham;
    mortadella; pancetta; prosciutto;
    sausage meat
potatoes
  anelli in mushroom and potato
    broth 23
  chestnut, pumpkin and potato
    gnocchi with butter and sage
    133
  for gnocchi 131
  minestrone 31
  minestrone soup from Genoa 32,
    33
  orecchiette with rocket, potatoes
    and cherry tomatoes 200
  paccheri with potatoes and mussels
    216
  pasta and potatoes Neapolitan style
    192, *193*
  pasta with potatoes and smoked
    provola cheese 190
  pizzoccheri with potatoes, cabbage
    and cheese 238, *239*
  potato gnocchi 132
  ravioli with potatoes, ricotta, lemon
    and marjoram 248, *249*
  spinach and potato gnocchi with
    cream, Parmesan and basil *134,*
    135, 136, 137
  trofie with pesto alla genovese,
    potatoes and green beans 324,
    325
Pradelli, Alessandro Molinari 295,
  320, 332
prawns
  fresh capelli d'angelo with prawns
    and lemon 62, *63*
  mezze maniche with courgettes
    and prawns 184
  scialatielli Amalfi style with
    shellfish, squid and tomatoes
    and breadcrumbs 264
Prezzolini, Giuseppe 42, 268, 327
prosciutto
  cannelloni in the Lazio style 58–9
  Romagna-style ragù 126
  tortellini, filled with pork,
    prosciutto, mortadella, served in
    broth 312, *313*
  vincisgrassi *333, 334, 335*
provola
  baked ziti with roasted peppers,
    provola and Parmesan 338
  pasta with potatoes and smoked
    provola cheese 190
Puglia 16, 19, 43, 82, 140, 194–5,
  198, 257, 340
pumpkin
  cavatelli with sage and almond
    pesto and salted ricotta 88
  chestnut, pumpkin and potato
    gnocchi with butter and sage
    133

  ditali and pumpkin 97
  minestrone 31
  pumpkin cappellacci 72, *73*
puttanesca see alla puttanesca

Q

quadrucci 240–43
  quadrucci and peas Roman style
    242, *243*
  quadrucci with spinach, butter and
    Parmesan 241
quantities 11

R

radicchio *223*
  pappardelle with radicchio, fennel,
    cream and Parmesan 222
Raffaella (pasta maker) 230–31
ragù
  baked tagliatelle with ragù 304
  cannelloni in the Lazio style 58–9
  fusilli with tomato and tuna ragù
    122
  lamb ragù with lots of herbs 120,
    121
  lasagna Bolognese style with ragù,
    béchamel and Parmesan 148–9,
    151
  pappardelle with onion ragù 219
  Romagna-style ragù 126
  spaghetti with rich tomato ragù
    273
  tagliatelle with ragù 302, *303*
  white ragù with pork, aubergine
    and fennel 47
ravioli 244–9
  ravioli with potatoes, ricotta, lemon
    and marjoram 248, *249*
  ravioli with ricotta and spinach
    246–7, *247*
reginette *see* mafalde
ricotta 260
  cannelloni in the Sorrento style
    55, *56, 57*
  cavatelli with sage and almond
    pesto and salted ricotta 88
  conchiglie with peas, bacon and
    ricotta 94
  conchiglioni stuffed with spinach
    and ricotta 95
  mafalde with tomato sauce and
    ricotta 174, *175*
  paccheri with broad bean pesto
    217
  ravioli with potatoes, ricotta, lemon
    and marjoram 248, *249*
  ravioli with ricotta and spinach
    246–7, *247*
  ruote with ricotta and pine nuts
    260

  spaghetti with tomato, aubergine
    and salted ricotta 279
rigatoni 250–55
  rigatoni with egg, guanciale and
    pecorino 252, *253*
  rigatoni with the sauce of
    Roman-style oxtail stew 254,
    255
Riley, Gillian 167
rocket
  orecchiette with rocket, potatoes
    and cherry tomatoes 200
Roden, Claudia 241
Romagna 124–5, 126
romagnola see alla romagnola
Romans 44, 140
Rome
  Il Bucatino 34–5
  cookery teachers 244
  Da Salvo 262–3
  Gatti & Antonelli 106, 107, *108,*
    109, 240
  history of pasta making in
    326, 327
  recipes and food traditions 107,
    131, 228, 242, 254, 267, 290–91
  Santa Maria dell'Orto 326, 327
  La Torricella 182–3
  Trattoria Perilli 250–51
Rosalba (author's friend) 229
rosemary
  chickpea and chestnut soup
    178, *179*
  lamb ragù with lots of herbs
    120, *121*
  pappardelle with duck 220, *221*
  pasta and chickpeas 144
rosmarino *see* orzo
ruote 256–61, *261*
  ruote with Gorgonzola, sage and
    walnuts 258
  ruote with mascarpone and
    walnuts 259
  ruote with ricotta and pine nuts
    260

S

Sabban, Françoise 42
Sada, Luigi 145
saffron
  bucatini with cauliflower, saffron
    and anchovies 40
  capelli d'angelo with leeks, cream
    and saffron 64
  fregula with sausage and saffron
    115
sage
  cavatelli with sage and almond
    pesto and salted ricotta 88
  chestnut, pumpkin and potato
    gnocchi with butter and sage
    133

ditali and pumpkin 97
fettuccine with chicken livers and
  sage 110
lamb ragù with lots of herbs
  120, 121
pappardelle with duck 220, 221
pumpkin cappellacci 72, 73
ravioli with ricotta and spinach
  246–7, 247
ruote with Gorgonzola, sage and
  walnuts 258
Salento 140, 145
Salimbene da Parma 245
salmon, smoked
  farfalle with salmon and
    mascarpone 104, 105
salsa 27
  bigoli with onion and anchovy
    28, 29
salt 13, 24–5
Salvatore (restaurateur) 262
sambusaj 245
sardines
  fusilli with tinned sardines, fennel,
    lemon and anchovy crumbs 123
Sardinia 35, 114
sausage meat
  cavatelli with sage and almond
    pesto and salted ricotta 88
  cavatelli with sausage, mint and
    tomato 86, 87
  ditali and pumpkin 97
  fregula with sausage and saffron
    115
  pasta with potatoes and smoked
    provola cheese 190
  penne with sausage, porcini
    mushrooms and leeks 226, 227
  spaghetti with rich tomato ragù
    273
scamorza
  anelli baked with tomato,
    aubergine and cheese 20, 21–2
  baked ziti with roasted peppers,
    provola and Parmesan 338
Scappi, Bartolomeo 66
scarpinocc 68
scialatielli 262–7
  scialatielli Amalfi style with
    shellfish, squid and tomatoes
    and breadcrumbs 264
  scialatielli with sea bass and lemon
    266, 267
Scoglitti
  Sakalleo 157
sea bass
  scialatielli with sea bass and lemon
    266, 267
semola 61, 83, 84, 107, 114, 140, 153,
    156, 195, 198, 208, 231, 263, 334
semolina 17–18, 83–4, 130, 194, 231,
    245
Sereni, Emilio 42
Serventi, Silvano 42
la sfoglia 294–8, 310–11, 312

shellfish *see* clams; mussels
soffritto 140
Sorrento 55, 136
soups
  chickpea and chestnut soup
    178, 179
  pasta and beans 92, 93
  pasta and chickpea soup with
    tinned chickpeas 142, 143
  pasta and potatoes Neapolitan style
    192, 193
  pasta with potatoes and smoked
    provola cheese 190
  see also brodi; minestrone
spaghetti 268–81
  frittata di spaghetti 281
  spaghetti with garlic, olive oil and
    chilli – midnight spaghetti 278
  spaghetti with rich tomato ragù
    273
  spaghetti with roasted tomato
    sauce 274, 275
  spaghetti with simple fresh tomato
    sauce 272
  spaghetti with simple tomato and
    basil sauce 270, 271
  spaghetti with tomato, aubergine
    and salted ricotta 279
  spaghettini with raw tomato sauce
    and lots of herbs 277
  spaghettini with raw tomato sauce
    and oregano 276
  see also vermicelli
spaghetti alla chitarra 282–7,
    287
  spaghetti alla chitarra in the style
    of Teramo 283
  spaghetti alla chitarra or tonnarelli
    with pecorino cheese and black
    pepper 286–7
  spaghetti alla chitarra with tiny
    chicken meatballs and white
    wine 284, 285
  see also pici
spinach
  cannelloni with pork, spinach and
    Parmesan 54
  conchiglioni stuffed with spinach
    and ricotta 95
  quadrucci with spinach, butter and
    Parmesan 241
  ravioli with ricotta and spinach
    246–7, 247
  spinach and potato gnocchi with
    cream, Parmesan and basil 134,
    135, 136, 137
squid
  scialatielli Amalfi style with
    shellfish, squid and tomatoes
    and breadcrumbs 264
stock *see brodi*
stracci 288–93
  stracci with peas, spring onion,
    guanciale and pecorino Carla
    style 292, 293

stracci with Roman spring stew of
  artichokes, peas and broad beans
  290–91
strascinati 19
stricchetti *see* farfalle
strozzapreti *see* pici
sultanas
  rigatoni with the sauce of
    Roman-style oxtail stew
    254, 255
Sumerians 42, 43
swordfish
  linguine with swordfish Messina
    style 157

T

tagliatelle 294–305, 299, 300, 301,
  305
  baked tagliatelle with ragù 304
  tagliatelle with ragù 302, 303
tagliolini 306–9
  tagliolini with chanterelles and
    datterini tomatoes 308, 309
  tagliolini with lemon, Parmesan
    and basil 307
Taleggio
  penne with four cheeses 229
Tanzi, Guido and Aurelio 118
Taruschio, Ann and Franco 332
Teramo 283
Terranuova Bracciolini
  Osteria Il Canto del Maggio 220
thyme
  pappardelle with duck 220, 221
timballi
  anelli baked with tomato,
    aubergine and cheese 20, 21–2
  baked ziti with roasted peppers,
    provola and Parmesan 338
Tomasi, Carla 244, 288, 292
tomatoes
  anelli baked with tomato,
    aubergine and cheese 20, 21–2
  baked macaroni with meatballs and
    aubergine 170
  baked tagliatelle with ragù 304
  baked ziti with roasted peppers,
    provola and Parmesan 338
  bucatini with tomato, guanciale
    and pecorino Romano 36, 37
  busiate with basil, tomato and
    almond pesto (*pesto trapanese*)
    48, 49
  cannelloni in the Lazio style 58–9
  cannelloni in the Sorrento style
    55, 56, 57
  casarecce with peperonata 80
  cavatelli with sausage, mint and
    tomato 86, 87
  conchiglioni stuffed with spinach
    and ricotta 95
  fregula with clams or arselle 116,
    117

tomatoes *continued*
   fregula with sausage and saffron
     115
   fusilli with tomato and tuna ragù
     122
   lamb ragù with lots of herbs 120,
     121
   lasagna Bolognese style with ragù,
     béchamel and Parmesan 148–9,
     151
   linguine with anchovies, tomato
     and breadcrumbs 160
   linguine with swordfish Messina
     style 157
   lumache with tuna, beans, tomato
     and basil 163
   mafalde with anchovies and tomato
     paste and breadcrumbs 173
   mafalde with tomato sauce and
     ricotta 174, *175*
   midsummer pasta 186, *187*
   minestrone 31
   minestrone soup from Genoa 32,
     33
   minestrone with tomato, and two
     kinds of beans 102
   orecchiette with bursting tomatoes
     and anchovy crumbs 201
   orecchiette with rocket, potatoes
     and cherry tomatoes 200
   orzo with tomato, basil and
     Parmesan 203
   paccheri with aubergine, two sorts
     of tomatoes and mozzarella
     214, *215*
   pappardelle with duck 220, *221*
   pappardelle with onion ragù 219
   passata 277
   pasta al forno 274
   pasta and beans 92, *93*
   pasta and chickpeas 144
   pasta with potatoes and smoked
     provola cheese 190
   penne with sausage, porcini
     mushrooms and leeks 226, *227*
   penne with spicy tomato sauce 228
   pici with tomatoes and garlic 233
   ravioli with ricotta and spinach
     246–7, *247*
   rigatoni with the sauce of
     Roman-style oxtail stew 254,
     255
   Romagna-style ragù 126
   scialatielli Amalfi style with
     shellfish, squid and tomatoes
     and breadcrumbs 264
   spaghetti alla chitarra in the style
     of Teramo 283
   spaghetti with rich tomato ragù
     273
   spaghetti with roasted tomato
     sauce 274, *275*
   spaghetti with simple fresh tomato
     sauce 272
   spaghetti with simple tomato and

     basil sauce 270, *271*
   spaghetti with tomato, aubergine
     and salted ricotta 279
   spaghettini with raw tomato sauce
     and lots of herbs 277
   spaghettini with raw tomato sauce
     and oregano 276
   tagliatelle with ragù 302, *303*
   tagliolini with chanterelles and
     datterini tomatoes 308, *309*
   tinned 272
   vermicelli with tomatoes,
     anchovies, garlic, capers, olives
     and parsley 330
tonnarelli *see* spaghetti alla chitarra
tortelli 68
tortellini 310–15
   tortellini, filled with pork,
     prosciutto, mortadella, served in
     broth 312, *313*
   tortellini with Parmesan cream
     314
Trabia 44
tracta 43–4
Trapani 48
Trentino-Alto Adige 226
tria 44, 140
tripolini 172
triqta 43
trofie 316–25
   trofie with pesto alla genovese,
     potatoes and green beans 324,
     325
tuna
   bigoli with tuna and peas 28
   fusilli with tomato and tuna ragù
     122
   lumache with tuna, beans, tomato
     and basil 163
   lumache with tuna, egg and capers
     164, *165*
Tuscany 18, 220, 230–31, 233, 288

U

Umbria 124–5, 230, 234, 340
umbricelli *see* pici

V

Val di Chiana 233
Val d'Orcia 233
Valle dei Mulini 208
Valtellina 236–7
veal
   cannelloni with pork, spinach and
     Parmesan 54
Venturi, Alessandro 36, 138, 322
Vera (author's neighbour) 66
vermicelli 326–31
   vermicelli with clams 328, *329*

vermicelli with clams, courgettes,
   almonds and breadcrumbs 331
vermicelli with tomatoes,
   anchovies, garlic, capers, olives
   and parsley 330
see also spaghetti
Veronese, Bartolomio 26
vignarola 290–91
Vincenzo (author's partner) 16, 34,
   100–1, 168, 170, 269
vincisgrassi 332–5, *333*, *335*
Viterbo 288
Viviani, Antonio 327
vrimzliash 44

W

Walnut Tree, The 332
walnuts
   cream of walnut sauce 321
   ruote with Gorgonzola, sage and
     walnuts 258
   ruote with mascarpone and walnuts
     259

Y

Yuge, Keita 257

Z

Zanini de Vita, Oretta 42, 74, 138,
   166, 327
ziti/zite 336–40, *339*
   baked ziti with roasted peppers,
     provola and Parmesan 338
   ziti with onion and beef sauce 337
zizziridd 340
zugolotti 340
zumari 340

Acknowledgements

It is true, as writer Laurie Colwin noted, that you never cook alone, that you cook with 'generations of cooks past, the advice and menus of cooks present, the wisdom of cookbook writers'. I felt this strongly and gratefully while working on this book, that I was cooking alongside the generations of women and men whose hands have shaped this immense edible patrimony.

Most strongly, when I was cooking and learning alongside the inimitable Carla Tomasi, Rina Poletti and Alessandro Venturi. Also Alice Carosi-Adams, Fabrizia Lanza, Enza Di Gangi and Giovanna Di Bella at the Anna Tasca Lanza cooking school, Francesca Fughelli and her family in Bologna, Andrea, Tomasi and Angela at Pastificio Passi, Raffaella Cova in Tuscany, Giada Ferrara and family at Ristorante Sakalleo in Scoglitti, Rosalba Pelusi, Liborio D'Aleo, my mother-in-law Carmela D'Aleo, Julia and Pino Ficara at the Grano & Farina cooking school, Daniela Del Balzo, Agusto e Andrea D'Alfonsi at Ristorante La Torricella, Maria Paola Sacco, Matteo Pezzana at Il Pesto di Pra' in Liguria. Huge thanks to the pasta makers, Massimo Mancini, Lorenzo Settimi, Paolo Mucci and Claudio Marcantoni at Pastificio Mancini in Le Marche, Sergio Cinque and everyone at Pastificio Faella in Gragnano.

Research and writing about pasta is no different to cooking it: it can be done thanks to the historians and scholars, past and present, who have synthesized the immense history. I wrote in the company of Giuseppe Prezzolini, Emilio Sereni, Silvano Serventi e Françoise Sabban, Oretta Zanini De Vita and her extraordinary *Encyclopaedia of Pasta*, Massimo Montanari. I am constantly grateful for the work and advice of Mary Taylor Simeti, Gillian Riley, Jill Norman, Simon Hopkinson, Anna Del Conte and Rosetta Costantino.

I am so happy this book found a home at Penguin with publisher Juliet Annan, whose appetite for the project propelled me. It was a joyful privilege to work with photographer Jonathan Lovekin. I have relished collaborating with everyone at Penguin, especially copy-editor Annie Lee, designer Saffron Stocker, managing editor Natalie Wall and production manager Charlotte Faber. Also

my friend Alice Carosi-Adams, who cooked with me for the photographs. Thanks to Linda Thompson for her diligent recipe testing, Rachel Rennie and Vincenzo for their eagle eyes on the Italian, and my parents Jenifer and Martin Roddy for reading and listening.

Thanks, too, to my agent Rosemary Scoular, and to Natalia Lucas, John Elek, Sophie Missing, and my colleagues at the *Guardian* – Mina Holland, Bob Granleese, Anna Berrill, Tim Lusher, Fiona Beckett, Yotam Ottolenghi, Felicity Cloake, Grace Dent, Meera Sodha, Thomasina Miers, Anna Jones, Tamal Ray, Liam Charles, Tom Hunt – and to readers of my column. And thanks to my family, in England, Rome and Sicily, especially Luca and Vincenzo, who ate the whole book.